IT'S WHEN YOU
SELL THAT COUNTS

Revised Edition

IT'S WHEN YOU
SELL THAT COUNTS

DONALD L. CASSIDY

McGraw-Hill

New York   San Francisco   Washington, D.C.   Auckland   Bogotá
Caracas   Lisbon   London   Madrid   Mexico City   Milan
Montreal   New Delhi   San Juan   Singapore
Sydney   Tokyo   Toronto

McGraw-Hill

A Division of The McGraw-Hill Companies

This publication is designed to provide accurate and authoritative information in regard to the subject matter covered. It is sold with the understanding that neither the author nor the publisher is engaged in rendering legal, accounting, or other professional service. If legal advice or other expert assistance is required, the services of a competent professional person should be sought.

From a Declaration of Principles jointly adopted by a Committee of the American Bar Association and a Committee of Publishers.

Library of Congress Cataloging-in-Publication Data

Cassidy, Don.
    It's when you sell that counts/Donald L. Cassidy.—Rev. ed.
      p.   cm.
    Includes index.
    ISBN 0-7863-1129-0
    1. Stocks.   2. Speculation.   I. Title.
    HG4661.C37 1997
    332.63'22—dc20   96-41901

Printed in the United States of America
   6 7 8 9 0 DOC 3 2 1 0

To Laura and Michael

TABLE OF CONTENTS

ACKNOWLEDGEMENTS

A book, like any product of the human mind, is an amalgam formed of conscious and unconscious experiences that affect the author over many years. Thus, a writer might well acknowledge almost anyone who has ever touched his or her life. Publishers prefer that such lists be brief, however. This imposes a discipline at once useful and harsh. With due apologies to others whose names fell off the short list, then, I thank, in chronological order:

Richard Randlett, a teacher of junior high school mathematics, who introduced me to investments: he will never know the horizons he opened in my mind.

Robert Scotland, a teacher of U.S. history at Wayland High School in Massachusetts: he demanded the best of good students. He allowed me to study the Great Depression as a history project and asked me to deliver a lecture to classmates; that experience built self-confidence.

The late Roger Spear, who founded an investment advisory firm later sold to Fidelity Management and Research Corporation: he patiently guided and taught an impetuous young man and let him learn on company time.

Charles Kline, a finance instructor at the Wharton School: his favorite expression was simple but profound: "Everything goes in circles and cycles."

Ellen Curtiss, for many years with Arthur D. Little, Inc.: she stretched me as a researcher, editor, and writer and convinced me that it can be done.

Richard Hurwitz, formerly Research Director at Boettcher and Company: he had the confidence and vision to hire as an investment analyst a management consultant with "no previous experience," a courageous act for a manager in today's myopic corporate culture. He was a tough and, therefore, valued mentor and remains a fine friend.

Heather White, a colleague at Boettcher and a dear friend: she taught me things about brokers that otherwise would have taken years to crystallize in my mind. She also told me I was good enough to undertake the perilous task of writing a first book. Then she led me to my publisher, saving much pain and frustration.

Robert Davis of Davis-Hamilton Associates, one of several research directors I served: his profound sense of proportion and cool, logical mind under stress taught me much more than he thinks.

Richard Follingstad, who invited me to speak at a public seminar in 1989 about the problems of a local company in Albuquerque: his stage provided me with a first vital direct exposure to how individual investors think about selling their stocks; that night convinced me this book was needed.

Scott Courts of Denver, a broker and now money manager wise beyond his years: he shared war stories, confirmed my worst suspicions, listened to and helped refine some of my concepts, and was excited for me.

Belita Calvert, who helped me in several little but important ways: from proofreading to listening to energizing and encouraging, she was always there. Now, as my wife, she continues patiently allowing me space and time for my work.

Michael Jeffers and Jennifer Lindsey, then of Probus Publishing: they made the final stages of my first book pleasantly smooth.

A. Michael Lipper and Evelyn Carter: they have generously and patiently allowed me to juggle my full-time employee responsibilities with the sometimes-hectic schedule of a writer and public speaker.

Finally, and not least, Wayne Baxmann of Houston: he has provided me with introductions to numerous local AAII chapters where feedback from my kind audiences has enriched my thinking and added fresh nuances for this revised edition.

INTRODUCTION

Several years ago, as an equities analyst for a regional brokerage firm, your author was in conversation with an experienced broker to discuss the recommended sale of a certain stock, of which the broker's client held 500 shares.

"Well," said the analyst, "a sale sounds nice since the stock is up several points here. He ought to be glad to take the profit."

To his surprise, the broker replied, "I wish it were that easy. You see, this guy is funny. He really hates to pay taxes, so I have an awful time getting him to sell to take a profit."

The analyst responded that he had heard that tune more than a few times and joked that maybe the broker should point out to the client that he ought to like paying taxes on thousands in profit rather than having a loss to worry about. The analyst then suggested some offsetting losses to close out, to help soften the tax blow and put the client's portfolio in better shape.

"Oh, no," said the broker, "he absolutely refuses to take a loss. I cannot even TALK to him about it; he's threatened to fire me if I do!"

In disbelief the analyst asked, "Are you saying that you have a client who is invested in the stock market but will not take a profit to avoid capital-gains tax, and who will not take a loss as a matter of pride? I'll wager lunch that he would refuse to sell a stock unchanged because it has not done what he expected."

At that point, the broker scheduled that lunch because her client, indeed, insisted on continuing to hold stocks if unchanged because he also hated paying commissions.

Whether the foregoing tale amuses or alarms the reader, there is a lesson in it. Here was an intelligent person, professionally successful, who owned a decent collection of municipals, as well as stocks and mutual funds. Not untypically, he had difficulty selling stocks whether they were up, down, or unchanged. Market participants like this always prompt that enduring question, "Why won't he sell?" The broker, too, was seemingly powerless to provide help.

There are many reasons investors have trouble selling their stocks. Brokers have their own distinct lists of hesitations about getting clients to sell. In fact, selling out of stocks is a universal problem. The inescapable conclusion is that people need help cashing in whether they are average, Main Street investors or professionals such as brokers or money managers. One of the reasons assistance is needed is that there is very little information on selling provided in the marketplace. Much more attention must be given the art of selling out stocks—whether at a gain or at a loss. And an understanding must be developed that today, many brokers are product marketers rather than investment experts.

Investors need to pay attention to the psychology of selling against human nature, to individual stocks and how they behave, to how both large and small investors think and act, and to brokers and the roles they play. Overwhelmingly, most books dealing with the stock market in any form focus on the buying transaction, neglecting the sell side of the equation almost completely. Selling may not be as exciting and is a narrower topic, but it is absolutely necessary and has its own very interesting twists and curiosities.

This book is divided into four sections. The first describes the external and internal problems and pitfalls that investors face when confronted with a hold/sell choice. These obstructions tend to be structural in nature. The second section covers several necessary aspects of the mind-set needed to approach the hold/sell decision. These problems are related to a natural avoidance of closure, which can represent with deathlike finality the mortality of an investor's judgment. The third section prescribes important strategies that should be applied to generate smart selling decisions. The fourth section explores micro-level tactics for executing a liquidation strategy more effectively and profitably.

The final two chapters provide readers with a checklist, to be used with each transaction, and with the ultimate sell-versus-hold test question, both of which function as learning devices.

There is no difference between a long-term investor in the classic sense or a short-term trader when it comes to stock market success: to profit and stay in the game, one must know how, and be ready, to cash in—to sell—when the time is right. Profits are made only when both a purchase and the subsequent sale have been implemented well.

IT'S WHEN YOU *SELL* THAT COUNTS

ROADBLOCKS TO PROFITABLE SELLING: REAL PROBLEMS, PHOBIAS, MYTHS, AND RATIONALIZATIONS

1

External Roadblocks

KEYS TO INVESTMENT SUCCESS

- Understand Today's Broker
- Accept the Four-Letter Word: Sell
- Acknowledge the Importance of Changed Fundamentals
- Understand Buying and Holding, and Other Conditioned Behaviors

TODAY'S BROKER

A description of broker skills as they have evolved over the past decade is not the focus of this book. However, an understanding of the broker point of view is essential for investors intent on making profits in the stock market. While some of the following observations about brokers may seem critical, they are intended to illustrate the broker point of view and to help the investor facilitate his or her relationship with a broker.

There are different kinds of brokers; to compound the confusion, each brokerage firm has its own broker terminology: "account executive," "registered representative," or "investment counselor" are some examples. Although the title does not matter, what does matter to investors is the training, experience, and basic professional orientation of their brokers no matter what they are called and no matter what firm employs them.

This is not simply to say, "get a well-trained broker." It is a recommendation to identify the broker's orientation and to find out how he deals with the investing public.

Note that the term *stockbroker* has not been used in this book; the term *broker* is favored. The choice of words has been deliberate: most of today's brokers, especially those younger than average, are not really stockbrokers in the classical, historical sense. And there are good reasons.

FALLOUT FROM THE FIDELITY PHENOMENON

With 20/20 hindsight, it is now possible to conclude that probably the largest single factor in the gradual extinction of the traditional stockbroker was the phenomenal success of Fidelity Management & Research Corp.'s money market funds in the mid-1970s. Fidelity's ability to attract billions of dollars, first to its Daily Income Trust and then to its lower minimum Cash Reserves fund (see Figure 1–1), triggered a chain of events that has led, over 20-plus years, to the relative scarcity of the traditional stockbroker—a lamentable consequence, but not one that Fidelity's management either foresaw or intended. The success of Cash Reserves—among other similar funds—rippled like a pebble dropped in a pond and widened into a series of tidal waves.

First, Fidelity's Daily Income Trust acted as a parking place for billions of dollars of investor funds during the disintermediation period of the mid-1970s.

FIGURE 1–1

Fidelity Cash Reserves
Asset Growth History

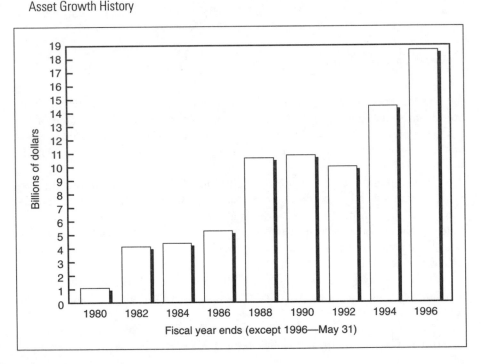

When interest rates later subsided, Fidelity encouraged and educated its money-fund holders to transfer assets to other mutual funds within the corporate family or "group."

The effect was not only to offer Fidelity investors a newly attractive equities climate but also—and much more importantly—to demonstrate to Fidelity managers and financial services industry competitors alike the success of asset-gathering as a corporate strategy.

Whether by brilliant forward planning or not, Fidelity executed a strategy of gathering and maintaining control of billions of dollars in investor assets. It was highly profitable—indeed, imperative—for Fidelity to maintain and extend its investment pool once the basic move had been made. And at the same time, it became obvious to competitors that they not only should, but indeed must, compete on equal footing by attracting their own client assets to a broad array of funds or "products."

Asset capture, then, became a competitive necessity for every company in the industry. Had Fidelity been able to continue playing the asset-capture game solo, it seemed plausible for it to have assembled "all" investable assets—clearly a massive threat to the jobs, egos, and incomes of thousands of investment professionals in all competing firms.

Not only mutual funds were affected; all financial services providers visualized their turfs invaded and captured by the asset-gatherers. Insurance companies feared that billions of dollars would be drained from their coffers, and new-policy sales choked off as investors soaked up the mutual funds offered by Fidelity and its like. Banks envisioned, accurately, both a permanent disintermediation of deposits and a likely diversion of assets from their money-management departments. Brokerage firms saw both a threat and an opportunity in the lure that mutual funds' professional management represented: it meant a probable drain on the assets held by individual investors in stocks and bonds, which generate periodic transaction revenues. By themselves entering the funds-management business, brokerage firms could stabilize their revenue and profit cyclicality by relying on asset-based fee income.

ONE-STOP SHOPPING

As a result of the asset-capture game, many financial organizations became supermarkets; the department store image fits equally well. Sears, Roebuck & Co., no longer the largest U.S. department store, became a financial supermarket. Starting with a distribution base (the customer list and the walk-in traffic) and with an insurance company (Allstate), Sears added a family of mutual funds and a brokerage firm (Dean Witter) and even got into real estate brokerage and financing. (In the 1990's, it would spin off some of these businesses to enhance shareholder value.)

Most financial services providers concluded, at roughly the same time, that the only survival strategy for long-term business success was to become a financial supermarket—the provider of essentially all services under one corporate or holding-company roof. By its nature, asset-gathering became an activity of prime importance because, once assets were captured, they were likely to remain under management or control until the investor needed them for spending. Annual or monthly fees accruing for the management of those assets grew large as the asset base rose from tens of billions of dollars to a few trillion (the amount in money funds alone, as of mid-1996, exceeded $815 billion). One percent of that pie as an approximate annual management fee had become an extremely attractive prize.

So banks and insurance companies bought brokerage firms and started their own mutual funds. Mutual fund firms created insurance and annuity products and started brokerage operations. And, most significantly, brokerage firms responded by marketing funds and similar products intensively.

The upshot was that individual brokers who had originally been "stock and bond brokers" now were trained to handle a wide variety of additional investment instruments or products, including annuities, certificates of deposit, guaranteed investment contracts, variable annuities, mutual funds of all descriptions, tax shelters, unit investment trusts, gold bullion, precious metal coins, and options and index futures.

Not only were existing brokers now re-educated in some or all of these new offerings, but the standard training programs for new brokers hired by nationwide brokerage firms soon included, and indeed emphasized, such specialized products. Smaller, regional firms, forced to compete on as equal a footing as they could create, followed in lockstep. Thus, an entire new generation of entrants into the brokerage business was conditioned to offer a full array of manufactured financial products.

These firms became the personal analog of the financial shopping mall, where ideally customers never leave the premises to satisfy any or all their investment needs. Asset capture became a way of life in the investment and brokerage industry. By the mid-1980s, standard training programs for new sales personnel had relegated stocks and bonds—once the staple of the business—to literally a 10 percent or less share of time and emphasis. A stock or bond became only one of a series of financial concepts or products that the newly trained salesperson learned how to offer to client-investors. A 1988 *Barron's* article estimated that 40 percent of the brokers in the business in 1987 had entered since 1980. Their training reflects this era of wholesale de-emphasis on stocks. Not only were individual stocks accorded less emphasis in training programs, but they also became palpably less attractive to the average individual investor.

This major development of the 1970s and 1980s was also, at least in part, a fallout from the Fidelity phenomenon. Huge pools of investable funds came under the control of professional money managers, whether in funds, pension plans, or insurance/annuity assets. The live marketplace became highly institutionalized as an increasing fraction of each session's trading was initiated by professional portfolio managers rather than implemented directly by individuals.

Individual investors—regardless of their age or Wall Street experience—became painfully aware that they were competing as relative rookies on a playing field dominated by giant players who, right or wrong, moved the market just by playing. This realization, brought home in a series of bear markets from 1973 to 1982 and coming again as no surprise in October 1987, convinced millions of individual investors to reduce their direct participation in stocks. In large numbers they quit altogether, went into hibernation, or turned their funds over to the professional managers, thereby accelerating the institutionalization trend.

These packaged investments or products are *sold to* investors; they are not actively *bought by* investors. So the operational dynamic is *not* that an individual investor goes to a broker who responds by identifying a product or service to sell to that investor. Now, in order to capture or "gather" assets in the new era, asset managers create packaged investment products to be proactively sold to an investing public by brokers who spend considerable time prospecting for new money.

NEW TECHNIQUES IN SALES

The most efficient way to sell a mass-produced product is to train a salesforce in a standardized and rehearsed technique. And because, for regulatory compliance reasons, certain representations must be made and certain caveats offered, a sales presentation is delivered essentially from a script. The extreme version is a verbatim or canned script or "pitch" that the salesperson is supposed to read from top to bottom.

The point? Prepackaged products and rehearsed sales pitches require persuasiveness and persistence, in contrast to the choosing of individual securities that required informed intelligence and incisive investment expertise. Played out through cold calling of fresh prospects, the sale of products results in successful asset capture. Prepackaged products also generate larger commissions than do stocks and bonds.

Imagine a securities broker with a prospect or existing client whose objective is safety of principal and income. He might place $10,000 in the Consolidated Income Fund, which is professionally managed and offers a 4.5 percent commission or perhaps a 0.5 percent annual commission as long as held. One or two individual income-type stocks, the alternative to the fund, pay an up-front gross commission of 1 percent. And at most brokerage firms, the broker's personal percentage of total commission is higher on packaged products than on stocks and bonds. Which products will the broker sell? The packaged products. Even if commissions were equal, the packaged products come with an easy, prepared script and the assurance of a proven professional management team; existing stocks do not. There is less post-sale "hand holding" with the packaged product because, presumably, it is less complicated. And many such products are one-decision (i.e., buy) in nature, further reducing demands on broker time for after-sale tending.

There is one more important broker aspect of the asset-gathering revolution: the nature of investment sales personnel. They are paid to distribute investment products created for the benefit of management. This process usually is performed most effectively with conservative, long-term-oriented investments. The salesperson of today is trained to help the client make a decision to *buy* a product. Professional training, mind set, and daily work habits all focus exclusively on a relationship in which the broker suggests instruments that should be bought and that the prospect then agrees to *buy*.

So the modern-era broker is not trained in the process of convincing clients that they should *sell* investment assets. This is, in effect, a structural "buy bias"— the concentration of the investment industry on the process of distributing packaged products designed to be *bought* by the public. Brokers are simply more practiced and more comfortable suggesting that clients buy something rather than that they sell something. This evolved because brokers became channels of distribution as a result of asset-gathering, rather than sources of investment advice.

One of the ways to identify a broker's professional point of origin—asset-gathering or investment expertise—is to find out how long he or she has been in the investment business and what prior career he or she had. If the person was previously an entrepreneur or franchisee or—the surest tipoff—a salesman of other products or services, this broker is at heart a hustling sales professional rather than—and not—an investment expert.

Another useful and revealing strategy is to interrupt the canned or scripted sales pitch with a question. Make the question really challenging. Ask the broker an off-beat question like, "What happens to the proposed investment if the Swiss franc rallies against the Japanese yen while the value of the dollar and gold both rise?" Brokers who actually are investment professionals should have some semblance of an informed opinion. Scripted brokers will be baffled.

Because of the buy bias, investors should expect little or no selling advice unless their brokers happen to be traditional or classic professionals from the old school. An investor must, then, realize that most selling activity is going to be virtually a do-it-yourself project. Clearly, going it alone is also standard fare for discount brokerage clients.

There is also a psychological bias against selling stocks: all buys are made in optimism, whereas not all sells conclude successful ventures. In buying, an investor focuses on how correct he or she may be; when selling, uncertainty centers on what kind of mistake might be committed. So selling is not a uniformly happy experience for investors. And virtually every sell, unless made at the historic high eighth of a point, at least sometimes *looks* like a wrong and irretrievably completed decision. Unhappy memories of such sales, reinforced multiple times, prompt avoidance behavior later.

THE FOUR-LETTER WORD: SELL

One of the reasons selling is a difficult proposition for a broker is the buy bias. It is easy to appreciate the more comfortable and optimistic sense that both investors and brokers have about buying, especially when buying is contrasted with selling. As stated before, buying is, by nature, a beginning based on hope and optimism. Selling is an ending that may not conclude in optimism, and it carries a lot more emotional baggage.

There are additional, very important reasons a brokerage firm almost never says "sell." All of them are logical if viewed from the firm's viewpoint. Individual investors must, therefore, center on their own profit needs when it comes to making a sell decision, not on the broker's desire for a commission or her sales orientation and not on the profit motive of the brokerage firm. A wise investor must adopt a strong do-it-yourself attitude and discipline about cashing in when the time is right, whether using a full-service firm or not.

The necessity for this go-it-alone investor orientation is that individuals are far from the brokerage firm's only client constituency. Usually, a brokerage firm's most important clients are public companies. This is because the investment-banking side of the brokerage firm is in business to raise capital for these companies, and it is a very lucrative business compared with retail commission revenues.

In fact, when an individual investor buys stocks or bonds in a new issue, the broker usually points out that there is no commission on the purchase. The broker may go so far as to say, "The issuing company is paying the commission." This is correct; and except for very small orders, the investment banking, per-share commission is well above what is paid on an aftermarket transaction.

So the level of commission dollars from companies issuing securities is high because the investment banking side of the firm has high fixed costs (salaries, entertainment, computers, legal and accounting consultants). Investment banking departments need to do underwritings for these large corporate clients, or they are not profitable. That means there is an inescapable tension within the brokerage firm between the investment banking side and the research side.

Because investment bankers need to do "deals" (i.e., bring out securities issues such as initial public offerings), naturally the firm's overall interests are best served if those stocks and bonds prove to be solid investments for the firm's clients. The firm's research analysts must make judgments on the available investment alternatives; they recommend those they think are best to the firm's brokers and clients through published reports and newsletters. A research analyst's job is complete only when he or she fully studies a company and its industry and makes *two* recommendations: when to buy and when to sell.

Unfortunately, individual investors almost never see a sell recommendation. Why? Sale advices are rarely published because of the negative impact they could have on the relationship between the brokerage firm and its investment banking clients. Think about these implications. Suppose that in January a brokerage firm brings to market a few million shares of a company called New-Issue Industries. The firm's brokers dutifully place the stock with clients and collect commissions. But suppose something goes awry in the company's affairs shortly after the offering is made: perhaps in March a competitor introduces a new widget or is acquired by a powerful conglomerate, or sales turn soft, or raw-material costs explode. The research analyst wants to point out the potential problem to brokers and clients, suggesting that the stock be sold.

But sell to whom? Most or nearly all awareness of the company is centered in the firm's own retail clients. How will the clients react if they bought in January and now in March are encouraged to sell because trouble lies ahead? At the least, they will suspect their brokers of churning their portfolios for commissions. At most, they may sue the brokerage firm over alleged misrepresentation or negligence.

What happens to the relationship between the investment banking department and the corporate officers at New-Issue Industries if the research department flashes the sell flag and the stock heads south? Future business between the firm and New-Issue Industries becomes highly unlikely. If word gets around the local business community that the brokerage firm recommends sales of stocks it brought public, other potential issuing companies are very likely to use a different underwriter for their upcoming issues.

For these reasons, the S-word is absent from the lexicon of most brokerage firms. It is considered a four-letter word; although institutional clients might hear that word over the phone, it does not appear in print.

There are several dimensions to the distaste for the word "sell," and one of the most important is the reluctance of a broker to activate the sale side of a security transaction. For that reason, consider any broker assistance a gift, and do not count on that help: brokerage houses almost never say "sell," so an investor needs to know the code words brokers use when they really mean "sell."

EUPHEMISMS

Other words for "sell," however, commonly do appear in the form of silence. Brokerage firms have devised a variety of ways to describe a corporate situation that indicates a sale is the best option. One of them is to write a report covering a corporate finance client, which is labeled a follow-up to the underwriting and carries no opinion or recommendation. Follow-ups need to be read closely. Even if the official policy is to give no recommendation, the tone of the report needs to be evaluated carefully. If it is less than glowing, suspect that the research analyst is not impressed with this stock and, while constrained from saying so, really thinks it should be sold.

Another approach is to give a recommendation other than buy that is kinder and gentler than sell. The best euphemism for sell, ironically, is its operative opposite: "hold." When an analyst does not want to say buy and is not allowed to say sell, the only option remaining is hold. *Consider hold almost always as a danger sign. In fact, "hold" really should generally be interpreted as meaning "do not hold."*

Common Brokerage Euphemisms for "Sell"

Hold

Accumulate
Long-term buy

Market performer
Market weight
Perform in line

Underperform
Underweight

Another way of saying sell is a carefully worded message like, "The stock is probably a worthwhile long-term holding despite some near-term uncertainties." That is translated by the cynic as, "If you hold for quite a while, maybe you will not lose." All these euphemisms are signals to cash in.

Make it a point to ask a broker about his firm's scale of rating words. For some very few it is "buy/hold." Others say "buy/accumulate/hold." Others may use words like "overperform/in-line/underperform" or perhaps "emphasize/underweight." Some even say "strong buy" as contrasted with "buy." Know the range of official analyst word choices. Anything less enthusiastic than the top choice should be interpreted as faint praise or outright damnation. If a broker does not verbally make a compelling case for the stock when the official advice is less than glowing, figure that the real message is to cash out your position.

POLITICS AND DIPLOMACY

Even when there is no current investment banking relationship between the issuing company and the brokerage firm, there are other important reasons research analysts are unlikely to advise a sale. First, there is the possibility of future business, so they do not want to poison the waters. And more immediately, the analyst needs to have the continuing, cordial, constructive, and prompt communication of senior management. Boston Chicken (now Boston Market), as reported by *The Wall Street Journal,* banned from future meetings an analyst who recommended selling its shares.

A sale recommendation, even if it is the correct conclusion, seldom warms up the company's management. They own shares themselves and so are never pleased by a price decline such as usually follows a sale advice. Also, the analyst may have legitimate reason to fear that an adverse recommendation might stifle management's future frankness of disclosures: the worst scenario is to recommend a sale that turns out wrong.

Finally, there is the numbers game. When an analyst writes a research report advising purchase, brokers can use that report to contact every customer whose investment objective makes the purchase of that stock appropriate. That means that a buy advice has a potentially wide audience. For example, suppose that a particular electric utility seems attractive to the analyst. The recommendation to buy can be presented to every client interested in income.

But a sale recommendation has much less business-generating potential. And a sale advice applies only to those clients who already own the stock (and to that tiny minority oriented to short selling). Suppose that our analyst now believes interest rates are about to rise or that fuel costs are a problem, and he decides to advise the sale of an electric company's shares. Perhaps only 1 in 10 clients acted on the idea when a buy was advised. These people are the only audience for the sale report. Worse than that, some clients may have bought at higher prices, and their brokers are hesitant to advise taking losses. So the sale report is not likely to be very effective in generating commissions. Research analysts are employed and compensated on the basis of the accuracy of judgment *and* on the amount of business their reports generate. So analysts have a buy bias too.

Brokers face another dilemma when making a sale recommendation. The investor tends to blame poor results more on a sale than on a buy. Ask any broker, Do clients remember bad buy advice given but not acted on, or do they recall a bad sell advice that was acted on? Overwhelmingly, scoreboard watchers watch the stocks they owned and sold—not those they never bought. That tendency can get brokers into trouble with their clients (and analysts into trouble with the brokers). Another way for a broker to get into even more trouble is to suggest redeploying the funds in another stock that goes down.

In summary, there are five ways a sale advice can backfire on a broker:

1. It can offend the client who is emotionally attached to the stock.
2. Selling can close out a painful transaction (a loss).
3. The sale can be followed by a price rally, which would have provided greater profit or a reduced loss if the stock had been held.
4. Funds liberated by the sale might be reinvested unprofitably, making the sale a double troublemaker.
5. Unless the sale price proves nearly perfect, the broker is resented for generating a commission by suggesting the action.

It is also worth noting here that penny-stock houses *never* recommend a sell unless it is to generate funds to buy something else. The major reason is that they themselves must buy what investors sell because they, virtually alone, make the market in the stock. And there is a parallel to guard against in non-penny brokerage practice as well. If an investor tells a broker to sell and the response is a pitch not to do so, this is a serious alarm signal. It may mean that the firm is concerned about the price and does not want to put pressure on the stock. Who would turn down an unsolicited sale order? Unless a broker gives solid, specific reasons to hold, insist on selling now, at the market.

The safest practice is never wait to hear sell advice. Assume it will not be heard, and plan to make personal selling-versus-holding decisions with the help of selling tools and rules that appear later in this book.

THE FALSE SECURITY OF LOW INITIAL RISK

It periodically becomes fashionable in investment marketing circles to emphasize avoidance of risk, particularly since the October 1987 crash. A balanced emphasis within the industry on risk avoidance—rather than on promising the moon in growth and profits—is healthy. That the investing public is taking this advice to heart is reflected by the noticeable decline in the number of well-known penny-stockbrokerage houses, so-called boiler rooms, and other similar operations that prey on investor gullibility, greed, and seemingly boundless optimism.

But even with the rebirth of emphasis on risk avoidance (which has receded somewhat in the great bull market of the mid-1990s), securities industry marketing efforts focus entirely on buying and virtually ignore the equally important second (selling) side of the transaction. In most public investment seminars, the selling aspect covered most often is the stop-loss order, but speakers rarely cover how and why to use this instrument adequately. Although stop-loss orders are useful, their routine use allows investors (and their brokers) to avoid confronting crucial selling decisions. Either a stop-loss order is triggered automatically or it is not activated at all, which neatly truncates the important selling thought-process. For brokers to advise using stop-loss orders routinely is also self-serving: if a client is stopped out of a losing position, the loss is relatively small, and use of these orders shows that the broker exercised diligence in trying to limit losses.

Of course, if stop-loss orders are placed too close to current prices, stops are triggered often; this increases turnover in the account for defensible reasons of caution but protects the client against possible major pre-commission capital loss in any one stock position.

Many investor seminars promise to highlight specific management techniques for protecting investor money to avoid risk. But "managing" is an active verb indicating an ongoing process. Managing a factory does not mean hiring workers, sending them through the door, and walking away. In the same way, managing invested funds means buying, watching, and selling. It consists of much more than an up-front, one-time allocation of assets or just a choice of purchases. Asset allocation—

among types of investment instruments, across industries, in world regions, and on a time horizon—is not a do-it-once activity. The strategies and tactics taught by many brokerage firms, however, merely list financial instruments rather than teaching specific, ongoing money-management techniques.

The lists usually consist of mutual funds, unit investment trusts (UITs), insurance, annuities, bonds, and stocks—none of which is a strategy or a tactic. They should be considered only the means by which to execute a strategy. Properly timed purchases *and sales* of these instruments are tactical actions. Of course, three of these six instruments are essentially one-decision (i.e., buy) investments: insurance, annuities, and UITs. Notice that not coincidentally these are packaged products created by financial institutions to be actively sold to the public. The broker is compensated at the start to get investors to buy, and there is no back-end action (selling or deliberate cashing in) built into the equation.

Generally, these six financial vehicles are properly described and positioned by the brokerage industry within economic cycles. But most brokerage seminars and reports focus only on identifying when a cycle is starting and how to take advantage of it by *buying* at the right time. So in the industry's eyes, managing and avoiding risk in the equities arena becomes a function of buying good stocks and selecting the right time to buy good stocks. What this nearsighted approach ignores is that risk is constantly present in varying degrees over time; managing investment risk must be an ongoing process that does not end when a purchase is made. Currently great companies cannot be guaranteed to remain so forever.

Before buying, therefore, assess all the opportunities and associated risks inherent in an investment package. Look at the upside and downside (seen and unseen) carefully. Then, shift focus after the purchase from the broad to the specific: the question "how?" becomes "which stock (among many) should be sold?" The notion that risk is avoided once a seemingly safe investment has been bought obfuscates the reality of future events.

Decision time for proactive entry into an investment is not the only juncture when risk is assumed or avoided. By now, the reader's awareness of the one-sidedness of investment marketing should serve to heighten sensitivity to the buy bias. Because greater external attention is always paid to buying, put more of your personal energy and work into selling. Although an investor can sit out an advised buy, once he owns an investment there is no way to call time out. The only way to end the game profitably is to sell.

UNDERESTIMATING THE SERIOUSNESS OF CHANGED FUNDAMENTALS

Today's institutional domination of the market and the increased leverage and fragility of the economy require that investors pay more attention to changed fundamentals than in gentler times past. Success now requires heightened attention to fundamental news about a company—and its industry and broader environment—when an investor owns its shares. If the news is less favorable than expected or if deterioration in the company's prospects is evident or suspected, the best action usually is to sell promptly. The reason is related to momentum: when things go wrong, it takes significant exertion of energy in the opposite direction to make them start going right again. That is true both in the management of the company's day-to-day business and also in the stock market.

In any speculative market, a snowball that starts going downhill tends to keep going. Prices swing emotionally from overvaluation to undervaluation. The extent of overshooting on each side is impossible to predict because it is driven by volatile emotions. So an investor's first job is to be smart enough to realize that the market gyrates and then to get out of the way before the pendulum swings adversely.

While stocks do not always accelerate in decline as a signal of having bottomed, it is true that an actual reversal to upside price action requires intervention by interested buyers. Such buyers must then be big enough and persistent enough first to stop the price decline and then to stabilize the price against the trickle of further selling that results from boredom. Finally, they must overpower sellers to push the stock's price higher.

STRATEGIES TO OVERCOME FUNDAMENTAL PROBLEMS

It is well known that running a business successfully takes a great deal of effort and attention. Few companies can be put on automatic pilot because external forces emerge or change, competitors enter the fray, or demand-side shifts require product or service changes. Management is paid to anticipate, monitor, and overcome difficulties to keep the enterprise moving ahead profitably. The same is true of investing in the stock market: the investor is paid for success in anticipating, monitoring, and acting. Those who merely react after trouble is obvious are paid badly or negatively.

The investor—as well as his money—is invested in the market. So he must be on guard to keep his hopes from overruling good judgment. This strongly indicates that an investor should read more than just the annual and quarterly reports; she should read the 10-Ks and the 10-Qs too. Study management's discussion of challenges and difficulties foreseen for the quarter or year ahead. Compare what happened against what management's earlier projections were. Compare the content and tone of current "outlook" statements against those of three or six months ago. Pay particular attention to unfavorable changes.

Remember that because of today's highly litigious climate, executives usually telegraph possible problems early on—to avoid being accused of withholding bad news. Listen to their warnings. If growth in revenue is slowing down or if margins are under pressure or costs are outrunning expansion, find out why. If management cannot identify causes, specific remedies cannot be taken—and that is a fundamental problem. Remember that problems seldom solve themselves.

For this reason, carefully examine what a company's executives say about their corporate problems and challenges. Look for discussion of solutions and actions, not excuses. Do not be readily forgiving; managements are paid to manage problems. If the president's report bemoans the fact that external forces are causing problems but offers no concrete corporate initiatives to reverse the difficulties, sell the stock. Fire this management team by selling the stock. Hire another team. Don't be patient when your money is on the line and in the hands of managers and directors who may be just drifting.

It is wiser to lean toward being overly harsh than overly forgiving. Be especially sensitive to the development of negative fundamentals. And paying attention just once a quarter, reading the interim report six weeks into the next quarter, is not enough. *If the price of liberty is eternal vigilance, the price of investment success is constant observation, evaluation, comparison, decisiveness, and a willingness to admit a mistake and move on.*

One undeniable reason to be up to date and relatively unforgiving is that institutions moving huge amounts of money into and out of stocks, unfortunately, have become very short-term oriented. Therefore, individual investors must be nimble enough to nip any potential investment problems in the bud. These smaller investors' inclination may be to give a company the benefit of a little more time to improve. But when a professional investor with a million shares gets impatient, share price will drop even if the patient, small investor later is proven correct about an eventual turnaround. Whether it seems right or wrong in a cosmic sense, developing impatience is actually a virtue for investors in our era of institutional trading domination.

It is apparent that taking losses quickly on important bad news or disturbing trends means falling into the pattern of short-term performance orientation. However, an investor must be realistic and do what is required to preserve capital. This willingness to be part of a growing short-term orientation if necessary falls under the broad banner of not fighting the tape. This approach means recognizing that while the market may be wrong in its approach, it is much bigger than an individual investor.

BUYING AND HOLDING, AND OTHER CONDITIONED BEHAVIORS

Investors buy stocks for a number of reasons, many of which are ill-advised. Purely from an investment perspective, there are only two reasons to buy common stocks. True equities investing consists of identifying those companies with undervalued stocks in terms of future earning power and buying them now because the projected earnings stream is expected to produce dividends. So the first objective is dividend income. The second objective is capital appreciation. Growth in price tends to occur over time if the fortunes of the underlying company improve, if interest rates do not move sharply higher, and if market psychology moves from negative to positive.

Some investment purists look down their noses and call the desire for capital appreciation "speculation." It may or may not be such, but investors buy stocks in order to sell them at a profit in the future, whether it be called intelligent speculation or investment. Whichever it is, to be successful a transaction requires both buying and selling. Both are required before the transaction's final result is established.

As stated in the introduction, overwhelmingly, published books dealing with stock market investing in any form focus on the buying transaction only and neglect the sell side of the equation almost completely. Selling may not be as exciting, and assuredly it is a narrower topic, but it is absolutely necessary and has its own very interesting twists and curiosities.

DIVIDEND INCOME

Investors who buy stocks for dividend income should consider the total package of risk and reward more carefully than most of them do. It is tempting to buy common stocks of companies in which the latest year's dividends represent a high percentage of the current stock price. The buyer believes that this high apparent yield will continue. What is often not fully considered is that the collective wisdom and expectations of all knowledgeable market players set current stock prices; therefore, an apparently high yield is usually a sign of high risk. So the buyer of a high-yield stock is accepting two risks: (1) that the dividend income itself may be reduced or stopped, and (2) that the stock's price might decline from the buyer's level if such an adverse dividend action occurs.

Almost continuously since the 1930s depression, common stocks have provided lower current (cash) yields than either long-term bonds or preferred stocks. In this environment, an investor requiring a high current yield should buy senior instruments. They are less likely than common shares to suffer reduced or omitted income payments, and they usually carry covenants promising to make up the withheld cash returns in the future if those events transpire.

If an income-oriented buyer has a serious need for current income, he should not take the incremental risk of common stock ownership; instead, he should stick to senior securities. Also, the buyer of common stocks for income should concentrate not on pure current cash income alone but rather on total return (referring to the sum of cash return plus realized or unrealized price appreciation). That appreciation, in turn, is caused by a rising level of dividends over the years. That rate of growth, expressed as a percentage per year, is added to the cash yield (dividend rate divided by stock price) to get total return. (See Tables 1–1 and 1–2.)

Thus, a stock currently yielding 7 percent with a dividend growth of 5 percent annually may, on average, be expected to provide a total return of 12 percent per

TABLE 1–1

Calculation of Annual Total Percentage Return on Investment
(pre-tax; assumes dividend raised 5 percent at year-end meeting)

Year End	Div Rate $	Yield Basis %	Price $	Cap Incr $	Total $ Retn	Total % Retn	Return on Orig Cost	
							Total %	Cash %
0 (Buy)	1.40	7.00	20.00					
1	1.47	7.00	21.00	1.00	2.40	12.0	12.0	7.0
2	1.54	7.00	22.05	1.05	2.52	12.0	12.6	7.3
3	1.62	7.00	23.15	1.10	2.65	12.0	13.2	7.7
4	1.70	7.00	24.31	1.16	2.78	12.0	13.9	8.1
5	1.79	7.00	25.53	1.22	2.92	12.0	14.6	8.5
6	1.88	7.00	26.80	1.28	3.06	12.0	15.3	8.9
7	1.97	7.00	28.14	1.34	3.22	12.0	16.1	9.4
8	2.07	7.00	29.55	1.41	3.38	12.0	16.9	9.8
9	2.17	7.00	31.03	1.48	3.55	12.0	17.7	10.3
10	2.28	7.00	32.58	1.55	3.72	12.0	18.6	10.9
Total:	18.49			12.58	31.07	Average: 15.5		8.8

TABLE 1–2

Calculation of Annual Total Percentage Return on Investment
(pre-tax; assumes dividend constant at 10 percent of purchase price)

Year End	Div Rate $	Yield Basis %	Price $	Cap Incr $	Total $ Retn	Total % Retn
0 (Buy)	1.40	10.0	14.00			
1	1.40	10.0	14.00	0.00	1.40	10.0
2	1.40	10.0	14.00	0.00	1.40	10.0
3	1.40	10.0	14.00	0.00	1.40	10.0
4	1.40	10.0	14.00	0.00	1.40	10.0
5	1.40	10.0	14.00	0.00	1.40	10.0
6	1.40	10.0	14.00	0.00	1.40	10.0
7	1.40	10.0	14.00	0.00	1.40	10.0
8	1.40	10.0	14.00	0.00	1.40	10.0
9	1.40	10.0	14.00	0.00	1.40	10.0
10	1.40	10.0	14.00	0.00	1.40	10.0
	14.00			0.00	14.00	

year. Actual results vary as the company's fortunes change and, significantly, as the level of prevailing interest rates shifts. Major capital gains can be achieved with the use of conservative instruments such as utility common stocks and growth-oriented real estate investment trusts (REITs) in periods when interest rates are declining. In contrast, even the best in quality among utility and REIT shares decline, in some cases severely, in the face of higher interest rates.

Most investors in quality blue chips, and especially in utility shares, consider themselves long-term holders. But because of the major influence that interest-rate cycles exert on stock prices, even blue chip stocks bought primarily for income also should be viewed as subject to sale to capture capital appreciation. (For example, a move from 6 percent to 7 percent in long-term interest rates is a 17 percent change in the valuation equation's divisor, which will swamp one or two years' dividend increases.) So, even for those investors whose stated strategy is a long-term "buy and hold," our subject of selling should not be given ostrich treatment. Knowing how to sell is an imperative discipline sooner or later.

CAPITAL APPRECIATION

As indicated earlier, the other legitimate reason for buying a stock is a prognostication that it will rise in price and thereby reward holders via appreciation in capital value. Some purists argue that any basis for expecting rising value other than higher dividends amounts to the greater-fool theory. Others say that hoping to capture a swing in psychology or interest rates in order to increase a stock's price amounts to speculation because such gains are not driven purely by increased earnings and dividend streams from the company. Suffice to say that very significant rises in price beyond what is driven by dividend streams *do* in fact take place, so capturing those increases is a legitimate subject for investor study and effort.

OTHER REASONS

Some people buy stocks for other reasons. For example, loyalty induces many investors to buy stock in the company for which they work or shares in a major employer in the community in which they live. But "loyalty buys" can result in major investment losses because there is a tendency for loyalty to override common sense and, therefore, to prevent timely sales.

Other market players buy a stock because of a perceived affiliation with the members of management or because they like the products offered by the company. These purchase decisions usually are not driven or timed on a price/value basis; they are not driven by the profit motive.

Other stock purchases are made because of excitement about some concept. In many cases, either the purchaser is ignorant of investment values and just feels good about owning a company that is involved in the subject business (environmental protection, humane research on new drugs, and AIDS are forward-looking businesses), or he has purchased this stock to feel trendy. There are also many people who buy stocks for the thrill of participation in the game. They play the market because it is socially acceptable to do so. Or they believe the market can generate the desired thrills and emotional drama of gambling—but legally and over a longer period of time before their money runs out.

A few psychologists who specialize in patients' money problems even find that some investors participate on Wall Street for deep-seated emotional reasons. Among the darker ones are self-destructive urges and a need to prove oneself to an approval-withholding parent, or even an Oedipal need to compete with father. Such problems lie well outside our intended range of discussion.

Finally, whether their conditioning is external or self-imposed, some investors really should be called collectors. These are people who gradually accumulate a variety of stocks over a period of years. But being a collector of stocks is similar to being a pack rat: it is most unlikely that a confirmed practitioner of either art can be reformed. Western society emphasizes acquiring things, not disposing of them. This conditioning supports a buy-and-hold bias.

Financial writers, advisors, mutual-funds advertisements, and brokers all constitute powerful external forces focused on buying. This emphasis is perhaps understandable, but it needs balance. Equal attention to selling—which is necessary to nailing down all profits—is required.

The balance of this book, then, is devoted to assisting investors who buy stocks for financial reasons. No remedy is offered to those who participate mainly for sentimental or psychological reasons. This book's goal is to provide guidelines about how to cash in profits when appropriate and to limit or prevent losses. A major emphasis is placed on understanding and overcoming the inertia that causes holding rather than selling.

2

Hidden Reasons
We Resist Selling

KEYS TO INVESTMENT SUCCESS

- Understand Subtle but Strong Psychological Impediments
- Learn and Implement the Difficult 180-Degree Reversal
- Battle Perfectionism
- Stop Trying to Protect Your Ego; Focus on Your Capital

Chapter 1 cataloged external influences that work against investors' selling their holdings. Those forces may not disappear from our lives just because they have been named, but at least they are readily recognizable when present. We can see and consciously work to neutralize such very visible enemies. Much more challenging are the numerous subtle psychological forces acting within our heads. Each investor is influenced by a different combination of these subconscious drives and motivations, which vary in intensity as well. At the risk of appearing to practice pop psychology, this chapter explores significant things going on inside our heads and our personalities. By identifying these forces, we can better understand why we feel as we do and why our first instincts in certain situations point us toward actions, or inertia, that can prove counterproductive in our investing lives.

Many insightful volumes have been written on human emotion and behavior; it is not the place of this one to attempt a comprehensive psychological examination of investor behavior, not least because your author is not formally trained in that field. A few works providing useful exploration into the psychology of investing are listed in the Appendix. Our attempt in this chapter will be to expose at a very high level those most central and overriding patterns in our human personalities that strongly influence investment action and inaction. Significantly, many of these appear to affect the selling side of investing considerably more than the buying side. That is why understanding and dealing with these mysteries inside our heads is such an important ingredient in becoming more successful at selling stocks well.

PAIN AND PLEASURE

Considerable agreement exists across various schools of psychological thought that humans are primarily engaged in finding ways to decrease their amount of pain and raise their amount of pleasure; however, those concepts need to be defined in greater detail. As testimony to how central this is, pain avoidance and pleasure or comfort-seeking are familiar concepts that certainly dominate marketing and advertising. While numerous other forces are undeniably at work as investors face decisions about selling, comfort-seeking and pain avoidance are extremely powerful.

At a most obvious level, it might be observed that making a profit represents pleasure, while suffering a loss equates to feeling pain (at least for all except masochists and neurotics). But our interest here is focused on a deeper layer in which forces that dispose us to certain attitudes and behaviors spring from our subconscious pain-avoidance and comfort-seeking tendencies.

WHY HOLDING FEELS RIGHT

Once we own a particular stock, inaction (holding) keeps us in or certainly closer to our zone of comfort than does taking action to change our circumstances (selling). Holding keeps us close to our past, to memories and feelings we cherish. Many investors hold stock in companies whose fortunes peaked years or even decades ago and cannot seem to explain why they resist selling despite obviously dim prospects for future recovery or gain. Maybe grandfather worked for the company, or we grew up in a town where it supported many families or sponsored the softball team. Perhaps ages ago we made a profit, or at least had a good paper profit for a while, in this old stock. Or our parents always spoke well of the company or confided they had made a small fortune in its shares at one time. Thus, nostalgic feelings surround the stock and we find it very difficult to end our association.

Without necessarily being rooted in the deep past, our positive association with a particular stock creates a bonded feeling. We have made a "good" profit (even if on a compounded basis the return is unspectacular, the total dollar or point difference feels pleasant), and so this stock is our friend. Held for a number of years, it has been virtually adopted as a family member. Thus, our primary inclination is not to sever such ties and terminate this comfortable relationship. "Why end a good thing?" we think at an unconscious and perhaps also at a conscious level. Being with, rather than without, that stock represents staying in a comfort zone.

Selling means deliberately walking outside that zone, which represents taking a risk, as summed up in a popular phrase about devils we know versus those we don't know.

In a world moving ever faster, in which technology both amazes and scares us and in which we've lost such pillars of security as lifetime employment expectations and permanently nurturing families, we look for and prize any anchors against the storm. Great (often, growth) companies whose stocks have treated us well and whose products and properties we see frequently act as a psychological bedrock to which we can hold firmly. We strongly resist as heretical any suggestion that such stocks ever be sold. No matter that they may have become grossly overvalued in a recent bull craze, or that perhaps their fundamental greatness is actually starting to fade, or that in a new competitive environment the company may survive and continue providing its service or product but at much-reduced profit. We cling to our old favorites no matter their current merit. From the late 1980s into the early 1990s, computer stocks (especially IBM) held such a power over their shareowners, despite a rapid sea change in technology, marketing, pricing, and other profit factors. But investors held IBM as a matter of nearly religious conviction due to its past merits (institutions held 50 percent when IBM earnings started declining in 1986 and held 50 percent in late 1993 when the stock bottomed below $40, down some 75 percent). In developing a mind-set to enable selling stocks successfully, meaning when the time is right, investors must battle against nostalgia and this tendency to cling to old lighthouses.

The common expression "what's wrong with this picture?" is one that refers to the psychological concept of cognitive dissonance. Here, a person is experiencing discomfort (and so may behave in strange ways) because new information and perceptions bring conflict with what has long and strongly been known or assumed as true. A spouse betrays our sacred bond of trust; an idol is accused of a terrible crime; a trusted teacher or clergy member is revealed as a pedophile. Our nicely ordered world crumbles in such circumstances, and our first response is to deny it could be possible. We seek to avoid dealing with this terrible new revelation. In investing, we wish that every tree planted in our portfolio should grow forever skyward. Alas, in reality it will not be so. But holding on to existing positions in defiance of newly introduced information enables us to avoid dealing with dissonance: what we choose to ignore might happily go away rather than hurt us. We would rather live with that questionable hope, or turn away altogether, than face the harsh truth that things have changed and we need to sell as a result.

WHY SELLING FEELS UNCOMFORTABLE

Selling requires of us a significant change in our thinking—indeed a complete reversal! When we bought that stock, its prospects were wonderful, and it represented value and opportunity. Now, whether our investment has since done well or faltered, choosing to sell represents adopting a 180-degree opposite stance. Issuing that order to liquidate means that what we once thought was correct now is no longer so in our minds. This company is no longer underpriced, or its prospects are not what we earlier imagined or expected. Or perhaps we have given up on its price/earnings ratio growing as we had earlier expected.

To say "sell" means that either what we once thought was right is no longer so and/or that maybe we've already been on the wrong side of the market for some time and are now admitting a change in opinion is warranted. Either way, selling is like saying we now believe what we earlier thought is no longer true. Most of us have great difficulty admitting we were wrong. If you place a very strong value on reputation or esteem in life, the reversal of position inherent in selling is likely to be an especially difficult battle zone for your ego and your comfort. Reversing a position is made more difficult if we have publicly or strongly espoused it. This is a very important reason for keeping our investment holdings secret: reversing ourselves and selling then involves no loss of face with others who have known our prior opinion.

As the old century turns to a new one, we live in a time of high expectations driven in part by ubiquitous computers and the rising speed of communications. Precision is possible and increasingly expected; we can all be monitored and our human fallibility documented and used against us. Time is telescoped, and we have become impatient with any delay or error. Seemingly everyone is suing someone else over anything that has gone wrong. We would like to require perfection just as it is expected of us. In our work lives we function in an environment that demands zero defects and expects immediate paybacks. Our children and grandchildren simply must gain entrance to that one best preschool or their lives will be on a path to ruin. Our favorite professional sports team is labeled a failure for not repeating as world champion. Perfectionism is that disease in our minds working to deny us enjoying any good or pleasure because it may not last forever.

Perfectionism makes us recoil from the decisions involved in selling our investments. Perfectionism makes avoiding such choices, and therefore holding by default, the least uncomfortable course of action. You know, both in terms of actual probabilities and as a matter of many experiences, that when you sell you will not receive the top price. That stock's very next tick, its closing price today or tomorrow, a possible piece of good news months hence, or a bull market three years ahead can easily bring a higher price than where you will sell at this moment. Thus, you feel doomed to being "wrong" sooner or later when you sell. By selling, we expose ourselves to yet another instance in which we can be proved less than perfect, in which we again stamp ourselves as fallible human beings. We feel pressure, either from our external world and/or from ourselves, to avoid such negative feedback, such failure labeling. Therefore, we tend to shun selling, which clearly sets a result as final (we gained or lost just so much, but we may well soon see that a higher price than ours was possible).

Buying represents the opening of possibilities of great things. Buying represents open-endedness; continued holding maintains such hope for gain and pleasure (or, when we have a paper loss, hope for recovery and the righting of a temporary wrong). Selling carries a finality with it because, by definition, it closes the book or ends the game and establishes a final score. We prefer to have our options open rather than foreclosed, to retain chances for improvement and betterment rather than to know that the verdict is sealed and no chance for change exists. We have great difficulty coming to closure since it cuts off further possibilities; it ends hope for any better outcome. Closure includes such experiences as cleaning out great-grandmother's attic; graduating and leaving school and friends; acknowledging a failed marriage by concluding a divorce; burying a dear friend or loved one; seeing winter come; leaving a company; retiring and therefore wrapping up business. Those are heavy and sad passages, so we resist voluntarily creating any closure experiences that we have power to avoid.

Holding keeps our options open, while selling clearly brings closure. (With surprising myopia, we ignore the fact that once we sell a stock we can just as easily repurchase it. Viewing repurchase as a very real antidote to our revulsion against closure, however, raises visions of again going through that agonizing process of reversing our opinion by 180 degrees, which is painful for all the reasons just given.) So we hold rather than sell because, at the very least, holding postpones coming to closure. Many a bad stock is held (into an uncertain yet not hopeless future) with palpable likelihood of further financial loss because the (presently avoidable) emotional cost of coming to closure is perceived as so heavy. Investors pay in dollar losses to avoid emotional pain from a closure process; often, as losses get worse, they will later need to pay a higher price in both lost dollars and eventual pain by imposing self-punishment over major mistakes. Selling as representing closure is a powerful deterrent, one requiring both strong will and courage to overcome.

BEHAVIOR PATTERNS THAT PROTECT FRAGILE EGOS

Holding protects our egos in several ways. When we continue to hold a stock that shows a profit, that portfolio position remains conveniently available to stroke us. We are smart; we are getting rich; we knew enough to hold through that nasty price correction and see a better day. Owning a good stock is having a rich wine cellar, owning a prestigious home, driving the right car, surrounding ourselves with beautiful artworks. A stock that is up makes us feel good. When it goes part way back down, we focus more on the remaining paper gain rather than the lost opportunity. A stock that is up strokes our egos. Holding it makes a good deal more subconscious emotional sense than pushing it away by selling.

Then there are stocks in which we have paper losses. Surprisingly, holding rather than selling these *also* makes us feel better. This is because of that closure baggage noted earlier. To sell a loser is to admit defeat and our human fallibility and to close off any possibility of later vindication or reward. If we sell what is down, it cannot recover for us, and we might actually compound our first mistake (should it rise) by having both bought high *and* sold low! So we preserve hope of ultimately being a winner and feeling better by holding. An objective, updated assessment of this stock's prospects may provide little to encourage optimism (in fact, by being down, the market price is declaring exactly that as indeed the current verdict of most investors). But we can hope for some healing, or perhaps a major miracle, as long as we hold: we can wait to see what comes next, and, if that is not satisfactory, we can wait some more to see what comes next after that.

To sell, we must be able to tear down any protective shields we've erected around our ego and stand the consequences of our actions and decisions. One of the worst aspects of losing in the stock market is that it reflects on our thinking. A loss not only leaves us poorer but also makes us feel foolish, stupid, or, at best, perhaps seriously inadequate to the game. Holding is less painful.

Quite a few books have been written on the subject of fear: fear of losing (failure) and, perhaps surprisingly, fear of success (winning). Clearly, keeping the issue open by holding rather than selling postpones any verdict and thus puts off fear (of either failure or success) to some undefined future time. In a nutshell, it appears that fear of success is related to at least two things: (1) some Freudians say that, to the male, great success represents bettering and thus replacing one's father, and (2) perhaps at a less complicated and threatening level, a great success sets a high standard that we may fear we can never again achieve. Thus, selling at a great profit may be a scary thing to do. Holding will allow our gain to run or at least will not officially set a new lifetime record we may never again equal. Thus, if fear either of failure or of success is a factor, holding works better for us than does selling.

A LOOK AHEAD

This chapter has surfaced some of the often subconscious or even unconscious psychological reasons why investors seem naturally to prefer holding over selling their investments. It is important, as part of the process of becoming a more successful investor by selling better, to recognize and understand these hidden drivers of our thinking and behaviors. The next chapter exposes some of the symptomatic rationalizations that investors exhibit, in effect acting out and justifying their often irrational predisposition to holding at any cost rather than selling. If you see some aspects of your own behavior there, now you will both know whence that stuff comes and be better equipped to battle against it. Success in investing is indeed a battle, and selling is a more challenging arena than buying. But your newfound knowledge will bring power to help you prevail!

3

Internal Rationalizations

KEYS TO INVESTMENT SUCCESS

- Overcome Commission Phobia
- Overcome Tax Phobia
- Overcome Specialist Phobia (a.k.a. Stop-Order Phobia)
- Avoid Holding with a Death Grip
- Be Careful of Wishful Thinking

COMMISSION PHOBIA

Most analysts hear the lament that investors balk at taking brokers' advice for suspicion their motives are driven by the prospect of earning more commissions. Frankly, most commission phobia is a smokescreen that is as dangerous to potential investor profit as it is illogical.

First, look at the logic of commission phobia. Like taxes, commissions are neither a surprise nor a rules change in midgame; therefore, paying them cannot logically be a valid objection at the time of sale. There is no way to sell stock without paying commissions except in a handful of very limited exit environments:

- The company receives a tender offer, so shares are sold for a net cash payment to the soliciting buyer, via its agent.
- The company conducts a share-buyback tender (a self-tender) in which some or all shares can be sold for a net cash price directly to the company.

- The company can purchase investor shares directly if the position is small (usually an odd lot). Sometimes firms solicit repurchases by mail.
- Company liquidation occurs, in which common holders receive a net cash payment.
- One individual can sell a stock certificate directly to another individual (perhaps within a family) through a transfer agent by endorsing the back of the certificate.

There is one other way to avoid commissions: if the stock becomes worthless due to bankruptcy and common holders get nothing, some brokerage firms buy back the stock certificates for a nominal price. This creates a transaction for tax purposes. In the absence of such a transaction, investors need to amend their tax returns for the year in which the stock actually became defunct and worthless. This extreme case is a wonderful example of how an investor can be penny-wise and pound-foolish about paying commissions to cash in; it is much better to pay the exit fee and sell at a partial loss before a stock goes to zero.

Commissions are more visible in stocks, commodities, and options than in most other products or services because securities prices are publicly quoted in newspapers, on quotation machines, and on television. Investors pay commissions to trade these vehicles as a way of rewarding the time or expertise of the people who actually do the trading for them. When other products are purchased, commissions are paid, but they are built into the purchase price. In fact, in percentage terms, built-in commissions for goods such as cars, shoes, or washing machines usually are immensely higher than Wall Street stock commissions.

Investors who purchase prepackaged products from brokers, say, front-loaded mutual funds, typically pay from 4.5 percent to 8 percent in commissions. Buy $10,000 in a "load" mutual fund, and only $9,200 to $9,550 is working for the client; the rest is commission. Cancel a variable annuity contract, and the exit fee is similar. These percentages are much higher than the typical 1 percent or 2 percent charged on stocks.

Investors most commonly display commission phobia when their investment has gone down, has done nothing, or has gone up so little that its tiny price gain is more than wiped out by round-trip commissions. When their money is doubled or when XYZ Worldwide Conglomerate creates a sudden gain by proposing a takeover of the company, investors seldom, if ever, complain about commissions. That shows why commission phobia is a smokescreen; it masks investors' pain at admitting to a mistake that caused a loss.

One fairly legitimate complaint about commissions, however, is the widespread gap between retail rates and how much big institutional investors pay per share to play the same game. The retail/institutional commission gap is even more upsetting when individual investors lose money. Although the hurt is painful when the buying decision was their own, commission phobia is most intense when the pain can be blamed on a bad purchase made on a broker's advice.

EFFECTIVE COMMISSION STRATEGIES

A possible remedy for retail investors is commission discounting, with due respect to account executives and their employing firms who need to make a living.

Formula-Based Commissions

One strategy is to negotiate commissions on a formula basis with the account executive. On the buying side, a full commission is paid when the broker presents an idea the client buys. When the client makes his own selections without service or information provided by the broker, some discount is arguably in order.

At selling time, if the trade results in a gain, the client should pay the full standard commission without complaint. If there is a loss, a two-tiered discount arrangement can work: the deepest allowable discount should be provided if the broker suggested the purchase; if the buy was the customer's idea, a smaller discount (maybe half the deepest allowable) is granted as a consolation/courtesy and as a psychological inducement to cashing in and moving on. This strategy works best with a small or regional brokerage firm; leading firms tend to be less flexible, except with large customers.

If an investor and his or her broker mutually agree to such a deal in advance, the commission problem usually can be eliminated. When clients continue to complain about commissions, however, it is then clearly a smokescreen to avoid making the decision to take a loss and move on.

Discount Firms

Besides failing to trade when it is expedient or negotiating routine broker discounts, investors also can limit commissions by moving the account to a discount firm. But in doing this, they give up access to research and a listening ear. Without taking sides on the sticky question of discount versus full-service brokerage firms' merits, it is clearly accurate that reducing commissions can be an important way of limiting the "cost" of changing one's mind. When that problem is addressed, full attention can be devoted to the primary issue: which way the stock is likely to move next. For those disposed to utilizing discount brokers, the American Association of Individual Investors (AAII) (see Appendix for address and telephone number) provides a valuable reference in the annual January issue of its Journal, which contains a comprehensive listing of discount brokerage firms and their rates. (See also Table 3–1.)

The one instance when a brokerage client should indeed worry about avoid-

TABLE 3–1

Listing of Discount Brokers
Charging Flat Fees under $30 per Trade

Firm	Flat Rate	Telephone
Brown & Company	$29.00	800–776–6062
Ceres Securities, Inc.	18.00	888–800–9311
CompuTel Securities	28.00	800–432–0327
E-Trade Securities	14.95	800–786–2575
Freedom Investments	25.00	800–221–1660
Pacific Brokerage Services	25.00	800–421–8395
Prestige Status Inc.	28.95	800–782–8871
Regal Discount	29.00	800–786–9000
Wall Street Equity	15.00	800–321–4877
Washington Discount Frequent	25.00	800–843–9601

Note: Rates shown were accurate as of mid-1996; some additional costs such as transfer/setup charges and inactivity fees may be imposed, and schedules may change over time. Check current rate card carefully before opening any account.

ing commissions is when a broker solicits a sale for the purpose of freeing funds to make another purchase. This is not churning per se, but it is an attempt to do two trades where one would do. And this sale generally is not suggested on fundamental or timing merits; it is only a means to enable another transaction and so may be justified on the basis of boredom or possibly greener pastures.

Most often, however, investors should ignore commissions and sell when the time is right because unwillingness to pay a commission in order to exit a losing situation is a self-defeating game. Unless the investor is dealing in a very small block of stock, the sale commission is likely to be a lot less than a point per share. If the stock is going nowhere or, worse yet, is going down, a commission saved by refusing to cash in is minuscule compared with the capital loss suffered by holding the stock.

Keep in mind that the capital losses resulting from holding too long include opportunity costs. Suppose a lazy stock is going nowhere—perhaps a utility with stagnant dividends. Resentfully, the investor refuses to sell because of the exit commission. The proposed replacement may have been a much better utility whose dividend is rising perhaps 5 percent a year and whose stock price appreciates as a result. In this case, refusal to pay a sale commission is very costly. Although these costs tend to be invisible compared with losses recorded on Schedule D, the effects of invisible and self-inflicted losses are, nevertheless, very real. Many investors might be persuaded to pay a small commission to take a loss if they focused on this: *a stock at a loss is worth its price plus one-third of its paper loss (the combined tax benefit) if sold, but only its current price if retained.*

TAX PHOBIA

However investors view the social, economic, or budgetary results of eliminating favorable tax treatment of long-term capital gains, the Tax Reform Act of 1986 had at least one positive result: it removed an artificial excuse for not selling stocks.

Until the Act legally erased the distinction between long- and short-term gains, many investors used the tax incentive to hold stocks for the long term as a justification for not selling. Unless an extremely large gain was involved and/or unless the time remaining to the start of long-term status was very short (thus decreasing the likely risk of losing paper gains), these reasons for not selling were foolhardy. But oversensitivity to tax treatment was nearly a religion for many market participants.

The converse of the hold-for-long-term-treatment philosophy on gains, of course, would have been a rule that investors should absolutely always sell a losing position before it went long term. As an arbitrary discipline, such an operating rule would have proven quite valuable as a capital preserver for many investors. However, this rubric seldom was observed, tending to prove that selective (i.e., one-sided) attention to the long-term-gain rule was more a psychological rationalization for postponing sale decisions than a useful tax-minimizing strategy.

Unfortunately, the existence of federal and state taxation on securities gains remains a stumbling block for investors even now that the distinction between long and short term has been eliminated. Objectively, this reason for not selling may appear to be illogical, but experience suggests that tax phobia is still very real to many investors.

Granted no one likes to pay taxes; but paying taxes on capital gains and on such taxable investment income as dividends and interest is a reality for all investors. It is not a surprise. Nor is it an unfair mid-game change of rules. Therefore, it is illogical to balk at selling a stock at a gain just because the transaction triggers a tax liability. There are only three logical extensions of refusing to take a gain on a stock to avoid paying income taxes. The investor must have bought the stock in the hope:

1. Of losing money (federal taxes are reduced 28 cents for only a dollar lost).
2. That the stock's price would not change.
3. That the stock would be held for the remainder of the buyer's life.

The first two alternatives are nonsensical and deserve no further comment. Despite tax reform, the third reason is a clever tax dodge because a legatee's basis is stepped up to the value on the date of the decedent's death. So an investor can "enjoy" the big loophole only by dying with capital gains unrealized. What a clever way to finally beat Washington!

The objection to paying income taxes due on realizing a gain is just another rationalization for not making a sale decision; it is especially appealing to the rationalizer because it is conveniently external to self. It can be blamed on "them," on the government, or on the "system." Most other excuses for not selling also reveal logical or psychological investor weaknesses.

TAX STRATEGIES

Income-oriented investors consciously choose among their alternatives: tax-free municipals and taxable interest or dividend generators are evaluated with advance attention paid to after-tax yields. (The tax-adjusted current yield and yield to maturity can be known in advance in the case of fixed-income instruments.)

In contrast, in the case of common stocks bought for capital appreciation, the tax outcome has to be imagined because it cannot be quantified. Therefore, an exact calculation of after-tax return is not made in advance. Because no calculation is made, the exercise of subtracting projected taxes is, conveniently in a psychological sense, omitted. But the future obligation is, nonetheless, real.

Although taxes are not avoidable, they are postponable—another pitfall for investors who complain about taxes. That postponability carries a chance at self-empowerment. Is beating the system a source of private satisfaction that gets in the way of rational investment action? The reality is that the price/timing of a sale decision should be made regardless of tax timing. The best time to sell a stock is at its highest price point; the next best time is as close to that point as possible. The best of all tax situations is to incur huge tax obligations, which accrue only from earning an extremely large capital-gains income.

Maximum profit should be the goal of every transaction made by every trader and investor, so taxes should be paid cheerfully when due. Remember, also, that the amount of profit *desired* before or after tax on a given stock position is irrelevant. The amount of profit realistically allowed by the market is a better criterion for timing a sale. Similarly, the amount of profit an investor can keep is always defined as the after-tax amount, so learn to live with that reality. Ten points is, of its nature, 10 points before taxes.

With the long-term tax distinction gone, at least half of the crutch for the nonseller has been removed. Investors must battle to remove the rest of this rationalization.

SPECIALIST PHOBIA (a.k.a. STOP-ORDER PHOBIA)

One popular objection to the use of stop-sell orders is that they tip off the specialist to investor intention and so become self-defeating. In this section, that argument is examined and laid firmly to rest. There certainly is one case in which a stop-order given in advance to the specialist affects the market. But that is only when the stock position to be sold is so large that it represents a significant percentage of an average day's trading volume. The solution is not to withhold any selling order; the answer is to avoid buying so large a position in the first place or to sell off the holdings in a series of smaller pieces.

The Overinflated Ego

Try never to get into the I'm-too-big-to-get-out bind because, in effect, the investor who says this looks like he is not ever planning to sell the stock. If he buys so much he is later too wide for the exit door, he will become a collector—he is neither an investor nor a trader.

Stock collectors—people who buy but never sell—inevitably defeat themselves because they usually end up with a long list of stale losers and eventually run out of cash. They are effectively out of the game and stuck with the sour results of past buying decisions. In most cases, as time goes on, the original reasons for buying either do not drive the price to the desired selling point or the reasons fail to work out altogether. Short of legacy at death, there are just two other possible exits for a trader or investor who accumulates a position too big to get out of: the takeover and tender offer (or the subcategory, the Dutch Auction repurchase offer). If an investor is big enough to accumulate a too-large block in advance of a takeover event, either he is dealing in inside information, or he is already wealthy enough to forgo reading books for investment advice.

Most dispassionate observers would suggest that the my-order-is-too-big syndrome is really just a disguised excuse. Most likely it is the product of an inflated ego and/or an overactive imagination. It tends to reflect the mind-set of a trader never satisfied unless he grabs the last eighth on every move.

Or it can reflect a market player who is actually involved more with the excitement and action of watching the market and thinking about making decisions than with that all-important goal of taking profits in a systematic way without the burdensome intrusion of emotion, second guessing, or looking back. Finally, of course, taking a too-big position might reflect subtle planning for a rationalization that will forestall closure.

The Persecution Complex

Another mind-set that masks making excuses is also worth noting. There are investors and traders who have a persecution complex about the market (and often about much of life). For these people, the market is a very personal struggle of the hapless individual against the world. They expect to be less than satisfied every time they take action—and every time they do not take action.

They also view market mistakes not as failures of their own logic or as examples of bad luck but rather as traps that were set specifically for them. The specialist system on the exchanges fits their world view of conspiracy. These investors know there is a person on the exchange floor who is privileged to see many future orders for a stock. They ask in horror why they should play the game with such a trader and let him take care of their personal interests when the game seemingly is so obviously rigged.

Stop-Order Strategies

However, the mechanics of the exchange floor should be examined to understand just how likely it is, in reality, that an order will tip the buy-sell balance to work against an individual investor. The alternative tactic, of course, is to stay ever at the ready with quote machine and telephone at hand, and surprise the market with an order when the designated price is actually hit.

First, it is not advisable to enter any stop-limit sell order at a round number or at a full dollar. This positions an investor with the crowd; a stampede could develop at the round dollar level. Any stop without a limit might in 20/20 hindsight result in a bad execution; a stop-limit could result in no execution at all if the investor is back in the line.

For example, if the selling price target on a stock is $50 per share, place the sell-stop an eighth or a quarter lower. Similar advice applies to any full dollar: instead of 18, use $17^7/_8$, for example. If the target is a half-dollar level, put the order in at an eighth lower, for example, at $7^3/_8$ rather than $7^1/_2$.

The guiding philosophy is this: if an investor believes that he is sharp enough to call the high on a stock's move accurately, he ought to be so concerned about getting out for sure that he would sacrifice a small amount per share as insurance against the slight chance that he is a bit off in his calculations or that perhaps some others are equally smart. He should be out in this case, instead of still in and sorry for insisting on that eighth or quarter.

The only way an order above the market can affect the price is if it is so large it scares away buyers who are so tactically active that they happen to ask about it at just the right moment. In listed stocks, the specialist on the exchange floor holds the GTC (good 'til canceled) stop-sell (and all other) orders in his book and exercises them as market orders when they are touched off. The book is not disclosed to floor traders except in a very limited manner.

The best (highest) bid and the best (lowest) asked prices are disclosed, along with the sizes of the total orders at those levels, on electronic quotation machines. These and only these quotes and sizes are also named by the specialist to inquiring brokers standing at the trading post. But an order at a price away from the best market (even an eighth away) is never disclosed until the moment it becomes part of the best next offer (to sell) or bid (to buy).

And even in this case, remember that the market is a big game with many players. Except in very thinly traded issues, it is highly unlikely that one individual investor's order will be the only order on the book at any given time. When he is trying to sell 500 or 1,000 shares at 24³/₈, there may be another 20,000 shares for sale at that price and probably a similar number to buy at 24¹/₄.

Suppose that the investor buys 500 shares of XYZ at 19 and targets a sale price of 24¹/₂. Following the earlier suggestion to avoid 50-cent multiples, he places a sell-stop order on 500 shares at 24³/₈. If the stock does trade up as high as 24³/₈, his order immediately becomes a market order (without limit) to sell.

Today, the stock is finally approaching his price. It is up, say, a quarter at 24 even. The market tone remains firm. The specialist's book shows 1,000 shares bid for at 23⁷/₈ and 600 offered for sale at 24¹/₈. That is the quote he provides to floor traders, and that is all. The specialist says, "23⁷/₈ by 4¹/₈, 10 by 6." He does not mention that there is a bid for 7,500 down at 23¹/₂, or that 1,200 are waiting to be sold at 24¹/₄ or that our investor has 500 for sale at 24³/₈. None of these orders are relevant yet, and so none are disclosed until they become the best orders. So our investor's order does not show until it is just an eighth or a quarter away from the last trade. Only when that time comes does his order start to show as the next limit sell order above the market.

Incidentally, he is in an advantageous position if he exercised the discipline of placing that order some time ago, such as, perhaps, when he bought the stock. Why? Stop-orders and stop-limit-orders are lined up on a first-come, first-served basis. So the longer our order has been in place, the earlier it stands in line, and the sooner it becomes a market order in the trading sequence. If our trader's 500 shares for sale are part of a total of 3,000 or 4,000 on the book at his price, his order is filled sooner if it was among the first placed.

Having a GTC order in place is better than putting in a day order at the same price every session until it is executed. Day orders die at the close, and each newly entered day order goes at the back of the line at its price. (Placing multiple orders also requires repeated discipline and frequent decisions.) A strong preference for stop-orders instead of stop-limit orders should be noted here. A stop-order says, "If the price reaches this level, I want to be considered a seller at market." A stop-limit order is less likely to be executed because it says to the specialist, "When the stock hits this price, put me in right away as a seller, but sell me out only if you can do it at the same price. Do it right away or forget it."

So if the size of position is generally in keeping with the pattern of average daily trading (i.e., the investor is not trying to sell a whole day's worth), he will not be big enough to disturb the day's supply/demand balance. Then he should not worry that his order might stand as a roadblock for the stock and will turn back its advance a fraction short of his level.

The idea is to be objective enough to recognize that the marketplace is so much bigger than any one participant that it takes no special notice of any individual order. If an investor's ego lets her imagine that her personal 500 or 1,000 shares is going to turn the tide against the stock's advance, she is too heavily involved in her own success or failure. Huge institutions may move the market or stop a trend, but you will not. Place the order where it should go, and let the market operate.

"They" Paranoia

Everyone who has heard whispers about the ubiquitous "they" needs to remember that "they" do not exist in the market. This is not to say that attempted—occasionally actual—market manipulation by individuals and/or firms does not exist at all. But when "they" get cited, it is critical to act against the dangerous assumption that "they" as a collective exist. Doing this is difficult because it requires leaning against the pressure of peers and brokers who give advice that is supposedly based on what "they" have allegedly decided will happen. Reject the "they" hypothesis, and act in an opposite, contrarian direction.

The underlying assumptions behind the "they" myth are that everything that happens (especially if it is bad) can be explained readily; that the world, and specifically the world of Wall Street, is ruled by conspirators; that bad guys cannot be reined in because they cannot be tracked down and brought to justice; and that a huge conspiracy is directed at relieving individual retail investors of their moderate wealth.

So "they" become a convenient scapegoat. Basically, anything that goes wrong in the plans or hopes of investors who believe in "they" is other-directed. This orientation absolves "they"-believers of mistakes in judgment and poor execution of strategy, at least in their own minds.

"They" is a moving target, whose identity cannot be known for sure, including, at various times: insiders (corporate officers), floor specialists on the exchange, corporate raiders, or, lately, program traders. In late 1989, the Japanese began to take on qualities often ascribed in the past to "they" as their national investment preference jumped from one to another of the foreign-stock, open-end mutual funds, and closed-end funds, causing wide price swings without apparent logic or pattern.

What is heard most about "they" is that "they" plan to move the market in a way that will trap small investors. Typically when the market whipsaws traders, the notion makes the rounds that "they" were to blame and had laid a trap. As the story goes, "they" planned to move the market up quickly to suck investors in at the top, at which point "they" would unload the stocks in question on the unsuspecting for a neat profit. Trapped with the stocks, small investors would suffer the next price drop once "they" pulled the plug on the rally. Then investors would get discouraged and sell out at the next bottom, presumably on a drop "they" would cause by either spreading negative rumors or shorting key stocks to drive quotes lower.

At the lows, "they" would step in and take retail customers' stock away for a bargain price, once again proving that "they" are in control and that investors are their fools.

In this scenario, every miscalculation is blamed on an outside force, not on personal bad luck or—more to the point—personal lack of expertise, discipline, or sophistication. Such thinking also postulates that there is an organized conspiracy to move the market. But keep in mind that the alleged conspirators would need billions of dollars to pull it off; "they" would need to trust each other totally so that none of them would cheat and step in or out at a better price than the others (or later turn state's evidence).

Strategies for Overcoming this Paranoia

The theory of "they," which neatly explains away all problems on the basis of an invincible and overwhelming outside force, has been discredited by all intelligent investors. Of course, if any rational investor really believes the game is rigged, he may question the first loss, but he would quit forever after the second. Firmly convinced that "they" have all the trump cards, the logical investor would see that folding his hand permanently is the only sensible course for an innocent.

Remember that, the next time someone tries to blame a reverse or a surprise on "them." And note who that someone is, to avoid giving them credence again. This someone is naive if they believe it themselves and dishonest if they are using "them" as a scapegoat for responsibility for the loss. Even if the rationalizer played the same stock and took the same beating, what he is doing is covering his own failing by blaming it on an invisible sinister force. Fault is being conveniently offloaded rather than accepted in an adult manner.

If any doubt remains, consider these questions: If "they" truly exist and are wealthy and powerful enough to pull off market coups,

- Why would they bother? They already have more wealth and power than they need; they should buy a country!
- Why would they take the risk of being caught at it and jailed? (They have more to lose than to gain.)
- Why would they choose to prey on small investors, who have relatively little wealth to pillage?
- Why is it never rumored *before* the fact that they are about to pull off a coup? (After all, even major takeovers are leaked in advance on occasion.)
- When they are blamed (after the fact, conveniently, after having disappeared), why are those who blame them not able to identify the villains specifically?

If a story is spread that "they" plan to run a certain stock up (or down) before it happens, run in the opposite direction. Whoever is spreading that story has no better reason to get an investor to buy the stock—or would give the reason. "They" theorizers are trying to unload the stock on the unwary. Sell, or sell short, rather than buy. There are three simple "they" rules to remember:

1. Do not believe people who adduce "they" as an explanation.
2. Do not accept "they" as a reason something will happen or did happen.
3. Do not rationalize that "they" were the reason for *your* failed trade or investment or even for just bad timing.

HOLDING WITH A DEATH GRIP

Investors tend to stretch their investment time horizons for two reasons. The first is that promised or expected hot developments seldom actually take place as quickly as hoped. But the second, and more insidious, problem is that human beings hesitate to come to closure, to wrap things up. Selling a stock has a finality akin to mourning a death. If one's stock position is kept open, hope for a better result is still alive. However, this hope can border on rationalization.

An example of this rationalization is a cynical Wall Street cliche that bad traders become investors. Unfortunately for legions of unsuccessful traders, this saying does not mean they have a religious experience, repent of their wasteful trading ways, and turn their attention to a value-oriented investing approach. It usually means that those owners of unsuccessful stock positions—originally intended as short-term situations—hold on for a long time out of stubbornness. These traders then become long-term holders through the back door; more accurately, they are self-trapped collectors of bad stocks.

It is important to recognize the trader-turned-investor syndrome as a classic symptom of switching objectives; this switch usually results from rationalization and fuzzy thinking. In fact, most traders do not even make a conscious decision to turn investor based on thoughtful consideration. That shift gradually creeps in through inertia.

An extreme version of the inertia and psychological baggage that can accompany losses is the investor who says, "I expect my stock could go down about 15 percent within the next month or two, but I plan to hold anyway." The logical rejoinder, of course, is to question whether, having that expectation and not already owning this stock, the investor would buy the stock today—before the expected 15 percent capital reduction takes place. Worse yet, why not double up now for the 15 percent loss?

In other cases, the investor may not perceive any imminent specific threat to stock price or to income stream; the investment may have gone bad last month and is currently in a price-dormant phase. Or it may be a recent purchase made for a specific reason—a scenario that has not matured as expected. Doggedly refusing to accept reality in the situation, this owner holds on; capital remains dormant, depreciates, or, at best, is less successfully employed than other available opportunities would allow.

This critique of the trader-turned-investor syndrome is not meant to condemn the conservative, longer-term, value-oriented approach to investing, nor is it an unabashed endorsement of trading the short term. But it does recognize that money has a time value and that investors mislead themselves dangerously if they allow a mistake or a badly timed purchase to lock up their portfolio contents until some hoped-for but nonspecific future return of better fortune bails them out.

Think about this aspect of time value and investment logic: the stubborn holder-on not only says he is willing to stand for perhaps a multiple-percent temporary capital reduction, he also says that a return just to current market value at some unknown future date is an acceptable outcome. Holding on for an imaginary nonloss is about as prudent as burying cash in the backyard. There is no return while one is risking loss of that principal.

That is not to say there is not a time to hold. Stocks should be held when market and company prospects are favorable and when the stock would be bought today if not already owned. When the investment strategy is not working out, it is usually a forceful signal to sell out because either the reasoning behind the purchase was faulty or the fundamentals of the situation have deteriorated since the stock was bought.

So if an investor would not buy the stock today, it should be sold because others who would potentially buy it ought to be in short supply if the investor is correct. This is a subtle trap for investors who like to hold. Instead of holding when something goes wrong, act like a successful business manager. Assess the situation without delay, and take warranted action. Short of actually selling the stock immediately, set a specific stop-loss limit, an upside goal, and a time window. Then, do not deviate. Although this addresses dramatic and sudden investment problem situations, it is only part of the remedy. In addition, also review holdings periodically to catch situations that have gone dormant. For sluggish stocks a disciplined, routinized approach is needed. Keep a notebook page on which to record stock prices at regular intervals and, for comparison, the major market average of choice. Do this no less than monthly and preferably weekly. When stocks drift, threatening to lull their inattentive investors to sleep, subject them to the tests suggested earlier for emergencies. This practice eliminates the cop-out, "Yeah, but I'm really a long-term investor."

WISHFUL THINKING

Tom Czech, in recent years the research director at Milwaukee-based Blunt Ellis & Loewi (now EVEREN Securities), says that "it's different this time" are the most expensive words in the investment business. They are a rationalization trap of the highest magnitude.

Recall that in the Old Testament the Lord promised Noah that never again would He cause it to rain for 40 days and 40 nights straight. It does not take an ecologist or an agricultural expert to presume that even half of 40 days' duration would do some pretty devastating damage. Those threatened with waterlog do not focus blindly on the difference between 39 and 40 days; a potential drownee tries to gauge roughly how much rain would be enough to do him in.

In the same way, by trying to measure the sameness or differentness of investment scenarios with exacting precision, investors can drive themselves to miss the point. What is important in comparing a current situation with the past is to recognize common patterns rather than waiting to act until an exact, 100 percent repetition of a precedent can be detected. In market comparisons, close enough usually is good enough.

There are two very different aspects of the "this-time-it-will-be-different" problem in investor thinking. One is an outgrowth of the "it-can't-really-happen-to-me" attitude that investors adopt when considering life's least pleasant realities. The second aspect is a logical jump from observation of very real differences to a conclusion that the implied outcome must or will be different.

Expecting "it" to be different involves a blend of reality and unreality that can be deceptive to the investor; "it" includes both the facts of a situation (fundamental news or trends) and the market's reaction to the facts. While history does tend to repeat, perfect replications hardly ever occur.

So even if it is literally true that "it" will be different this time, investors should not lull themselves into complacency over minor differences. To focus on the divergences while failing to note significant similarities is to miss the big picture. By not seeing important parallels with past events, investors can make an erroneous decision to hold based on misfiltered information.

CONFRONTING REALITY

Although business situations are seldom if ever identical, success in business can be analyzed; patterns of managerial behavior are recorded, categorized, and taught in graduate business school classes. In the same way, there are common contributors to failure that are discernible in deteriorating investment situations. Following is a list of some of the danger signs:

- Heavy promotion of the stock by management or agents.
- Projections of unusually strong/lengthy growth.
- Use of round numbers for predictions (e.g., 50 percent growth or a "$10-billion market").
- Questioning the motives or expertise of reasonable doubters.

- Strong claims of being the best, unique, or exclusive in a business.
- Defining the market narrowly so that, by definition, one is the leader.
- Ready excuses that fault outside forces when performance falls short.
- Lateness in reporting earnings (against either prior practice or Securities and Exchange Commission (SEC) filing deadlines).
- Change in outside auditors.
- Change in lead banker without improvement in interest cost and/or size of credit facilities.
- Substantial insider selling of the stock.
- Resignation of key (especially financial) officers or of directors.
- Sales or margins trends diverging negatively from competitor or industry patterns.
- Inconsistent management statements.
- Identical (seemingly rehearsed) management statements.
- Stonewalling when trouble is obviously present.

Faced with some combination of perhaps three or four of these signs, an investor reasonably and prudently can conclude that something is wrong and should get out of the stock. To insist that a particular combination of adverse events as seen in another situation can be fully repeated before concluding the stock is in trouble is naive and will probably prove costly.

As already indicated, things do not get better by themselves. When a company's affairs appear to be deteriorating, even if certain negative events have not been reported, investors are well advised to assume the worst by projecting that the situation is likely to continue worsening.

The point is, investors should be looking diligently for disturbing similarities to other problem situations rather than watching for comforting differences. The objective is to detect trouble as early as possible, thereby preventing or limiting loss of one's capital. There is an analysts' cliché that the first earnings disappointment will not be the last. Similarly, be suspicious at the first signs of any type of trouble. Unless a neutral or skeptical observer can be convinced that all is well, exit before things have a chance to become worse. Ask dispassionately whether, in light of today's facts, you would call it a good idea to buy now.

As indicated earlier in this chapter, there is a real but subtle difference between the "this-time-it's-different" rationalization and the "this-can't-be-happening-to-me" thinking. If what is going wrong is like something that went wrong once before, there is probably a reason. Putting it bluntly, many investors tend to make the same mistakes repeatedly. Wishing something would not have happened again, however, is barely across the reality/denial border from "this is not happening." This indicates a need to deny that anything is wrong, a blocking of the pain caused by a mistake. And, of course, when a mistake is public knowledge (the broker knows, and, at year's end, the spouse and tax accountant will know as well), the distaste is all the more deep and embarrassing.

What usually happens in these situations is that the investor focuses in the wrong direction by turning subjective and inward. But the reality is that whatever is happening (collapsing earnings, a dividend cut, executive stock sales, or resignations) is happening to the company—not the investor—in the objective plane, entirely unconnected causally to this particular investor's current ownership of the stock. It is happening, period.

The personal internalization that says "it is happening to me" and eventually "this can't be happening to me" is a rationalization. Sometimes an investor grasps at the discernible differences from a disastrous past investment experience and uses them to tell himself shakily that things will be all right, that it is not at all the way it looks.

Instead of rationalizing, sell the stock on the first price bounce after trouble struck the company, and reassess the situation from a cooler distance. Remember that things do not right themselves. And realize that some serious buying power from many other investors will be required to get the stock back up to higher levels.

A smart investor asks this key question, "If I did not own the stock, with today's knowledge would I be a buyer now?" When trouble first appears, prepare for the worst. This includes developing a mental scenario of what other shoes might drop, how long it all will take to play out this situation, and how market psychology will react to the problem. The most important aspect of performing this mental exercise is to examine prior situations in search of their similarities rather than differences. Then, from a big-picture standpoint, remember that history does repeat.

DEVELOPING THE PROPER MIND-SET FOR PROFITABLE SALES

4

Acknowledging Mistakes

KEYS TO INVESTMENT SUCCESS

- Handle Mistakes
- Keep Records of Actions
- Use Checklist to Reassess Stocks
- Use Master Tally Sheet to Detect Patterns

How an investor handles mistakes is more important than how many mistakes he or she makes or even how extreme they turn out to be. And one's handling of errors actually affects future frequency and severity as well! There are three guidelines to remember when contemplating inevitable investing mistakes:

- Expect to make mistakes and learn to live with them.
- Mistakes will have a greater or lesser net cost in the long run, depending on what an investor does or fails to do with them.
- Make the most of mistakes by turning them into learning experiences; keep detailed, real-time records of every transaction from start to finish.

HANDLING MISTAKES

Investors are human beings and therefore fallible. So it follows that, to avoid a downward spiral of self-criticism and emotional depletion, all investors must learn to forgive themselves for the mistakes they inevitably will make. The object of the game is to be right more often than wrong and to be right big and wrong small. The means to winning is to keep mistakes under control and in perspective. Put ego aside by remembering that the competition is not the market, the broker, or the guy next door—it is the investor's own record.

If an investor does learn to perform better over time, such improvement occurs precisely because he is learning not to make the same mistakes repeatedly. He also learns to control and channel his intensity, to concentrate on the stock at hand rather than on internal feelings. Another principle that must be learned in order to profit consistently is not to let market results have an enduring effect; if one can avoid the emotional scars of mistakes, subsequent moves can be made rationally and more skillfully. A good analogy is a baseball player in a hitting slump, who must concentrate on the next pitch rather than on the past five hitless at-bats in order to regain success.

The beginning of "mistake wisdom" is acknowledging and taking ownership of investment errors and then letting go of them. As in all of life, we must forgive ourselves or be unable to live with ourselves. In investing, of course, the object over time is to make fewer mistakes in proportion to total transactions and, if possible, to make mistakes less costly and successes more profitable.

People who are accustomed to winning consistently because of their brilliance and hard work are likely to be frustrated in a very fundamental way by the stock market; intelligence and diligence are helpful but not sufficient for achieving market profits. Examples are "A" students, successful lawyers, and A-track corporate executives. In the same way, people who succeed by precision or by rules are likely to be disappointed that investing cannot be totally controlled or predicted. Examples are computer programmers, engineers, and civil servants. Similarly, people whose lives involve exercising power often find trading stocks psychologically frustrating since they possess no such accustomed control. Examples would be military officers and police.

On the other hand, people who have routinely felt life's ups and downs are, by conditioning, psychologically better prepared for the realities of a mix of winning and losing on Wall Street. Salespeople, for example, know the frustration of bad weeks and do not expect perfection; their understanding that winning means just a higher-than-average success rate—not 100 percent perfection—gears them more effectively on an emotional level for the stock market.

Once the psychological art of living with mistakes is mastered, those mistakes must be turned into sources of opportunity if an investor is to profit from them. In fact, mistakes *must* be used as building blocks for the next transaction. Think of each buy and sell transaction, both gain and loss, as the tuition required to make progress in the learning process. Like a college student, an investor always pays tuition; the important question is whether he pays attention in class and gets his money's worth by learning something.

Investment success can be built on both right and wrong past moves; those behaviors that result in pain (loss) need most to be understood so they can be changed. One of the most costly sources of error is the tendency to repeat mistakes. And the most costly and troublesome mistakes are those of which the investor is unaware. Many such mistakes are driven, often at a subconscious level, by psychological forces, such as unresolved guilt, narcissism, unvented rage, and grandiosity.

Unfortunately, brokers and investment advisors are too often unwilling or unable to help investors become aware; realistically, they should be viewed only as technical experts in the market and not behavior-modification teachers. They may run money better, but they do not teach clients how to do it. So investors are on their own, with the challenge of learning from past mistakes. They need to overcome rationalization and avoidance behavior in order to focus on this learning opportunity.

Following are the two most important steps investors can take to analyze their own investing behavior:

1. Face up to errors instead of ignoring or minimizing them.
2. Categorize mistakes, and work toward avoiding repetition.

RECORD KEEPING

The most productive way to face errors is to record all investment behavior, analyzing what worked and what did not work. In this way, personal behavior patterns emerge that can be changed. It is helpful to create a notebook and record every transaction, even computerize the facts if so inclined, for future analysis. If honest, real-time records are not kept scrupulously—saving confirmation slips until tax time does not count—the result is to lose the learning potential in mistakes. In effect, the investor who is unaware of his mistaken behavior is still flying blind.

Note the suggestion that records be kept *in real time*. This has four positive effects. First, memory tends to fail when it must process mistakes, so recorded hard facts are a necessary component for accurate analysis. Second, real-time records eliminate cumbersome back-checking, a big task that can be an extremely effective barrier to keeping the analysis up to date. Third, real-time records preclude fudging or minimizing errors, which tends to occur when an investor wants to look back through rose-colored glasses. And finally, if an investor takes time to actually write answers to specific questions he or she asks both him or herself and a broker about tactical mistakes, it is easier to identify mistakes before making another ill-conceived move.

Following is a worksheet geared specifically toward catching the most common investor mistakes. These questions are shortened to emphasize key words that identify the most common points in time when mistakes are made. It may be helpful to photocopy this worksheet into a notebook and add blank pages for lengthy answers.

Investor Mistakes Checklist

Record the following information when each stock is bought:

- ☐ Whose idea was the purchase (self, broker, advisory letter, friend)?
- ☐ How long was the stock actively studied before taking action?
- ☐ Why is the stock expected to perform as projected?
- ☐ Is the general market in a major uptrend or downtrend?
- ☐ What was the prior-day closing level of the Dow-Jones Industrial Average (DJIA)? The recent few days' trend?
- ☐ What was the execution price of the stock purchase (excluding commission)?
- ☐ What was the prior-day closing price of the stock? Its recent few days' trend?
- ☐ What was the month-earlier price of the stock (was it a case of chasing strength)?
- ☐ What was the week-earlier price of the stock (was it a case of chasing strength)?
- ☐ What is the price objective for the stock, including the implied price/earnings (PE) ratio?
- ☐ What is the time of expected workout (date and number of months from now)?
- ☐ What is the implied return in percent per year?
- ☐ Where is the chart's breakdown point (support, trendline)?
- ☐ What is the actual or mental stop-loss price point?

As indicated by these questions, it is very important to establish not only a price objective for each stock holding, but also an associated timeframe. To record this data, mark a calendar or tickler file at the projected workout date. Do it when each stock is purchased. This creates an effective reminder to look at that time at every position and reassess it. This practice helps you to avoid drift.

Stock Reassessment Checklist

At the tickler or projected-workout date, record in real time the following information:

- ☐ What is the closing level of the DJIA?
- ☐ What is its percentage move since the buy date?
- ☐ What is the stock's closing price?
- ☐ What is the percentage move since the buy date (compare with DJIA)?

☐ Is the overall market still in a bull, bear phase?

☐ Is the stock in a major uptrend?

☐ Has the stock not moved to the established price goal? Why?

☐ Why continue holding the stock? Cite specific reasons, not wishes.

☐ What is the new price target (and implied P/E)?

☐ What is the new workout date (put in tickler file again)?

☐ What objective change, not failure or prior scenario, justifies extending the workout date?

Sale Checklist

When the stock is sold, record the following in real time:

☐ What is the DJIA at sale date? (Compute percent moves from buy and review dates.)

☐ What was the sale price (compute percent moves from buy and review dates.)

☐ Did the purchase rationale come true?

☐ If not, when did failure become apparent?

☐ How long was the time between failure and sale date?

☐ Was the stock held for a longer/shorter time than planned? Why?

☐ What was the high price of the stock while it was held? (Compute the percent down from that point to the price at which it was sold.)

☐ What was the low price of the stock while it was held? (Compute the percent down from the price at which it was bought, to that low.)

☐ Did the stock ever sell above the price target while it was held?

☐ If yes, why was it not sold then?

☐ Was an above-market GTC sale order ever placed? If no, why not?

☐ Was a stop-loss order ever placed and then removed or lowered? Did that reduce profit or extend loss?

☐ Was the sale execution planned or impulsive?

☐ Was the stock sold on strength, weakness, boredom, company news (good or bad), or general market action?

☐ Whose idea was the sale?

An investor who truthfully answers all the questions in these checklists can expect to be uncomfortable. Good! (Discomfort leads us to modify our behavior.) Those questions that cause the greatest discomfort usually identify where the most recurrent mistakes are made or where performance is less than optimal. To learn from prior mistakes, note those portions of the investment sequence, and review them the next time a purchase is made. In fact, highlight the problem questions on the checklists and refer to them often—before, during, and after subsequent positions are in place.

Tally the mistakes noted, scoring one point for each occurrence, on a master sheet (an example is shown at the end of this chapter), for example, a tendency to hold longer than planned, to raise the price objective without solid reasons, or to develop a pattern of selling from boredom. High scores for the most personally troublesome problem areas will emerge. That is where to concentrate improvement efforts in order to become more profitable in the market.

While analyzing mistakes, it is important to disregard the delusion that any investor can ever "bat a thousand" (even professionals have error rates around 40 percent), but do believe that improvement in performance is possible, indeed likely, if systematic effort is applied to noting and correcting mistakes.

BUY/REVIEW/SELL EVALUATION SHEET

Complete this section at the time of purchase:

Stock _____

Buy date _____

Study period _____

Whose idea? _____

Reason bought? _____

Major market trend? _____ DJIA prior-day close? _____

Stock prices:

    Buy price _____

    Prior close _____

    Week ago _____

    Month ago _____

Was this sale a case of chasing recent strength? _____

Price objective:

    $ _____

    P/E _____

    By date _____

    Elapsed months _____

Implied return *per annum* as a %? _____

Stop-loss point? Mental/actual? _____

Complete this section at the tickler/review date:

DJIA close? _____ Change since buy date (%)? _____

Stock close? _____ Change since buy date (%)? _____

Satisfied with relative performance? _____

Major trend:

   Market? _____ Stock? _____

Was the price goal reached? _____

   If yes, why held? _____

   If no, what went wrong? _____

Revised target:

   $? _____

   P/E? _____

   By what date? _____

Why holding? _____

Complete this section at the time of sale:

Date? _____

Was hold period longer/shorter than planned? _____

DJIA close _____

   Change from buy date (%)? _____

   From review date (%)? _____

Sale price _____

   Change from buy date (%)? _____

   From review date (%)? _____

Satisfied with relative performance? _____

Did buy reason work out? _____

   If no, when apparent? _____

Time between visible failure and sale? _____

High price while held ($)? _____

Giveback to sale price (%)? _____

Low price after buy ($)? _____

Percent overpaid (%)? _____

Reached target while owned? _____

   Why not sold if not? _____

Used GTC target order? Used stop? _____

Stop pulled/lowered? _____

Why? Helped or hurt net result? _____

Sale planned/impulsive? _____

Sale trigger/circumstances? _____

   Whose idea? _____

MASTER TALLY SHEET

At Buy Date:

Stocks Scored to Date	1	2	3	4	5	6	7	8	9	10	11	12	13	14	15
Whose idea	☐	☐	☐	☐	☐	☐	☐	☐	☐	☐	☐	☐	☐	☐	☐
Good reason	☐	☐	☐	☐	☐	☐	☐	☐	☐	☐	☐	☐	☐	☐	☐
Study period	☐	☐	☐	☐	☐	☐	☐	☐	☐	☐	☐	☐	☐	☐	☐
Market trend	☐	☐	☐	☐	☐	☐	☐	☐	☐	☐	☐	☐	☐	☐	☐
Chased strength	☐	☐	☐	☐	☐	☐	☐	☐	☐	☐	☐	☐	☐	☐	☐
P/E target	☐	☐	☐	☐	☐	☐	☐	☐	☐	☐	☐	☐	☐	☐	☐

At Tickler Date:

	1	2	3	4	5	6	7	8	9	10	11	12	13	14	15
Major trend	☐	☐	☐	☐	☐	☐	☐	☐	☐	☐	☐	☐	☐	☐	☐
Exit-at-goal failure	☐	☐	☐	☐	☐	☐	☐	☐	☐	☐	☐	☐	☐	☐	☐
Stock trend	☐	☐	☐	☐	☐	☐	☐	☐	☐	☐	☐	☐	☐	☐	☐
Conviction re holding	☐	☐	☐	☐	☐	☐	☐	☐	☐	☐	☐	☐	☐	☐	☐

At Sale Date:

	1	2	3	4	5	6	7	8	9	10	11	12	13	14	15
Held too long/short?	☐	☐	☐	☐	☐	☐	☐	☐	☐	☐	☐	☐	☐	☐	☐
Relative performance	☐	☐	☐	☐	☐	☐	☐	☐	☐	☐	☐	☐	☐	☐	☐
Scenario right?	☐	☐	☐	☐	☐	☐	☐	☐	☐	☐	☐	☐	☐	☐	☐
Decisive at failure?	☐	☐	☐	☐	☐	☐	☐	☐	☐	☐	☐	☐	☐	☐	☐
Percent given back	☐	☐	☐	☐	☐	☐	☐	☐	☐	☐	☐	☐	☐	☐	☐
Percent overpaid	☐	☐	☐	☐	☐	☐	☐	☐	☐	☐	☐	☐	☐	☐	☐
Exit-at-goal failure	☐	☐	☐	☐	☐	☐	☐	☐	☐	☐	☐	☐	☐	☐	☐
GTC order at target?	☐	☐	☐	☐	☐	☐	☐	☐	☐	☐	☐	☐	☐	☐	☐
Stop tactics	☐	☐	☐	☐	☐	☐	☐	☐	☐	☐	☐	☐	☐	☐	☐
Sale planning	☐	☐	☐	☐	☐	☐	☐	☐	☐	☐	☐	☐	☐	☐	☐
Circumstances/trigger	☐	☐	☐	☐	☐	☐	☐	☐	☐	☐	☐	☐	☐	☐	☐
Whose idea?	☐	☐	☐	☐	☐	☐	☐	☐	☐	☐	☐	☐	☐	☐	☐

5

Keep a Clear Head

KEYS TO INVESTMENT SUCCESS

- Recognize Crowd Psychology
- Take Time Out

Winning on Wall Street is a difficult game, or at least one that seems easy only late in major bull markets. Following the secondary crash of October 1989, a survey taken for *The Wall Street Journal* indicated that the majority of the investing public saw the deck as stacked against them: insider trading was perceived as an institutional advantage over individual investors, market manipulation was widely suspected as a result of the scandals and celebrity prosecutions of recent years, and program trading by huge investing institutions (and brokerage firms for their own accounts) was viewed as an investment barrier for the little guy. Such perceptions had changed but little as of late 1996.

Whether an investor is right or wrong about a stock or about market motivation, multi-billion-dollar investors do move the market in whatever direction they think it will go simply by acting. (See Chapter 10.) Therefore, investing is a difficult game for individuals, even when they play on a relatively even playing field and even if information is fully and equally available to all market participants.

Harsh reality is that not every investor functions in the stock market with equal efficiency or earns equal returns. The disparity in market performance generally boils down to how well each investor—individual or institutional—can master, or invest against, his emotions. So keeping a clear head means the difference between profits and losses. It means staying clear-headed when everyone else is not, especially during market swings from panicky lows and price despair to manic euphoria.

Statistically, it is known that most market participants in one cycle are again around for a re-enactment of the drama the next time around. Almost incredibly, a majority fall prey to the same mistakes in the subsequent cycle. Most such mistakes have to do not with fundamentals but with investors' emotional reactions to news and price volatility. So it pays to remain emotionally clear-headed.

It is the nature of all speculative markets that they move from one extreme to the other. For example, in a recession, the U.S. economy might show a 3 percent to 5 percent drop in real gross national product (GNP). Corporate earnings may slide 20 percent or 25 percent. But the major stock averages might fall 30 percent to 40 percent in a year, as if economic life were about to disintegrate.

In this scenario, some individual stocks will fall 80 percent to 90 percent—and that includes only the survivors; some other companies inevitably go out of business, and their stocks become expensive wallpaper.

CROWD PSYCHOLOGY

What takes hold of investors in this kind of extreme market movement is crowd psychology, a total loss of self-control. What ought to be governing is a high awareness of the patterns of one's very recent market experiences, and the reason is simple. The degree of recent success or failure has a powerful influence on the success of subsequent market moves. Success enables more success, until a point when inhibitions disappear. Failure takes its toll in future failures generated by faulty, irrational, or incomplete thinking.

CASE STUDY

To illustrate, following is a hypothetical stock chart on which are overlaid the buying, holding, and selling decisions—and the emotional reactions—of a hypothetical investor who can, in all respects, be considered real and representative. In fact, this investor is so real in composite as to be the force that moves the stock on the chart the way it is illustrated. (See Figure 5–1.)

The actions and reactions demonstrated, multiplied by thousands of active buyers and sellers in millions of shares annually, create the type of price gyrations seen in the exhibit. The chart follows XYZ Corporation; its time scale covers several years from the start of one bull market to the bottom of the following bear market. The price scale is in a range typical for many actively traded common stocks. Given the volatility of individual issues in recent years, the relative rise of 200 percent followed by nearly a 70 percent collapse is not at all unrepresentative of reality.

Specific price points on the chart are marked with the letters A to Z, capsulizing the hypothetical composite investor's thoughts, feelings, and actions in the comments that follow.

FIGURE 5-1

XYZ Corporation
The Emotional Roller Coaster

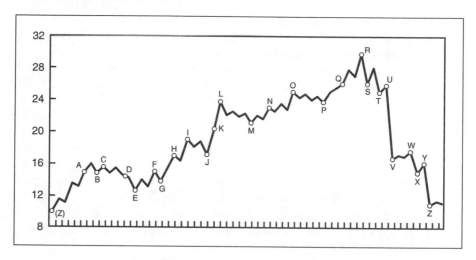

Trace the price movement from one letter to the next, moving from the beginning of the price action to point A for example, and then read the comment corresponding to that letter. Then observe the price movement from there to point B, and look at the relevant comment. In that way, you can follow the thoughts and feelings generated by a typical stock's action in a telescoped view.

A. Looks like a winner; up 50 percent from the panic lows. Good relative performance. Buy 500 shares at market.

B. Just a little consolidation. The earnings-per-share forecasts are good. Not worried; plan to hold.

C. Alright! Finally back above original cost. Now it's really ready to go.

D. Glad I sold here. It both broke down and triggered the stop. That's two strong signals, and I didn't miss them.

E. Knew I was right about that dog. Glad I'm out.

F. I've seen this price before. That stock isn't worth it. Short 300.

G. See, I knew it! Now I've got this one figured out. This baby is headed for nine or even lower!

H. Aha! A false breakout if I ever saw one. Short another 200.

I. Can't believe it. This turkey's got a P/E of 22 and it's going up? Another point and I have to take cover.

J. That's better. Now I'm even on my second lot short.

K. I've seen this before: another false breakout. I won't be fooled because I know this rally can't last.

L. I can't stand it anymore. Cover all 500 at market!

M. Wish I'd had more guts and stayed short. Look at this downtrend.

N. Hmmmph. Not bad—flat earnings despite recession talk.

O. Look at this uptrend. I've gotta get on board. Tape's saying something's happening that's not apparent. Buy 400.

P. I'm scared by this break. Can't afford a big loss. Sell half.

Q. Guess I was wrong (but that 50 percent sale still felt prudent). Gotta buy back that 200 shares since the market is firmer again.

R. Terrific! $30 and going north. I'm not greedy: 32 and I'll be gone. That's a reasonable 25 percent profit.

S. Just a correction. Darn market's off 240 points. But there's gotta be a fifth up-wave. I'll take 30 when it gets back there.

T. Well, it makes no sense to see the stock way down here. Look how high the yield is. That'll support the price. It just can't go lower.

U. That's better. The market's stabilized too. We've seen the worst.

V. Dividend cut 60 percent? Who could have seen that coming? Can't sell now. Too big a loss.

W. Guess the worst is over. I'd average down if I had the cash. No, on second thought this one's hurt me enough. Can't trust it.

X. Margin call? Sell half. I love this stock at these prices but just can't put more cash into the market.

Y. Glad I didn't sell it all. Should have met the margin call and held it for the rally since it was so darn cheap!

Z. Here we go: down again. I can't stand it anymore. Get me out; sell at market.

This hypothetical chart reflects a very confused investor, it is true. And the sequence may seem too long to represent any single investor/stock relationship that had gone so badly. But many an individual investor tends to make several, if not all, of these flip-flop mistakes before quitting, and for three reasons:

- He has made a profit on the stock before, which generates an affinity for playing it again.
- He feels he knows the company or the industry and so believes he understands the stock as well.
- He wants to get even, or reach breakeven, before letting go here to engage with another stock.

All of these mind-sets are representative of unclear thinking. Not only do many investors dig in their heels and insist on coming out of the stock "relationship" whole, but the bad feedback creates more confusion, which makes them dig in their heels even deeper.

Comments associated with this chart include five highly significant reactions to price behavior that indicate typical investor mistakes when emotions take over:

- Swings back and forth between fundamental and technical explanations and rationales.
- A tendency to follow and mentally project continuation of the recent trend.
- Uncontrolled swings toward extremes of emotional reaction.
- Beliefs that the market is out to trap the individual investor.
- Prior bad experiences with a stock that create damaging and confusing effects on the investor.

TAKING TIME OUT

One useful way to short-circuit the negative thinking spiral listed in the preceding section is to quit playing a stock—or industry group—after one or two losses. Whether or not there is such a thing as unfavorable chemistry between a stock and an investor, playing again only deepens the destructive pattern and increases risk of additional mistakes. In the same way, if there is a pattern of consecutive losses or whipsaws across several stocks, quit all of them for a period of time.

This does not mean selling everything (long-term positions that are working well and would be bought again today need not be disturbed). Just stop trading and clear the mind. Draw up lists of the stocks that are most solid and those that are shaky, and describe why. Set price targets. Write down firm resolves not to sell on weakness or buy on strength. This pause in the action allows an investor to control his actions before a return to the market; his or her tendency to follow crowd hysterics will be diminished.

This pause, however, is best accomplished when some selling has taken place and a cash cushion exists. If an investor stops while fully committed, there is an urgency about getting back to the action because there are still positions causing active worry. A key question to ask is, "If action absolutely could not be taken for a month, which stocks would I still be most comfortable to own?"

Also note that it is a mistake to take a head-clearing pause after every loss. But when there is a run of mistakes, say, three or more, seriously consider calling a halt. Those errors count whether in the same stock or across several. Then ask a broker to take a dispassionate look at current positions and make independent suggestions with which to compare. Ask him to mail a copy of his suggestions on a specified date. If the broker has difficulty helping in this way, the investor has received a telling warning about the broker's usefulness.

The clearest heads do prevail in the market. A losing streak that the investor does nothing to correct can become self-sustaining as personal confusion gains the upper hand over reason. Psychologists say that losses act to disrupt one's sense of self-unity; losses further cause shame, which also causes disorientation or loss of one's bearings. So call a halt before your downward mental spiral can set a precedent for future trading failures.

6

Transform Denial into Action

KEYS TO INVESTMENT SUCCESS

- Learn from The Schuller Corporation Case
- Prevent Denial

DENIAL AND LOSS

The process of deciding to sell a stock is a difficult one at best unless an investor has developed a discipline or methodology and adheres to it faithfully to avoid inevitable internal mental battles. When a loss is involved, the sell decision is even more difficult because the issue of pain avoidance is now present. It is human nature to seek self-preservation, and pain signals to us a danger to our well-being. Some investors may be obsessed with safety, while most are reasonably balanced in their tolerance of the risks involved in seeking to earn a profit. But every investor has some threshold at which pain must be avoided, sometimes at ridiculous cost.

One of the most convenient ways to avoid the pain of loss—or even of profit squandered—is denial. Dealing with an investment or trading loss involves not only financial pain but also ego pain, a blow to our self-sense of value. A majority of stockholders at some point attempt to avoid both pains by failing to deal with the reality of their losses. They prefer not to think about it, or they minimize it. When specific stock positions go bad, the pain avoider becomes a longer-term holder, who is more accurately a collector of stocks. He has no real investment motive or astuteness of value judgment and is, in fact, simply denying the pain of potential (or already apparent) loss.

Unfortunately, most investment brokers are of very little or no help to their clients in dealing with losses—they are unwilling or unable to break down client denial or avoidance behavior. Part of brokers' inability to help stems from the bias of their training, which is strongly focused on gathering new assets and then persuading clients to buy, not sell, securities. But the broker problem goes much further.

The broker, too, as a human being is a pain avoider. He or she needs to remain on cordial and constructive terms with clients. A successful sales person must listen to customers and act on all resulting feedback. So, naturally, when a customer indicates an unwillingness to deal with losses, his or her broker hears that message loud and clear—and heeds it. An unspoken contract between investor and broker develops: "I will not complain about my problem if you will please do me the favor of not reminding me of it."

There are several rationalizations that investors use to deny losses, or the importance of their losses. One relies on the rubric of the U.S. Tax Code. Investors are well aware that, for tax purposes, no loss is recognized as having occurred until a closing transaction actually takes place (and the 31-day "wash-sale rule" is not violated). Using this tax reality as a psychological crutch, many investors actually talk themselves into believing that they do not have a loss until they actually take one. On objective examination, of course, such reasoning is absurd. Few such investors, holding a pleasant 200 percent paper gain, would say they have no profit!

It is, of course, possible that price might recover and today's paper loss might be reduced or recovered—or might even become a paper (or real) profit in the future. But the truth is that if the stock is quoted below what was paid, there is a loss of capital because wealth is measured by the current value of assets less liabilities. Liquidate investments under duress, value an estate, or switch investments to obtain maximum current income from available assets, and reality prevails. A stock is currently worth only what it can be sold for now—not what it was bought for, what the owner wishes it would be, or what he thinks it should sell for. If current price is below cost, a loss exists. Period.

If an investor is too smart or too logical to attempt self-deception with the "paper-loss-isn't-real" farce, he may rely instead on a less disprovable assertion: the stock will come back given enough patience. Hope springs eternal, and once in a great while a terrible loser does reverse and rise phoenixlike from the ashes. Then, the investor who has sold out at a loss and later sees the price recover says, "See, if only I'd been smarter or more patient and followed my instinct and held on, I would not have had that loss."

Closing out a position, especially when at a loss, represents the process of coming to closure. Optimistic by nature, we prefer to see our options remain open rather than have them closed off. Buying a stock involves the grand opening of new possibilities, but selling closes the final chapter. As noted in Chapter 2, many closure processes in our lives carry sadness: graduating from and leaving our alma mater, admitting a failed marriage via divorce, burying a departed friend, cleaning out great-grandmother's attic. These represent some pretty heavy baggage, of a kind we'd prefer to avoid lifting if possible. Selling a stock conjures up such feelings, at least at a subconscious level. Holding it allows us potential for greater profit or reclaiming a current loss. If our stock is down, selling brands us with a sign of failure, which we'd like to avoid.

Actually placing a sell order and taking the loss on a final basis (the trade confirmations and the Schedule D entry are lasting souvenirs) goes even further in that it sets up our investor for a second source of pain by being "wrong again": watching the stock move higher without being on board for its recovery. This possible double horror show can be avoided by refusing to take the loss in the first place, says the denier.

What psychologists call denial is, in the investment arena, an umbrella description for a variety of rationalizations and self-deceptions. All are designed to allow possessors of losing investments to justify doing nothing about them.

There are several variations on the denial theme. One springs from the memory of the purchase price, the highest price ever reached, or the best achieved since purchase. Old best price levels can each act as a high-water mark that becomes a once-was, a could-be-again, a should-be, then a will-be, and all too often a gotta-be. It does not matter how many months or years ago that high-water mark was made. It does not matter that the company's fundamentals or general market psychology has been eroded seriously. It does not matter that a rise of several hundred percent from current prices may be necessary for full recovery. To avoid accepting and dealing with the loss, the denier waits (and waits and waits some more) for recovery, denying the long adverse odds.

THE SCHULLER CORPORATION CASE

A specific example, albeit an old one, of how extreme and irrational the predisposition to denial can be is in order. In 1988 after more than six years under Chapter 11 protection, Schuller Corporation (previously Johns Manville and at that time simply Manville Corporation) announced that it would complete its reorganization soon and, in the process, issue a very large number of new common shares to settle the claims of creditors and asbestos-injury victims.

Official company documents filed with the SEC indicated that the exiting holders' equity would be diluted 94 percent to 97 percent. Following local Colorado media coverage of the good news that Chapter 11 status would end, the then-Manville common (old) stock rose from $2.00 to $3.00 on extremely heavy trading volume.

Management even took an extremely unusual step by issuing a statement, in response to market action, in which it repeated previous written warnings that its stock involved a high degree of risk.

Part of the reorganization was to be a reverse split on a one-for-eight basis. (Reverse splits are designed to cut the number of shares outstanding and to return a stock's price to a more respectable price-per-share level.) The long and well documented history of declining value following reverse splits compounded the prospective negative effects of massive dilution from the bankruptcy settlement.

As a local brokerage analyst, your author issued a very strong, urgent recommendation to brokers that they contact all clients who then owned Manville common shares to sell their old stock at market without delay. A dual-trading market existed in the then-Manville shares. The old stock retreated a few days later to $2.00 per share. But the post-split shares were trading at the very same time on a when-issued basis at $8.00 each.

There were technical and mechanical reasons, internal to the market's rules (not relevant here), why such a spread in prices could exist. In fact it did exist. The simple fact was that an investor holding old shares would see a certain loss of 50 percent in capital: 800 shares currently worth $1,600, for example, would in a few weeks become 100 shares worth $800. It was like being able to read a future *Wall Street Journal* and check the quotations in advance. A holder of old stock had an opportunity to sell his or her existing shares, simultaneously replace that position with one-eighth as many when-issued new shares, and pocket the difference after commissions in cash.

Neglecting to sell, therefore, represented a fully conscious acceptance of a known penalty to capital: not a tiny marginal loss but a whopping 50 percent loss! To the broker community's (and this analyst's) amazement, some clients could not be convinced to sell their stock even to avoid absolutely certain further losses. Some said, "I've held the stock for a long time and see no reason to abandon hope now." Others did not want to create a wash sale, even if it would preserve half the capital involved. One client wanted $2.50 per share and would not sell for less. One client repeatedly swore he "didn't care" about his loss.

DENIAL PREVENTION

This example demonstrates that investors must somehow set up their own ways of dealing with reality, even if that requires what seems like unnatural or artificial devices: stop-loss orders entered at purchase, rigorous periodic reviews of each position, even filling out a questionnaire to justify continued holding.

Another denial-prevention strategy is to sell one stock periodically—perhaps quarterly to avoid too much churning—whether it seems needed or not, just like routine auto maintenance. Do so dispassionately and regularly, and in the process your most mediocre stock holdings can be sloughed off much more easily. The added practice in making sell decisions will make future ones easier.

Think back for a moment to recall the virtual chaos and near-paralysis on Wall Street after the crash of October 1987. Many brokerage firms were far behind in calculating margin calls to clients; therefore, investors had an unusual opportunity—but fleeting—to assess their positions and take action before they were absolutely forced to. One of the more insightful client thought processes went something like this:

1. I expect the world to go on.
2. I expect to remain an equities investor.
3. The decline has created some wonderful values right here at today's prices, so I don't want to quit now and return later only to buy back at higher prices.
4. I know I will face a margin call within days or hours. I do not have the courage (or the cash) to put up extra money, so I must do some selling.
5. It is in my best interests to keep those stocks whose prospects seem best *from current levels.*
6. Therefore, to raise the needed cash my only logical move is to sell those positions that I would least likely buy again today.

A self-imposed thought process or exercise something like this, developed for an imagined crisis such as a possible future crash, can be helpful by forcing the reluctant investor to focus quickly. It helps him recognize which stocks are not going to be the best choices to hold. Those are the ones to sell. After going through such a mental exercise several times on a theoretical basis over a period of months or a year, losses generally can be dealt with more easily. The first time through, do it on paper. Then pick up the phone, and issue an actual sell order. Eventually, this new-found ability to sell without pangs of remorse will improve investment results as tired dollars get repositioned into more promising situations.

7

Require Realism to Support Hope

KEYS TO INVESTMENT SUCCESS

- Learn Fundamental Psycho-Mechanical Realities
- Understand the Aftermath of a Crash
- Make sure the Hold Decision Is a Decision

It is true that a positive attitude helps produce positive results and, conversely, that believing something to be impossible can be a self-fulfilling prophesy. However, while wishing may be a necessary component of success in endeavors over which the investor has some degree of control, in itself it is not sufficient. In the stock market, where an individual is too small to exert a meaningful influence over price for very long, wishing simply will not make it so. For investors with high self-esteem, one's inability to control the market can act as a subtle source of nagging discomfort; we all need to accept what we cannot change and make the best of it.

Thousands of investors—optimistic by natural temperament and encouraged in their buy bias by brokers—spend more energy in hoping than in logical and coolheaded analysis. Their continual wishing is actually counterproductive: in baseless optimism, they deceive themselves and ignore reality by holding a stock that is not working out. Falling into such a trap is quite easy since the stock's price, more than a barometer of wealth, comes to measure an owner's ego; giving up represents admitting defeat, and defeat makes us feel stupid, which evokes shame.

FUNDAMENTAL AND PSYCHO-MECHANICAL REALITIES

There are two reasons that hoping against hope fails: one reason is fundamental, the other reason is psycho-mechanical (as distinguished from a technical reason, to use the conventional market vocabulary that contrasts with fundamentals). (See Figure 7–1.)

If a company is not producing expected results, profit disappointment sets in for shareholders. Fundamental results—an expected product announcement, a technology breakthrough, patent award, sales increase, earnings turnaround, or dividend boost—must occur to generate stock-price profits. If this does not happen, the stock loses needed supporters and, eventually, its price takes a deep decline (particularly if positive expectations had been high and/or had persisted for a lengthy period). In strong bull market phases such as those seen from late 1994 through mid-1996, investors readily become impatient with underperformers and dump them for more appealing, faster action elsewhere, This can lead to one more reason hope must be realistic; if it is not, it will be loss-creating.

When fundamentals fail, the implication is very clear: sell the stock, do not hold it. It can always be bought back later if or when those hoped-for fundamentals do come through. After disillusionment has become the dominant attitude, early signs of fundamental progress will be disbelieved, thus providing ample time to buy back in at a price not too far up from the lows. That's the good news.

The bad news, ironically, is that fundamentals might actually be going according to plan, which naturally encourages optimism. But even though fundamentals may be good, the often-fickle market may cease to be willing to pay up for those fundamentals. All too often, investors are lulled into misguided overconfidence because the company's story works out as anticipated. Therefore, they expect the stock to respond favorably, which sets up a trap. It might be up *already*.

FIGURE 7–1

Stock Price Driving Factors

		Fundamentals	
		Good	*Bad*
Psychology	*Positive*	Price up	Price perhaps even
	Negative	Price likely down	Price down sharply

An old market proverb says stocks fall of their own weight, but it takes buying pressure to boost them up. At first, it may seem obvious why technicians say that for a stock to remain strong it must rise on increasing volume and that a price advance occurring on declining or low volume is suspect. But there is a second and more profound implication about the difference between fundamental realities surrounding the company and the psycho-mechanical forces or factors that drive its stock price. Do not assume the two will necessarily operate in the same direction.

Let's go back to the distinction between *technical* (which describes a stock's price and volume action) and *psycho-mechanical*. The latter encompasses all those non-fundamental factors actually operating in the stock market in real time—things that drive investors to place actual buy or sell orders for a stock. This difference must be explored to understand why stocks can go down while their fundamentals are positive.

A logical investor sells unless a positive decision can be justified to buy the stock. This is supported by the contention that stocks should always be presumed suspect and constantly subject to sale unless there is positive justification for actively deciding to buy. Holding can be logical only if others reasonably can be expected to buy.

Why hold a stock at all? There are only two income-based objectives: dividend potential and interest rate volatility. With an income objective, hold the stock if its dividend is secure and is being regularly increased. With interest rate changes, hold only if interest rates will not move adversely enough (i.e., sharply higher) to reduce the market value of the expected dividend stream. Since rates move faster than dividends (a move in long-bond rates from 6 percent to 7 percent is a 17 percent rise in the valuation divisor), this implies being ready at the sell trigger even with stocks bought for income.

If your objective is capital appreciation and not income, the only justification for holding is a belief that price will begin, or will continue, to rise. Just expecting a stock not to decline is not a good reason to hold it. That is the equivalent of putting money into a checking account and leaving it there. Actually it is worse because one's stock-price expectation or overall market-tone assumption might prove overly optimistic, and the stock could decline anyway; but the (insured) bank deposit is presumed risk free.

This leads to the key element: hold a stock only if it is expected to rise (enough to compensate for opportunity cost and risk). Then logically examine the basis for any bullish expectations by envisioning realistically the stock's positive psycho-mechanical factors. Only a combination of psycho-mechanical factors—added to positive fundamental news—can drive the price higher; both are required for a price rise. One alone is not enough, except briefly near runaway market tops. At such times, general market enphoria will temporarily reduce selling urgency. But such circumstances must not be assumed to persist long.

THE AFTERMATH OF A CRASH

Even lately, a number of years since the 1987 market crash, it remains clear that there is a need for positive upward (buying) pressure ("sponsorship") to keep a stock's price from falling. The market for a stock is not like the market for food, for example. Stock demand is psychological, not based on necessity. To compound the effect of a lack of compelling stock demand, there tends to be an ongoing supply of shares that, if not matched, pushes prices lower over time. Included are unending sources of selling pressure: settling an estate; retiring and living on one's assets; paying for a college education, vacations, or medical expenses; raising capital for a business or to buy other stocks; boredom and disappointment—all of these create a supply of shares. Those are individuals' reasons for selling. Institutions face redemptions and periodically switch to other holdings that seem more attractive. If this supply is not met by equal demand, prices decline.

The central issue then, is the source of buying power or demand for a stock. It is true that at some point a stock can become so compellingly cheap that it finds support. But the problem is that a truly cheap price level may not yet even approximate yesterday's closing price—especially when viewed from bull market heights. Thus, a logical corollary exists: do not hold a stock unless it would be a prudent purchase today. If an investor is not willing to buy it for his own portfolio, who else would? If he buys it anyway, this is the greater-fool theory at its worst.

Therefore, look objectively at how purchase decisions favoring a stock are likely to be generated. Think in terms of sponsorship for the stock. For sponsorship to exist, it is necessary that corporate management be involved in the process of providing information to the professional investing community and to the public. This does not mean an investor should look for a company that is actively and aggressively promoting its stock; in fact, those situations are suspect and usually best avoided. Sponsorship refers to credible executives giving their time and honest answers to research analysts who want to follow the company and who may wish to recommend its stock to their clients or to place or keep it in managed portfolios. Institutional sponsorship is important; its loss can be devastating to share price.

Remember, demand for a stock does not occur in a vacuum. With the exception of a magazine story or news event, themes that catch the public's attention (pollution or AIDS or the Internet), or word-of-mouth recommendations, most retail demand for stocks is generated by stockbrokers who call clients and suggest reasons to buy. With so many other prepackaged (and lower maintenance) products available to recommend, most brokers today do not find their own stock stories; they rely on research department recommendations for ideas. Clients of these brokers then buy stocks that have sponsorship. Other stocks are neglected.

This description of stock sponsorship might seem to be useful as a screening device for identifying promising stocks to buy. But remember that our primary focus here is on how to make decisions about holding or selling a stock already owned.

Although the Dow Jones Industrials in late 1988 had rebounded to above 2000, it was a dreary period for common stocks. As a result of the 1987 crash, many individual investors quit the market altogether and remained too leery to return. Large numbers of those who remained had losses and refused to take any action because they felt "locked in." The result was a very low level of participation by individual investors. The minimal speculative tendency that did exist was centered on takeovers when the news seemed plausible, or when the reason to buy was based on more than hope or theory.

Starting at that time, many brokerage firms reduced staffing, and many retail brokers left the business because of declining customer activity. Even more important was the reduction in research coverage. This meant the public was far less frequently prodded to buy stocks. Those analysts who remained employed generally concentrated more heavily than ever on large capitalization issues. The reason is clear: an analyst's time costs the firm money. And that expense must be justified by trading activity that generates commission revenue dollars.

Since the investing public was in a timid frame of mind following the 1987 and 1989 crashes, it traded for several years in familiar names more than in smaller, fledgling enterprises. As a result, many stocks have narrower brokerage sponsorship than they had earlier, and some others have lost all research coverage. The research department's reasoning goes, "If clients will not buy it, why should we bother to recommend it? And if we don't plan to recommend it, why should we even continue to follow it?"

The resulting implication for stocks in the early years after a bear market is apparent: increased urgency surrounding the hold/sell decision, especially in smaller capitalization issues and low-priced stocks both listed on the major exchanges and on NASDAQ. It was widely noted (although roundly denied by brokerage firms) during and just after the 1987 crash that the trading market in many unlisted stocks virtually disappeared for a day or more. Market-making firms reduced their exposed capital, causing a lack of depth in the market. While the problem has become less acute with the passage of time and the broadening of automated electronic trading systems, it remains present.

The penalty suffered by low-priced issues is compounded by margin rules (and to some extent by investors' caution). Most brokerage firms extend credit (margin) of up to 50 percent of the purchase price on stocks priced at $5 per share or higher (some firms have adopted a $3 standard). When a stock declines below the stated level, it becomes worthless for purposes of calculating margin-account equity.

Therefore, a price decline through these levels snowballs downhill. Such a decline triggers margin calls, causing further selling. Aware of this, market makers become wary of carrying over the counter (OTC) inventory, and tactically savvy investors relinquish their lower priced stocks. Further into a risk-averse climate, most brokers understandably became hesitant to call clients to suggest that they buy low-priced, more speculative stocks. In the giddy and buoyant atmosphere of mid-1996, such conditions are easily forgotten, but they return with each bear market cycle.

This change illustrates psychomechanical factors in the market that, together with fundamentals, determine stock prices and trends. Part of the immediate aftermath of the October 1987 crash was a real change in the mechanical inputs that constitute the market for individual stocks. Simply put, many stocks came to have less sponsorship than they previously had. Therefore, for any given disappointment in fundamentals (or general market hesitancy), the resulting decline in share price is likely to be more sudden at first, more substantial in extent, and more extended over time than would have been the case before the crash.

Today, the number of active, risk-taking individual investors is down. The number of brokers and analysts offering buy advice also is down. As a result, hoping against hope is more dangerous than ever. In addition to assessing whether fundamental news supports an advancing price (remember, just staying even is not good enough), also judge whether current psycho-mechanical forces in the market allow the price to advance. In a negative, cautious post-crash type of environment, lean more heavily than ever toward a "guilty until proven innocent" attitude. The burden of positive proof must now lie on the stock. Likewise, although it seems intuitively strange, in very strong market phases expect the slightest disappointment to be met with swift and sure price punishment as performance-driven investors abandon an offending stock for greener pastures.

Remember that stocks fall of their own weight, but it takes buying pressure to move them higher. One way to judge a stock's prospects is to look at recent price charts (now available from several sources either free or at very low cost via the Internet): if the price is not in an uptrend—particularly if it has broken down—it means that demand for it has weakened. If that is the case, your invested capital will shrink if you hold on in hope. Viewing a stock's price not simply as so many dollars per share but directly as a measure of your wealth will add a degree of urgency to your hold/sell deliberations.

Be coldly objective: *is* there going to be buying pressure to move this stock up? Where will it originate? If likely sources of continuing support cannot be identified (as distinguished from the reasons the stock "ought" to go up), a decision to hold will lose money. If there is no specific reason for ongoing optimism (on price action as well as regarding underlying fundamentals), an investor is literally hoping against hope.

In these circumstances, not to sell is to make a wager against the odds. And remember, a decision to hold is like a decision to buy again today—it is a reinvestment of its holder's capital for another day in the same stock. Holding is more subtle and does not involve a phone call to a broker or a transaction cost. But that decision to hold should be a decision made consciously and actively, not a default as a result of doing nothing or (worst of all!) of not even *thinking* about doing something.

THE HOLD DECISION OUGHT TO *BE* A DECISION

The hold decision often results from an investor's bias toward a positive outlook on the future, justified by a standard of living that has been generally rising since the Great Depression. This subtle bias can persuade Americans to take enormous personal, career, and financial risks in pursuit of reward. It might well be supposed that as demographics work to gray the population, willingness to tolerate risk may decline. Such a perspective may seem foreign after a multiyear bull market, but that context will not persist forever uninterrupted.

Investing in the equity market certainly requires a degree of optimism, but that upward bias must be supported by fundamentals in the industry and company, by thoughtful personal judgment, and sometimes also by the judgment of suitable advisors. It is appropriate for an investor to take some risks in search of a stock that doubles or in search of the next Intel or Compaq. But if that risk is too high relative to her personal tolerance, she should put her money into certificates of deposit (CDs) or choose a growth fund with a long-established superior record and accept a lower rate of return.

A word about reliance on fundamentals is necessary at this point. All too often investors make the mistake of transference by projecting attributes of an industry, product, or service onto a specific company. Such an error of lazy thinking is especially common when an essential service or product is involved. An example might involve telephone stocks. We cannot conceive of a world without their wares. But just because telephone service is necessary does not mean that any particular company providing it is guaranteed to do so profitably enough to keep paying dividends at today's rates, or even to survive. Some companies may endure fierce commodity price competition and come out as winners, but the winner may not necessarily be the one a particular investor has chosen. Work to ensure that lazy thinking about such matters does not creep into your hold/sell equation.

Unfortunately, investment brokers make their living by catering to that aforementioned investor optimism, which supports the buy bias described earlier. Investors lose billions of dollars every year because of the optimism and casual thinking they bring to daily living. Money is lost not only on fraudulent too-good-to-be-true, get-rich schemes but also in the buying and too-patient holding phases of legitimate securities transactions.

To offset that tendency, proper buy timing and pricing can help reduce the pressure that inevitably surrounds the selling decision. There is a natural tendency to fall victim to excitement and buy a stock when it is already hot. Only the most disciplined of traders and investors consistently refuse to buy stocks on good news, on stories, or on excited rallies. Instead they demonstrate self-discipline by staying with buy limits placed below those market prices prevailing at the time a buy deci-sion is first made.

Buying too high on a burst of excitement is the first source of optimism-in-duced losses for traders and investors. But even greater damage results from hold-ing onto positions because of excessive or unjustified optimism. One major diffi-culty in overcoming this problem is that declining stocks occasionally do rally. An occasional burst of counter-trend strength in a weak stock does its diehard owners more harm than good.

To illustrate, suppose an investor buys a stock (Figure 7–2) at $100 a share and then watches it decline by exactly $1/8$ of a point every single day. In eight weeks, the stock eases to $95, and in 16 weeks it trails off to $90. The erosion is gradual but relentless. Every day this investor picks up the newspaper or calls his broker for a quote, and the story is always the same: down again, down just $1/8$.

Now imagine a second stock (Figure 7–3), also bought for $100 a share. This one also heads south, but in a different pattern, actually in a way that accurately re-flects true market tendencies. Some days it drops $1/4$, or $1/2$, or even a full point. But on other days it rallies. In fact, sometimes it rebounds consistently for maybe a week or more at a time. Overall, however, its net rate of decline is the same as that of the previous (daily $1/8$) decliner: every eight weeks it falls by the same net five points.

FIGURE 7–2

Constant Decliner

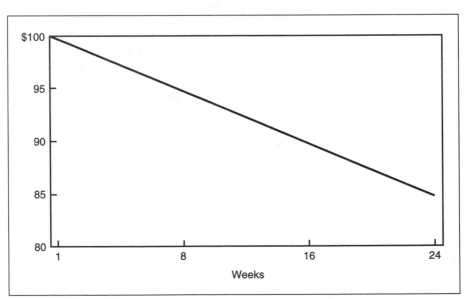

FIGURE 7–3

Jagged Mover

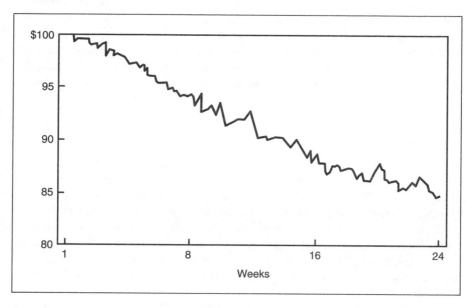

Most investors probably would have a more positive frame of mind toward this second stock—when it reaches 90 or 85 or even 80—than about the first—on the same dates and at the same prices. Why? Our second stock, by rallying—sometimes for several days in succession and occasionally by a nice point or more—has provided positive feedback more recently and immensely more often than that constant ⅛ decliner. Each time the stock turns up, a flicker of hope is kindled. The major problem here is that even bad (declining) stocks have their good days (or weeks).

Not only does daily price action in the market sometimes renew hope, there can be positive fundamental news as well. A reasonably good quarterly earnings report or an optimistic brokerage recommendation will generate a renewal of optimism in the heart of any investor. Recognize that, as the holder of a specific common stock, you are not an entirely objective human being. Every positive wiggle in the stock price, every time the quote holds steady against a 35-point drop in the Dow, and every good piece of news is a source of positive psychological feedback. Anything that goes right is a vindication of personal judgment, a welcome boost to the ego, and a source of renewed feelings of grandiosity.

Thus, if the dominant price path of the stock is downward, each and every cause for renewed optimism is actually a false signal. In the cold light of reality, those false signals should be viewed as uninvited distractions from the truth rather than as rays of hope.

When hope springs eternal, the investor must separate the facts of the situation from the fiction. This discrimination process must include not only the hard news background—what is actually true about the company and its industry versus what is rumor and hope—but also the equally important personal psychological environment, in which the investor has linked his or her state of mind with a company and its stock. Guard against being trapped by a personal, renewed sense of optimism when hope springs eternal.

USING CHARTS

The best way for an investor to calibrate his state of mind against the market is to rely on stock price charts. Putting aside that unending debate about the virtue or logic of technical analysis, a chart can be useful as an accurate road map of price movement history. The most accessible and useful charts for the big picture are those included on the front side of Standard & Poor's Individual Stock Reports. A mere couple of inches provide a 10-year motion picture of stock movements. (Some analysts argue that a 10-year analysis is questionable because too much fundamental and economic background change occurs, and the data may, therefore, lose some relevancy.) Fortunately, the Internet age has brought multiple sources of on-line charts, often at little or no cost, that are updated daily and even during market hours.

Without any expertise in charting techniques, an investor can spot whether the stock is still in a downtrend or whether its price action has overcome negative momentum for the better. Only rarely will it be true to say, "I am not sure; it seems to be right at the point of reversing." If that is true, resolve to look again in a week, and make a yes/no decision then, refusing to take another time extension.

To make this process truly useful, impose a self-discipline by writing down some decision guidelines the first time—something like, "The stock seems to be right on the edge of the top of the down-channel at its present price of 39. If it moves up to at least 40, I will be convinced that it has really broken its downtrend, and I will hold. But if it fails on this move by backing down to $37\frac{1}{2}$, that will be a sign that this latest rally was a false hope. In that case I will sell at market."

Any investor who needs a nudge should mail his or her broker a copy of this decision rule with a note asking to be called in 10 or 14 days to do the follow-up chart reading jointly. Note that what is written should be confined entirely to the action of the stock and not include anything about feelings, cost, desired price targets, or gains or losses. Focus entirely on the factual reality of the stock, and give up hopeful desire.

Above all, do not back into a nondecision by default through the insidious process that consultants call "analysis-paralysis." The market keeps moving with or

How Do You Feel?

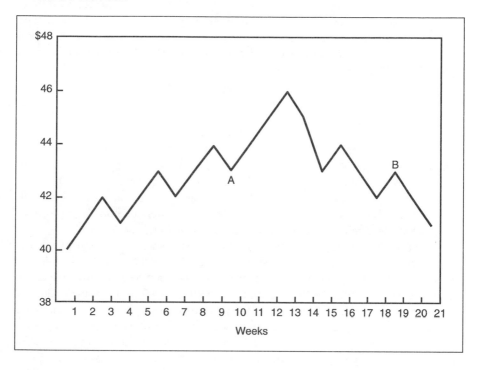

without an investor. So do not wait open-endedly for just a little more news or tech-nical confirmation. There is never going to be a final answer or a point of total clo-sure. So exercise discipline: make an evaluation, and take action accordingly.

If your stock declines and then rebounds, take note of a change in personal optimism level. (See Figure 7–4.) Keep a daily notebook in which to write down the stock's price and what feelings arise about it; then decide whether a revival of optimism for the stock is truly justified by new facts. Bear in mind that when a de-clining stock has rallied back to a given price level, it feels better to the owner than when it had earlier fallen back to that same price. The most recent feedback creates hope (and today has more saliency), while the earlier move produced fear. Watch the emotional difference, even at the same price. (See $43 in the graph above.)

The price you pay for a stock can get in the way of prudent selling because it influences later willingness to sell in terms of both timing and price. So buying well is important—but it is only half of the transaction. The investor also must exit skill-fully. Failure to buy well not only puts all the burden of possible net success on the exit execution, but it also colors the holder's thinking in ways that are damaging.

First, an investor can expect little broker support to sell if he did not buy well (i.e., cheaply). Brokers are paid on their volume of business generated, and, in the last few years, this income generation has been under increasing pressure. In these circumstances, they skew their efforts more strongly than ever toward clients and investment suggestions that are likely to generate transactions. As a result, calling an investor to engage in a discussion of a stock that was bought badly is not high on most brokers' to-do lists.

The Broker as Devil's Advocate

Just as a CEO is best served by subordinates who think for themselves and have the courage to speak their minds, investors are best served by a broker who acts as a devil's advocate. What the client does not need is a rubber stamp to simply confirm his or her own thinking. Many of today's brokers are salespersons rather than seasoned investment professionals, so the hunt for a good devil's advocate is difficult because most account executives, if indeed they pay much attention at all to individual stocks, fear being fired for making investors uncomfortable.

A broker's tendency to act in a consensus or status-quo mode is strongest exactly when it is least helpful: at market extremes. When the crowd is unanimous that a big rally has further to go or that the world is about to end, brokers feel the greatest pressure to conform since they are figuratively swimming in the middle of a raging tide every minute. Although it is dangerous to generalize, they often do not dare express with any conviction a heretical contrary view. Therefore, to increase your chance of market success, select a broker who operates on a contrarian basis. That way if the impulse to act contrary to the crowd at market extremes fails to arise in you, this rare breed of broker can save the day for having been selected on his or her ability to be a disciplined contrarian.

There are two significant aspects to the reluctance of brokers to sell stocks that were not first well bought: time and price. Suppose a broker's research department has advised the purchase of XYZ Widget. It is possible that an investor got on board late because his broker paid little attention when the stock was still near its lows, the broker did not develop confidence in this analyst recommendation until after a good rally already had taken place, or the client did not become convinced until the broker had pushed it after it was already clearly going up.

The stock has risen from 30 to 40, and the client bought at 38. Now what happens if (1) the research analyst turns bearish, (2) the company's fundamentals deteriorate, or (3) the overall market signals it is time to move to the sidelines?

Our broker is embarrassed to report the analyst's about-face just after his client got on board, and he well may worry that the investor suspects account churning. The broker also may believe that the market is consolidating before a further rise, as many would in this case. In any event, the broker is subject to an ever-optimistic buy bias, so phoning the investor about selling is not attractive to him.

Finally, our broker knows that since she just got in at 38, the investor is less prone to selling quickly at 40 than a luckier or more decisive client who entered at 32 several months earlier. Deep in his gut, the broker hopes that the stock will rally further, allowing the lower-priced (early) buyers out here or higher and getting his late-entry client a few more points' profit and more time from her entry point so that he can phone her with better news later (higher price).

The client should not expect a quick call when the rating drops from "buy" to "hold" or (rarely!) "sell." So one aspect of buying badly is short timing between entry and the new, less bullish recommendation. Of course if the buy was the investor's idea, the barrier is even higher: the broker will expect indignant "price" resistance (actually driven by a defensive ego) upon daring to call with a suggestion to sell.

The second problem is a price-driven sell, which occurs on a loss. Suppose that the investor gets in at 38 on the way to 40, and our analyst is right in thinking that things have gone sour. The price is now 37. Not only does the *broker* feel squeamish about calling now (an easy criticism is to say he should have called when it was at 40), more bad tendencies result from the *client's* own mind-set.

A typical client does not sell readily at a one-point loss, especially having first tasted a quick, two-point paper profit. So the investor compounds the broker's weakness: if one of them is inclined to sell, the other probably is not; the phone call may not be made by either party. So both the timing aspect of having entered late (bought recently) and the price aspect of having suffered a loss (bought too high) are dangers to the investor's financial health. A change of mind soon after a buy is an ego embarrassment because it inherently involves an admission of error. Taking a loss is a second blow to self-esteem. It is evident then how both the timing and price of a badly made buy render any selling decision more painful and difficult than it would be on a big gainer.

The truth is that when it is time to sell before the price goes down, it is time for everyone to sell, no matter what the timing is or what the cost at entry. But human nature somehow seemingly prevents investors from factoring *out* in their sell decisions a stock's initial price. And the shorter time an unsuccessful stock has been held, the less an investor is willing to switch mental gears and say "sell."

What alone should determine your decision is whether this stock seems likely to go down from here and now; if it does, it should be sold as soon as possible. The central question that should decide the hold/sell dilemma is, "Would I buy this stock today?" Many investors fail to ask that question at all. Rather, they fall back on hope, their initial price target, memories of better past prices, or similar factors having no realistic bearing on future potentials.

There is no denying that buying better helps most investors cash in more effectively when the right time comes. Most buying mistakes (aside from acquiring inflated "hot" new issues and penny stocks) occur not in buying bad stocks but in buying mediocre or even good stocks too late—again, because investors tend to be crowd followers. They wait for confirmation because they lack sufficient courage to act without a feeling of overwhelming optimism. They are most ready to jump in only sometime later, when the overall market, the individual stock, or both have already become overbought.

While our main focus is on successful selling, there are three places in the book that help investors contain and overcome their tendency to buy too late (too high): Chapter 11 on contrarian thinking, Chapter 14 on emotional red flags, and the checklist on common investing mistakes provided in the Appendix.

If a stock is held only because of perceived positive potentials for the whole market, it should be sold. Throughout this book, one acid-test questions appears: "Would I buy today?" A similarly revealing question is whether an investor would consider selling it here if he had bought better. If there is even a hint of an affirmative answer, he must recognize that cashing in is the right thing to do.

A WORD ABOUT BROKERAGE COMMISSIONS

Throughout this chapter's preceding pages, use of a full-service, full-commission brokerage firm has been assumed. For many readers, this may not be accurate, implying a heightened need to operate in a go-it-alone mode. Investors who are self-starters and do their own research and maintain their own discipline need not pay full *advice-can-be-useful* commission rates. While stock-skilled brokers' and their attention to breaking news is sometimes quite important, many investors prefer to trade away these benefits for significantly lower transactions costs.

Those who find themselves frequently considering commission costs as a factor in hold/sell decisions should seriously consider the true, deep-discount brokerage alternative. As of late 1996, more than a dozen firms offered flat-rate commissions regardless of size and type of order, at $30 or less each way. One processes odd-lot orders for $20. Several allow electronic order entry by telephone, personal computer modem, or Internet for $15 to $19. An excellent source listing such choices for self-directed investors is the annual January issue of the *AAII Journal* (see Appendix for address and telephone). A striking example of the mind-freeing power of low commissions costs is this: if you pay $30 for 500 shares, your round-trip cost, at $60, is less than one-eighth per share. In that context, the cost to change your mind, or to buy a little insurance or peace of mind, is so small as to be irrelevant; your only remaining point of mental debate is which way the stock seems likely to move next.

8

Forget Your Cost Price

KEYS TO INVESTMENT SUCCESS

- Accept the Irrelevance of Your Personal Cost Price
- Know the Few Cases When Cost Price Might Matter
- Cease to Misuse Personal Cost Price

Traders and investors alike unknowingly attach enormous subjective importance to their own cost price in a stock. When this personal history takes on its a life of its own, it colors future thinking. Awareness of this historical cost-price point is a subtle, powerful, and dangerous influence on a selling decision. Therefore, this chapter exposes and seeks to correct such thinking.

THE IRRELEVANCE OF PERSONAL COST PRICE

Humbling though it might be, the first reality that must be established regarding history is the total insignificance of any one investor's purchase event. In the markets of the middle 1990s, on average more than 350,000,000 shares are changing hands daily on the New York Stock Exchange alone. Similar or larger trading volumes are seen daily in NASDAQ's listings. A 300- or 1,000-share purchase, which may be a financial event of note and an emotionally charged decision for an individual investor, is lost in that avalanche of daily Wall Street activity. Even so, the historic accident of one's buy price becomes psychological baggage of great personal magnitude. And almost always, its effect is detrimental to the eventual execution of a successful sale. (It should be noted that a successful sale does not necessarily mean a profit. It can, under some circumstances, mean a deftly timed exit that prevents a loss or a greater loss from developing or that frees capital for some other more productive use.)

A good sale point is a time/price combination on the stock's historical chart that, when viewed in hindsight, evokes the reaction, "Wow, that sure was a good exit point right there!" The successful sale point is, therefore, defined only in terms of what occurs *after* it in time—not at all in terms of the historical fact of any one owner's related purchase price.

If a stock is to collapse from 50 to 30 in the next week, a sale at or around 50 now is a good sale for anyone, regardless of whether the stock was bought at 52, 48, 75, 20, or $50^1/_4$.

This is a key point, so it bears re-emphasis: a good price or time at which to sell a stock is defined by what happens to that stock *after your sale occurs* and has nothing to do with any prior event (the purchase date or price). A good sale is advantageous in hindsight context, regardless of whether it closes out a small or large gain, breaks even, or nets a loss. It is a good sale if it sidesteps a subsequent decline or if it avoids a loss of money's time value (a prolonged sideways market or a period of serious relative underperformance; see Chapter 12 for more detail on this concept.)

All too often, however, the irrelevance of an investor's cost price is not reflected in the way she views her holdings. She has in mind that she owns 200 Chrysler at $58^1/_4$; in fact, she simply owns 200 Chrysler. But her cost price per share, unfortunately, has become a figurative line in the sand and, therefore, a historic hook. When the stock is above personal cost price, she feels smart, superior, and vindicated (increasingly so as the margin of paper profit widens). But when a stock trades below cost, our investor feels insulted, cheated, ashamed, stubborn, or deprived. Ideas of celebration or bragging have disappeared.

When this stock's price is once again at her cost point at a date subsequent to her entry, that coincidence can trigger any of four conditions:

1. If the stock has recovered from an interim decline, she feels relief and ego vindication: relief because the pain of having suffered a reversal has been alleviated (ignoring the time value of her money, of course); vindication because once again she can look into the mirror and know she was right.

2. When price rallies back up to her buying level, she experiences excitement: now the action is really going to get started. If the stock happens to hang around her personal cost-price level for quite some time, each return to that level is likely to trigger some degree of boredom or frustration. But at the same time, prolonged trading at her cost level is likely to reinforce in her mind the concept that such a price is reasonable, represents demonstrably solid value, and is deserved by the stock (or, more dangerously, by the holder personally). But unfortunately such

cathexis, or strength of feelings about a price (in this case, created by frequent reinforcement), is likely to intensify our investor's later difficulty in selling if the stock price moves lower. Conditioned to expecting a given price level and holding out for its reattainment, an investor can become fixed by her own perception.

3. The opposite emotional reaction occurs when a stock after purchase has risen and then subsequently falls back to one's cost-price level. The greater the price distance of the now retraced move, the more intense is our investor's emotional reaction. There is a very empty feeling of having given it all back—a sense of sadness and emotional emptiness or loss that anyone who has gambled away a temporary profit will remember all too well. The primary reaction is one of shame or disappointment with one's indecisiveness or lack of discipline. But a stubbornness also takes hold. One recalls previously reached high levels and believes that the company's stock deserved to sell at those quotes and therefore should return to them. Our investor then resolves to hold on for that rally, even though it is one merely fantasized out of hope or desperation.

4. Paradoxically, as an alternative, that decline back to cost price may actually plant the subconscious seeds of resignation to loss. Having done so badly by failing to sell at a profit, our investor begins to feel maybe she is doomed to having a bad experience with this stock anyway. Of course, depending on the size and tenderness of the ego involved, the now-disappointed investor may try to cover up feelings of self-criticism over failure to nail down that earlier paper profit. She can blame it all on bad luck, on a broker or an advisory letter, on the overall market, or even on "they."

Therefore, be very wary of the psychological trap that the memory of cost can represent. The greatest single problem it creates is that mental line in the sand—the dividing line between gain and loss, between wisdom and foolishness, between mental celebration and remorse. Remember that an individual trade is an insignificant grain of sand on the market's beach. To quote an old cliché, the stock doesn't know you own it!

WHEN MIGHT COST PRICE BE RELEVANT?

There are only four cases in which price paid actually may have some significance in the market at a later date. But even in these instances, that price's importance is totally coincidental and is not caused by or related to a personal purchase action. What these four circumstances have in common is that they each involve price levels to which large numbers of *other* investors attach meaning. It is those large numbers, not your participation in the equation, that make this price have significance.

The first significant price level at which an investor coincidentally or accidentally may establish a cost is when a primary or secondary offering takes place. That level, by definition, involves a large number of shares and a large number of other investors. If a new issue comes to market at $10, that level becomes the mental mark in the sand for thousands of individuals—a win/loss inflection point. Such a point later may be viewed as the level to "get out and get even," as a trigger point for a stop-loss order, or as a point where some investors may double up. Whichever kind of reaction the crowd has in relation to this price level, the historical pricing level of a primary or secondary offering can have a significant effect on future price action.

An investor may buy into that offering or, just coincidentally, buy at some other time but at the same price. While the price he paid actually does have some significance in the market, in this case it has nothing to do with his few hundred shares. It is the distribution at that price of perhaps several million shares to many investors that matters; they attach psychological weight to that price and are likely to take buy or sell actions related to its return.

The second event that can make any price important is the so-called price gap. Much has been written by market technicians about the theory and importance of chart gaps in the history of a stock's price action. However, our point here is not to arbitrate that debate.

Briefly summarized, the market lore of price gaps is that all gaps tend to be closed. Actually, it is probably more accurate to say that upside gaps (except in cases of successful takeovers) tend to be retraced and filled. Some downside gaps are caused by such powerful negative fundamental news that they literally may never be filled. So do not be lured into a false sense of optimism about all gaps being filled. The company might not recover, and, in some cases, it may eventually disappear following a devastating chain of events triggered by whatever news caused the downside gap. As this was written, ValuJet's future viability seemed hanging in the balance following its tragic Flight 592 crash in May 1996. Corporate survival would have overriding impact, not the fact that a downside price gap existed between 17 and 13.

The point about gaps is this: whether or not an investor is a technician or believes that price gaps are important technical phenomena, large numbers of other traders and investors active in the market undeniably *do* hold that viewpoint. Their collective actions or inactions, based on their beliefs, do have an effect on market-price action. So the gap price itself becomes important in later market behavior.

Say an investor buys right at the moment the gap developed. While the market, in this case, does attach significance to his price, it is for reasons unconnected to him. It is like having a December 25th birthday.

Round numbers also may be significant price points, but for reasons that bear little objective relation to rational investment theory. In the same way that a primary offering or a gap price level creates a memory in the minds of investors, a round number can become a trigger for action. Many recall saying, "If IBM ever corrects back to 100 (or 75), I am definitely going to buy some." Or, "If stock X hits 25, I will take my profit there." In the case of lower-priced issues, it is any full-dollar figure that becomes a target. When large numbers of people act on these targets, such price levels actually do become significant because of bids and asks that cluster at or very near them. Again, however, it is not because of any single investor's 200 shares acquired there.

Finally, any of several technical chart-price patterns may render a particular price level significant. Tops and bottoms of channels, tops of rising triangles, the apex or "breakout point" of a triangle, a neckline in a head-and-shoulders formation, or that price at which multiple tops or bottoms have occurred can all become significant price points.

It is randomly possible that your own purchase price level might coincide, whether it is established before or after those events. Subsequent market action may call renewed attention to this particular price level, fixing it even more firmly in mind as important. But its relevance derives from that price level's larger technical importance, created by many other participants (some of whom *do* believe in charts) who attach meaning to that level.

Therefore, avoid building a strategy on an imaginary foundation that your personal price is important to the market just because it seems important to you. In addition to defining the very real (at least pre-commission) dividing line between profit and loss, one's cost price sets up several other private mental constructs that have no operative importance in the marketplace.

MISUSING PERSONAL COST PRICE

What these constructs all have in common is their being linked to your cost price as a starting point—an accidental moment that then becomes subjectively important history. Personal cost forms the baseline for some calculation that exists only in your head. For example, your goal may be to make five points, 15 percent or 20 percent before commissions, or an ambitious 50 percent gain or even a double. Or you might set either a mental or an actual stop-loss point designed to limit a loss to some predetermined amount in points or percentage. All these formulae share the commonality of a personal entry-price level. But the market is not conscious of any such formula!

If technical analysis has any meaning, the chart pattern itself defines reasonable resistance and support levels that relate to the stock's overall recent or long-term past history but do not in any way have cause-and-effect ties to any individual's particular entry point.

For example, suppose that some investor's stock is locked in a lengthy and

FIGURE 8–1

Locked in a Price Channel

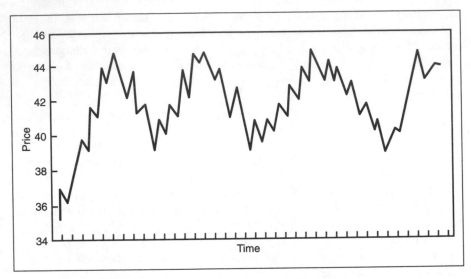

well-defined price channel between 39 and 45 (see Figure 8–1). Assume he is lucky or smart enough to have bought at 40. By setting an arbitrary upside goal of 15 percent above cost (before or after commissions), this individual will be frustrated by repeated retreats from the 45 level, just about a point short of his personal target of 46. If, on the other hand, he sets a 10 percent stop-loss error margin, his trigger will be 36—three full points below a very obvious breakdown level of 39 on a decline.

Setting any formula based on one's entry price could easily be self-defeating in this case. Triggers should be based on the chart's evidence regarding realistic near-term price targets and significant support levels, or on reasonable longer-term fundamental valuation measures, not in relation to some accident of personal cost.

Here is another reason not to base a stop-loss order on a rigid percentage away from personal cost: suppose you believe in setting a 10 percent limit on losses. Selling at whatever price that implies would make the concept of bargain hunting at the same price appear wrong. If it is correct (showing patience and discipline) to buy down at a certain price, selling down at that price must be wrong. In Figure 8–1, a protective stop at 40 to protect a poorly-timed purchase at 44 would be an example.

In summary, the "memory-becomes-history" syndrome based on personal cost can be highly detrimental to later execution of a good sale. Cost-price history causes a host of psychological reactions to subsequent price action in the stock, most of which battle against a good sale decision and most of which are probably quite unrelated to what the market collectively perceives about that stock.

A personal entry point and any formulae it generates are not as relevant as the stock's own demonstrated price history and fundamental valuation parameters, which are totally unrelated to your individual entry point. Keeping these psychological and factual perspectives in mind requires deliberate suppression of ego, which may feel humbling when first implemented. But that effort may actually prove easier than what is theoretically more helpful but in practice seems virtually impossible: forgetting what was paid and letting the stock's future action alone indicate when and where to sell.

9

Understand That You Sell the Stock, Not the Company

KEYS TO INVESTMENT SUCCESS

- Separate the Stock and the Company
- Realize that Price Equals the Changing Level of Esteem

To legitimize becoming a long-term holder, an investor must find a comfort zone; there is none better than fundamentals, he or she will say. When price behavior in an intended shorter term position becomes unexpectedly negative, the investor rationalizes a flip from the technical to the fundamental orientation: "It's a really good company so its stock is bound to come back." In fact, the more one knows about a company and the stronger the ties that are felt with it, the more danger there is of switching from a trader/selling mode to an investor/holding mode. A switch of investment objectives is a major warning signal; alert, well-disciplined investors must take pains to guard against any such switches.

SEPARATING THE STOCK AND THE COMPANY

The invention of a new reason to hold rather than sell is confused thinking. In the same way that weak decision making causes a trader to become an investor (collector) by default, another confusion can creep in that just as easily prompts holding: the mistaken idea that the stock is the same thing as its company. Although a stock certificate legally does represent some fractional share in the corporation, a company and its stock should never be considered identical.

Often when a holder's position begins to erode, he changes tactical identity by default from trader to long-term holder. What he has done is to mistakenly associate the stock with the virtues and strengths of the underlying company. This is a subtle but critical mistake that must be strenuously guarded against. A further danger arises when our trader then fails to perceive that such confusion of identities has taken place, for this lack of perception only reduces any chance of correcting the situation.

No stock goes up forever, no matter how strong its issuing company. Even during a raging bull market, not every stock price advances. Among those that do score increases over a year or more, none progress in price at a steady rate without interim fluctuations or setbacks. Sometimes even the greatest growth stocks experience meaningful interim declines. While a given company may prosper consistently over time—such as American Home Products or Coca-Cola with their lengthy records of consecutive quarterly earnings advances—its stock often acts independently in the short to medium term. The reasons are usually completely unrelated to company fundamentals; they can include an adverse trend in the general market, temporary factors such as group leadership rotations, or simply a short-term correction of an overly exuberant earlier advance.

Therefore, a stock and its issuing company often do not move in harmony: there are times when a firm's business prospers but its shares decline in price; at other times the stock's price can even be advancing, seemingly against all logic, when fundamentals are in a decline.

Traders most often tend to equate the stock with the company when its share price has fallen since purchase. The trader becomes an investor through the back door by falling back on fundamentals or generalized faith in the company when its shares decline. Seeking justification for the decision to hold rather than sell, our investor now waxes enthusiastic about the company's virtues (or even its industry's great prospects) rather than focusing on prospects for what is most important to making a profit: stock price performance.

Usually the symptoms of this misguided switch in investment status are rearview-mirror in nature. Examples are, "They have reported 47 consecutive quarters of rising sales and earnings." Or, "You know, they are ranked number so-and-so in the Fortune 500 now." But, in actuality, something clearly has gone wrong because reputation and Fortune ranking have not helped the stock to rise since purchase.

An even more dangerous influence is a relationship between the stockholder and the corporation. Emotional ties (such as employment, enjoyment of company products, or warm feelings about company community involvement) are difficult to keep in perspective. Exactly when the time is most critical, such loyalty ties usually stand in the way of a tactical sale of the stock. When a stock is up, we praise its technical strength and/or our wisdom in buying and holding it; after a decline, we seek fundamental anchors in support of holding on.

The difficulty in keeping stock and company conceptually separated is compounded when the shareholder's ownership position has been publicized to others. If people around him know that he owns stock in his own or a relative's employer, he feels in a bind when it is time to sell the stock. This psychological complication is avoidable, but only with deliberate effort. It is also a persuasive reason not only for mentally separating any company from its stock but also for never divulging personal investment positions.

PRICE EQUALS THE CHANGING LEVEL OF ESTEEM

Another subtle but critical factor in an investor's decision to sell or hold—or, in this context, to separate the company and its stock—is awareness of some common terminology used when buying. A broker or investor might casually say, "I think we ought to own some Microsoft," or "Our General Electric really has treated us well." Buying with this personalizing attitude, namely, of owning some of the company and its essence, subconsciously encourages the investor to identify with that company as an emotional partner/owner. In an increasingly depersonalized and fast-changing world, we all tend to seek affiliations. Downsizing has taught employees to reject old-time concepts of loyalty to companies; shareholders need pay no greater duty of allegiance, especially when international competition and emerging technologies now change even major companies' prospects faster than ever before.

If an investor cannot sharply distinguish his separate personal identity from his position as shareholder and thus somehow partner, the investment is essentially pre-ordained to become a long-term collector's item. It is critical, then, to focus at all times on the concept that a stock is purchased in anticipation of taking advantage of the expected rising esteem level at which other investors hold the company; you are merely a passive rider on the stock's price coattails and do not truly purchase a share of ownership in the sense of buying into a medical or law partnership or some other active business venture.

In reality, a company may reach new heights of prosperity while you as individual stockholder own a bit of it, but you still can lose money. Why? You and other temporary owners have bought merely rights to cash in on whatever changing level of *perception* other people (taken as a whole, the market) may hold about that company. They may like it less tomorrow because of buying in too late (too high), because interest rates are rising (making all equities less attractive relative to bonds or Treasury bills), because of adverse public opinion about its products, because of press publicity over high corporate executive salaries, because general corporate reputation might deteriorate, because investment tastes shift in favor of other industries, or because of a rising fear of recession.

Other investors collectively may be right or wrong about the company over the short to medium term. And you as an individual may prove correct, while the majority are incorrect, about fundamentals. As Benjamin Graham noted in *The

Intelligent Investor, markets act as voting machines in the short term but in the long run function as weighing machines. Thus, actions and opinions of the crowd determine share price in the short to medium term, which is the most important factor because that share price determines whether you have a gain or a loss, and when. So buy and sell not just on personal judgment of a company behind a stock but on your studied assessment of what other investors think of the company and how that thinking seems likely to change.

In the same way, making investment decisions involves mentally and emotionally separating the facts—or the facts as they are perceived or expected to be—from what the market (i.e., the collective opinion of investors) believes and will come to believe. The company may, indeed, continue to be profitable and to grow. But when or if it falls out of investor favor, no matter how valid or invalid the reasons for that change in collective esteem, its stock price will suffer.

To determine whether now is the time to hold or to sell, focus on changes in perception rather than on fundamentals. An investor can be dead-on right about fundamentals. But if the market collectively decides that it no longer is willing to pay as much for this company's reputation or earnings, its share price heads south. Eventually, an individual's logic may be vindicated again as value reasserts itself and other investors resume their willingness to pay for it. But in the interim, the individual is going to suffer a loss for fighting the tape.

The tape reflects market reactions and perceptions translated into buying and selling decisions; it does not reflect the truth about a company's fundamentals. So keep in mind that the company and its stock are separate. You ought to buy a stock out of willingness to bet that others will pay a higher price because of whatever good reasons you perceive in advance. Purchase is a bet based on your judgments of market perception, company reputation, and collective psychology—it should not be perceived as acquisition of a piece of the company. Stocks are best used when bought and sold for profit, not when held as nostalgic or affiliation talismen. (See Figure 9–1.) Holding a stock near interim high point "A" bets on your fortitude at "D" and wastes time until "B" when future value will catch up with today's overoptimistic price.

Being able to keep a company and its stock strictly separate in your mind has become ever more critical in recent years. Excellent companies such as Xerox, Compaq, or PepsiCo may suffer single-quarter earnings shortfalls against analyst estimates or might even experience actual interim declines in earnings. As will be discussed in Chapter 10, such minor stumbles usually call down immediate massive institutional selling. While such selling may be vastly disproportionate to any long-term true fundamental meaning of the event, it does signal a period of more cautious appraisal by major investors. If you maintain the mental agility to view a stock as an opinion barometer because you have separated it from the company's fundamentals, you will be able to sell without costly hesitation. Fail to separate a

FIGURE 9–1

Market Timing versus Holding Long Term

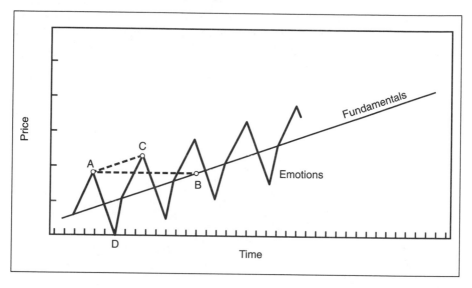

company and its stock in your mind and you will have great difficulty over separa-
tion and loyalty issues and will be less successful in your investment moves.

Figure 9–1 could have substituted the word "Esteem" for the usual price scale
on its Y axis. Unless you plan on holding forever, which will produce merely average or even sub-par returns, you need to buy and sell. Swings in market psychology
drive prices to fluctuate around true long-term value (if only the latter could ever be
known accurately today!). Another way of viewing these price swings is to think of
them as changes in the consensus of esteem given to a company by all investors
taken together. When esteem runs up above reasonable valuation of fundamentals,
price will eventually correct downward to redress that temporary mistake. Above-
average profits accrue to those who capture such positive differentials of esteem minus reality. (Similarly, on the buying side of the equation, handsome profit opportunities can be captured when reality minus esteem is a positive number, meaning
that the stock in more common terms is temporarily undervalued by the market of
opinion.)

When you sell a company's stock, no one else except your broker (who, these
days, might be a computer!) need know—unless you are an insider or 5 percent
holder required to file a Form 13-D with the SEC. The company is an inanimate object; it will not be hurt since it will not feel any sense of desertion or disloyalty on
your part. By keeping a company and all it represents to the outside world clearly

differentiated in your mind from your ownership of its stock, you will free yourself to sell without looking back when price rises to your objective or when fundamentals change and render your prior price objective now invalid. Yes, you certainly should want to buy stock in good/strong companies rather than feeble/failing ones since that difference will raise your odds of cashing in on rising esteem. You should view the world's collective esteem for a company as something to take advantage of rather than to fall in love with and be enveloped by.

10

Adopting Survival Tactics for the Institutional Jungle

KEYS TO INVESTMENT SUCCESS

- Survey Today's Investment Scene: It's a Jungle Out There!
- Learn How to Survive in the Institutional Jungle
- Take Action to Avoid Being Trampled

In times past many market analysts, advisors, and investors considered large holdings by institutional investors a positive factor in evaluating a stock. If those big players like it, such logic said, it must be good. Perhaps that remains valid in terms of longer term fundamental merit. However, this chapter makes a case for viewing high institutional ownership as a distinct threat to near-term price stability. And price means wealth to any stock's owners, so sharp, sudden price risk should be taken very seriously. When a stampede gets going, the smallest creatures are at risk of being trampled—unless they are able to move very fast!

SURVEYING TODAY'S INVESTMENT SCENE: IT'S A JUNGLE OUT THERE!

The past four decades, and particularly those years since 1987, have seen increasing dominance of securities markets by institutions. Today mutual funds get much of the attention, but insurance companies and pension plans also remain major factors. As illustrated in the accompanying graph (Table 10–1), derived from data supplied by Lipper Analytical Services, Inc., assets controlled by mutual funds investing in

T A B L E   10–1

Rising Importance of Institutions

Year	Value of All NYSE-Listed Stocks ($ Billions)	Value of All Stocks Held By Equity Mutual Funds ($ Billions)	Ratio
1975	885	37	1:25
1980	1,349	49	1:23
1985	1,950	124	1:16
1990	2,820	263	1:11
1995	6,013	1260	Under 1:5

stocks have grown almost 35-fold, from $37 billion in December 1975 to $1.26 trillion as of December 1995. In the same 20 years, the value of stocks listed on the New York Stock Exchange (admittedly, no longer the uniquely dominant trading market it once was) grew less than sevenfold to just over $6 trillion. With more baby boomers coming into their primary asset-accumulation years and also realizing that they must invest to avoid financial disaster in retirement, market participation will rise. Millions of these boomers are not especially interested in the market and/or are afraid to handle serious money on their own. Thus, institutional control over assets and trading in the stock market can only grow.

The New York Stock Exchange estimates that institutional activity accounts for about 70 percent of the value traded on an average day. Such dominance on the trading floor presents both a problem and an opportunity for individual investors. In a nutshell, the problem is that institutional buying and selling de-stabilizes the market, especially since many large investors are increasingly short term in orientation, often chasing price or earnings momentum rather than focusing on long-term value. Lately, the slightest deviation from analysts' consensus estimates triggers major and rapid price movement. Usually such price adjustments are more extreme on the downside than on the upside, primarily because fear is a stronger motivator than greed.

This environment presents individuals with three choices. First, as so many millions have already done, they can abandon individual stocks and place their money in mutual funds. This route, of course, merely makes institutional dominance even greater. Program trading, widely publicized as an alleged cause or at least an aggravator of the sudden October 1987 meltdown, was an excuse for many to take exactly this approach. Such investors add to the problem, but who can blame them if they are basically passive and fearful in their investment lives?

A second choice is to ignore the whole problem and let the market do as it will in the short as well as longer term. Here, an investor admits that he or she cannot predict where institutional lightning will strike next but still feels or concludes that ownership of some great (highly institutionally held) growth stocks is a necessity. Choosing to attempt no protective action is the equivalent of deciding to "grin and bear it."

A third choice attempts to break the cycle of victimization for individual investors. It involves knowledge, preparation, and a proactive approach rather than passive acceptance of short-term price damage compounded by, even worse, reactive panic selling. This approach requires independence of mind, decisiveness, and, at times, a degree of healthy suspicion about how Wall Street works. Here, an investor includes in his or her assessment of every stock its exposure to ravaging by institutional jungle animals.

Increasing, even accelerating, dominance of daily trading by huge players makes choosing action rather than passive victimhood a growing and urgent necessity for individual investors holding stocks directly. Those unwilling to do the preparation and work, and then actually take necessary action (by placing sell orders!), would be much better served by abandoning individual stockholding for mutual funds than by remaining involved directly in stocks. Why? Funds move much less erratically than do individual stocks and, therefore, are less likely to generate emotional reactions such as selling in panic when institutional dumping causes sharp and sudden price damage.

HOW TO SURVIVE IN THE INSTITUTIONAL JUNGLE

Knowledge, evaluation, and action are the three essentials for surviving and prospering in today's institutionally dominated markets. The critically important facts are as follows:

- The proportion of your company's stock held by institutional investors.
- The normal level of trading volume (especially in comparison with institutional positions).
- Timing of the next earnings announcement.
- The strength of the stock's recent performance.

Knowing institutional ownership is one item absolutely integral to a buy decision because it helps define price risk. Three readily accessible information sources here are Standard & Poor's *Security Owner's Stock Guide,* individual company reports by S&P (commonly known as "tear sheets"), and *The Value Line Investment Survey.* Knowing precisely updated levels of ownership by the elephants of Wall Street is not necessary; 60 percent and higher should act as a sign that strong attention must be paid. As percentages rise into the 80 percent to 90 percent range, risk of price volatility becomes extremely great. The following is a listing of mid-1996 institutional holdings in selected well-known stocks:

Stock	Percent
Avon Products	84
BankAmerica	57
Compaq	64
Digital Equipment	69
Exxon	40
Federal Express	78
General Motors	59
Humana	62
Intel	54
Johnson & Johnson	56
Kimberly Clark	67
Louisiana Land & Exploration	80
Mesa Air Group	70
National Semiconductor	82
Oregon Steel	63
Pitney Bowes	82
Questar Corporation	74
Reynolds Metals	79
Seagate Technology	76
Toys 'R' Us	60
Union Pacific	69
Valero Energy	77
Whirlpool	78
Xerox	77
York International	79
Zebra Technologies	54

Average trading volume is also important since it must be related to institutional ownership. Keeping those annual stock and mutual funds table sections published in early January by *The Wall Street Journal* and by many major-city newspapers will provide a handy source of trading volume information. With markets open 250 trading days annually, calculating average daily volume is easy since multiplying an annual total by 0.004 (four-tenths of 1 percent) can be done readily. Again, an S&P stock guide provides a fair approximation because it tracks monthly trading volume (divide by 20 as a fair approximation, but realize that this source is based on a statistically less reliable one-month sample). Even more prone to error is a quick reference to a weekend newspaper, which provides an even smaller, although recent, data sample. Those using computerized databases can readily find volume information for longer periods as desired.

The institutional position must now be related to average trading volume. Suppose an adverse news development, including a company missing the quarterly earnings estimates that analysts have convinced themselves are accurate, should occur. Suppose that perhaps just 5 percent of the institutional shares should be sold in response to bad news. How much stock would that throw into the market, and how many times an average day's volume would that represent? The higher the number of average days' volume, the more likely a stock is to drop severely and sharply for several days. You should not own a stock unless you have done this calculation and envisioned this scenario. It is not theoretical; on the contrary, it is all too common! Institutional money managers are short-term oriented and are driven to perform. Unless professed and practicing contrarians, they sell stocks at the slightest hint of trouble, which they believe will render those stocks continued underperformers in the few months ahead—and a few months is long term in too many of their views!

Not only must our proactive investor know that important ratio of institutional holdings versus average volume, he or she must also be aware of when quarterly earnings are due for publication. Twenty to 45 calendar days after quarter's end is the common range, but that is hardly accurate enough! Value Line, S&P, and other similar sources publish due dates. Except for annual results (which require an audit and thus take longer), each quarter's results are usually published about 90 days apart. An electronic news database will reveal the prior quarter's date. To be most precise, phone the company's investor relations office and simply ask.

The final crucial puzzle piece is how well your stock has performed lately. Quite simply, the greater its recent price strength, the larger the price risk if bad news occurs. Strong short-term price action means positive anticipation is high, so anything short of expected will not do. In bull markets (such as in 1995–1996), investors impatiently and greedily require continued and preferably rapid gains. Disappointment will not be allowed; any stock failing to maintain momentum is thrown overboard for the newer, hotter group or concept. As an example of how institutions produce a herd mentality, one major Midwestern-based mutual funds complex requires its portfolio managers to sell 100 percent of any stock immediately if its quarterly earnings undershoot the in-house analyst's estimate by even $0.01/share. This is an equivalent of shooting first and asking questions later. Their selling will, of course, prompt liquidations by aggressive fund managers whose computer models detect a reversal in price momentum. This, sadly but truly, is the jungle in which individual stock investors must operate.

The listing of crucial factors given earlier does not include what the consensus quarterly earnings estimate is. The reason is that it matters little if at all in an absolute sense. Falling short is a crime punishable by massive selling, no matter what the target was. Those interested can find estimated earnings per share (EPS) in *Value Line*, on S&P tear sheets, or in many electronic databases and several chart services. Extremely strong expected percentage gains probably raise the odds of failure, and its consequences. But any level of earnings estimate, if not achieved, will be met with swift and sharp price declines. An individual investor need not know what the estimate was; market price reaction will immediately reveal whether the actual earnings made the grade. Thus, knowledge of the estimate is less relevant than preparation for the possible consequences of "failure." By analogy, it does not matter exactly what kind of high winds are approaching your property—a hurricane, cyclone, or tornado. You can expect damage if in you are their path, and you must prepare your defenses.

TAKING ACTION TO AVOID BEING TRAMPLED

As any consultant will say, all the information available is worthless unless analyzed and acted upon. How critically true this is in investing! Knowing how heavily exposed a stock is to possible ravages from institutional herd selling will only generate bad headaches unless you take remedial action. The worst action to take when an EPS disappointment makes the big players run for cover is to join them. Their selling creates maximum downward pressure on price and, therefore, peak emotional strain on holders. Unless you monitor your stocks constantly every trading session, you will be late when you see the EPS and price-change news. If you place market orders after the bad news, you are likely to be making an emotionally driven tactical mistake. The best course is to take anticipatory action based on your previously described analysis. (Chapter 26 covers in more detail how to assess the seriousness and impact of bad news and what holding/selling strategies are implied.)

Four courses of action are available. In a bull market, wherein expectations are already high, positive earnings surprises in major, highly institutionally held stocks tend to generate little upside price action. Everyone was already on board. In that context, it can be said that the most prudent course could be to sell such stocks at market on any rally shortly before quarterly earnings due dates. This means stepping aside to see what happens. For those using deep-discount brokers, this is very inexpensive and provides peace of mind as well as capital insurance. It amounts to clearing out of the jungle just before the predictable stampede season. On the whole, and especially with low commissions, it represents more to be saved than missed.

A second course of action is to place a stop-loss order fairly close to the current price shortly before the week when the company is scheduled to report its earnings. Stop placement is discussed in Chapter 23, so it will not be covered in detail here. Basically, the purpose of placing this stop is to guard against the greatest possible amount of potential damage in case those wild animals become unhappy. Here you should be less concerned about the virtues of staying in a good long-term position (a looser stop) than about preventing loss (a tighter placement). A temporary but closely placed stop can easily be removed after the EPS news, assuming no damage was inflicted. Good placement would be at the height of the recent uptrend line, at the price support zone, or down just a couple of points. A stop-loss order placed too far away provides little protection against loss and may actually sell you out very near the short-term bottom, entirely defeating your purpose. Two rules to follow in placing such EPS-time stops: (1) do not use a stop-limit order because, in a fast decline, you will be passed by and thus your order will have been useless, and (2), do not play too cozy a game in timing your order entry: if the company reports after the close or before the open, it may already be too late to enter an order since a bad report will result in a deep downside gap opening, and the damage will already be done. Therefore, have your order in several days ahead of that expected announcement date.

A third approach, and one advocated in the chapters on order placement in Section IV, is always to have a sell order in place above market. This has the virtue of selling you out on strength rather than on weakness. Thus, it would be wise to have a sell order placed at a price above current levels. Where? Just below the upper line of a rising channel or just below the level where selling resistance has previously been found. Don't be greedy for that famous last eighth of a point: a half point or so is little to leave on the table if you are being sold out well on a good upward price move. While above-market sells are generally preferable to stop-loss orders, in the case of quarterly EPS-risk time, the latter also must be in place. If your brokerage firm will not allow both orders on the books simultaneously, place an against-the-box, short-selling order above *and* a stop-loss below, both at technically important levels as just described.

A fourth way to handle this quarterly problem with heavily institutionally owned stocks involves using options. Several good books are available describing options strategies, so no such detail will be attempted here. You need to be prepared; open an options account and sign all necessary forms in advance. It never hurts to have such facilities in place even if they are never used. When a price emergency is already occurring, it is too late to begin options paperwork! The two choices are buying a put option with a strike price below current market (to reduce your premium outlay) and selling a call option with a small in-the-money strike, which will get you some premium earned but not risk much loss in case unexpectedly good news follows. Once the outcome is known for a few days, closing out the put option is generally advisable since time will erode its remaining premium. In addition, bad news will put maximum temporary selling pressure on the stock, raising a put's value and increasing the chance that the next move will be a mild price recovery.

SUMMARY: BEWARE OF THE STAMPEDE

This chapter has warned of the occasional acute price pressure likely in institutionally dominated stocks and has given the reader lists of necessary information to gather and analyze in advance. It has also described order-placement strategies for protecting capital. As you first force and then allow yourself to sell more frequently, the process will come to feel easier and more natural. Buying back is nothing to cause shame. Often a round-trip commission (particularly with a deep-discount broker) is inexpensive insurance against the injuries to be suffered from being trampled by the jungle's herd. The dangers the herd brings are not only avoidable capital losses but also present the risk that you will succumb to emotional strain and sell just as its selling causes a bottom.

SECTION

MASTERING THE
CONTRARIAN APPROACH

11

Be a Contrarian

KEYS TO INVESTMENT SUCCESS

- Define the Contrarian Approach
- Master the Contrarian Approach

Nearly everyone who invests looks to the professionals for advice. The hope, of course, is that the alleged "secret" of professional successes can be learned. But it is not evident that investing success can be learned by anyone who aspires to it; some people have reasonable investing potential and some do not because investing is an art and not entirely a science. As in sports and the creative arts, a certain amount of innate aptitude is required.

For those who have some aptitude, there is no better guru than the man who was reported to be the richest man in the world. Three-time-billionaire J. Paul Getty once said:

Buy when everyone else is selling and hold until everyone else is buying. This is not merely a catchy slogan. It is the very essence of successful investment.

Because this is a book on *selling* investments, Getty's advice should be slightly reworded: "hold until" means "sell when. . . ." The essence of that message is the gospel of contrary opinion. Like any other prescription for investment success, the contrarian approach is never quite as simple to apply as its truth is obvious. This is because there are no exact yardsticks that unfailingly indicate exactly when a trend is overdone.

But this is no reason to abandon all attempts to apply contrary thinking to the investment process. To ignore its wisdom because of a personal inability to catch absolute tops and bottoms by using it is like refusing to eat healthy foods because death is inevitable anyway.

This chapter explains why it is necessary to maintain a contrarian mind-set in both buying and selling stocks. Statistically, it is known that the majority of investors lose money. Only a minority get richer. It is also well documented that a large majority of professional investors, on the order of 75 percent to 80 percent of mutual funds, for example, fail to match their index benchmarks. Professional money managers are known for crowdlike behavior; they prefer to own popular stocks and possibly still lose money comfortably rather than come up short by some less conventional means.

But it is also well known that an investor can be successful despite losing more often than winning, provided that his losses are cut short while profits are allowed to run. To become more successful at investing, then, it is necessary to act less like the majority and more like the minority, more of the time.

DEFINING THE CONTRARIAN APPROACH

Although the zero-sum-game hypothesis in economics is mostly rejected, secondary investment markets taken in isolation and as a closed system are a finite-sum game. Assume that a company is going to sell a certain number of widgets this year, achieve certain margins, pay a given tax rate, and deliver some specific earnings per share regardless of its stock price. The fundamentals help determine price action, as does industry-related and general market psychology.

Given that a stock will move from one price to another, will retrace some or all of that change, and will arrive at a third price or just back at the starting one, and that only a certain amount of trading volume will occur in the process, then some people make money; others lose or forego equal amounts of gain. The entire net price move, in dollars per share, multiplied by the number of shares outstanding equals the increased or decreased combined wealth that all shareholders experience collectively (before commission).

Those who buy at the top lose. Those who sell to them win. Those who scalp three points on the way up take potential profits from those who sold to them. Those who hold on and ride the entire price merry-go-round end up back where they started. They have lost the time value of their money and have failed to accept profits while prices were up. (They also have failed to learn the contrarian's skill of selling high and have probably done themselves some self-image damage in the process.)

Others who did cash in at higher prices have taken profits and can now buy in again at lower prices. Those to whom they sold are now holding higher-cost securities. So it is basically a zero-sum game, where one person's gain is equal to the losses or missed gains of his or her counterparty in buying and selling transactions. Only one side of each transaction on the exchange will prove profitable. Therefore to be successful, learn to play the game better and/or more nimbly than the other players: do *not* follow the crowd.

There is so much emphasis on the buying end of the investment equation that there is plenty of available evidence to monitor how overheated a market is becoming. Bullish pressure can be palpable if an investor looks and listens, and that is useful and valuable input. If one can sense when the clamor to buy is getting out of hand and out of touch with reality, then he or she is recognizing a classic contrarian signal.

MASTERING THE CONTRARIAN APPROACH

To succeed as a contrarian, always look for these signals. Many can be detected by observing events in the world outside that of daily quotations and trading:

- Is the market front-page news in the general local media?
- Do television programs or movies use stock market jokes or plots?
- Are people talking about stocks over lunch more than usual?
- Are brokers making more calls offering "exciting opportunities"?
- Are there numerous IPOs, many doubling or more right away?
- Is corporate or personal prosperity widespread, and are expectations of continued expansion the norm?
- Are many more investment advisors and letter writers bullish than bearish?
- Is the percentage of mutual fund cash in equity funds low or fast declining?
- Has there been an historically very strong net inflow of money into growth-oriented mutual funds?
- Do investors commonly say they expect to get historically unrealistic annual rates of return such as 20 percent or more?
- Are people focusing on potential rewards and ignoring or downplaying risk?
- After a major rise, when skeptics pose troubling questions, are bulls saying "it's different this time. . ."?

These signs of a major long-term top tend to accumulate gradually over a period of months; therefore, they never appear as a major, sudden, shocking cluster. No one rings the bell and declares a bull market over. It happens, literally, when people least expect it. So the would-be winning investor's job is to out-smart and out-think the other players. It is impossible to hit the exact top (that perfectionism issue covered in Chapter 4), so stop worrying about that or trying it. Almost all major market tops occur as rounding-over patterns when viewed on a chart, not as one-day flagpoles. (Chapter 13 will list a few signs of short-term exhaustion tops, but our focus now is on the big picture rather than on tactics.) The losers have absolutely no idea that they are helping to create a top by their classic overenthusiastic behavior. They miss selling at top by a mile, just as they grossly miss the bottoms as buyers.

Savvy investors catch the greatest percentage of the move by cashing in somewhere near the top and are entirely content to sell to a potentially greater fool who tries to hold for the top.

But make no mistake: it is not easy to lean against the tide. It is unfashionable to be a worrier near the top; if an investor starts selling early (the best time), she is written off by others because she looks wrong for a long time. She may have regrets (seller's remorse) and second thoughts against selling stocks as they get increasingly overvalued.

In the short run (usually quite near the frothiest point before a top), one is tempted to reverse field and jump back in to chase "just one more hot one" while it looks inviting. That impulse should be resisted above all: it is a classic final signal to cash in rather than buy more. In the long run, however, one proves right with a contrarian attitude.

The key to success is to do what is *not* easy. What seems very easy will probably prove a mistake. Almost invariably when a buy looks compelling and overwhelmingly obvious, the investor actually is getting in too late. The best bargains are purchased when the investor has to struggle and debate, afraid even to tell his broker about an idea under consideration. When he loves the stock because it has treated him so well and wants to stay on board longer to maintain that highly comfortable association, he has overstayed the market. Thomas Herzfeld, a Florida-based brokerage executive and closed-end fund money manager, told a *Wall Street Journal* reporter in late 1993,

> "We buy [on] wars, earthquakes, coups, assassinations, and devaluations. We sell on peace, free-trade agreements, and all that other good stuff."

Buying and selling that way is how to succeed, but it always feels like facing into a 100-mph head wind at the time.

Remember that the majority always feel that they are right, even when they are not. The crowd can be correct during much of a long trend, but always overstays and proves itself wrong at turning points. When the feeling of bullish rightness becomes universal and powerful, a top is immediately at hand. Being successful in trading means leaning against that powerful tide, which then creates psychological, financial, and social stresses and strains not everyone can handle. Humans banded together for mutual protection for centuries, so our in-bred natural tendency is to feel uncomfortable when deliberately walking, alone, to a different drummer.

If by nature an investor is passive, a follower, he may lack sufficient courage to do what is required for trading success. But if one can stick to contrarian principles despite probable early suboptimization of profits, he acquires a bucketful of cash near the top (plus some interest) for use later when the panic phase arrives.

Perhaps the most forceful statement on the need to act in the contrary mode appears in *Confessions of a Wall Street Insider* by the self-named C.C. Hazard:

> (T)he stock market is built on a necessary foundation of error. You make money on the market mainly by living off the errors of other players. You become a predator, in fact, a carnivore, a beast of prey. Others must die that you might live. . . (T)he stock market requires an endless supply of losers.

By refusing to act like and with the crowd in either its manic or panic stages, an investor immensely raises his or her chance of not being part of that pool of losers. Bernard Baruch, who enjoyed impressive Wall Street success, summed up his most important advice in a mere four words: "Never follow the crowd!"

12

Focus on the Time Value of Money

KEYS TO INVESTMENT SUCCESS

- Remember the Rule of 72
- Note the 9.2 Percent Long-Term Rate
- Understand Why Avoiding Losses Is So Critical
- Examine the Anatomy of a Loss

Throughout this book there is a bias in favor of pushing the reader toward selling out positions instead of holding. The inertia behind holding is powerful and, combined with other psychological factors, often prevents investors from feeling comfortable about selling. There is a deliberate effort here to make a strong case for selling, in as many ways as are relevant to individual investing. One of the best, and perhaps most relevant, arguments is the unstoppable march of time.

Although time works against an investor in many ways, it can be a very powerful ally when money is put to work in ways that generate high, compounded returns over a long period. But precisely because of the magic of compound interest, the value of time is great, so the cost of lost time can be staggering. Understanding the somewhat natural inertia that disguises itself as patience should have a great enough impact that investors learn to become impatient with underperforming investments.

Probably the most widely cited study of long-term market performance

109

was conducted by Roger Ibbotson and Rex Sinquefield;[1] it examined returns on financial instruments over a half century. As brokers who know about equities are fond of pointing out to hesitant clients, the conclusion of this monumental study was that over a very long period of time common stocks provide higher average returns than the other investments covered. They generated, on average, 9.2 percent per annum, including both capital appreciation and dividends.

This is not high compared with inflation since the late 1960s, or compared with the rapid increase in the Dow Jones Industrial Average from 1982 to the 1987 pre-crash highs. And following the +16 percent compounded returns over the period from 1985–1995, many analysts are now using an upward-revised 10.5 percent annual Ibbotson bogey for equities. But taking a longer-term perspective, it seems more realistic to expect that recent equity return rates will prove extraordinarily strong when seen in hindsight from the year 2025, for example.

Therefore, for our purposes the longer-based assumption of a 9.2 percent rule of thumb remains a useful starting point for evaluating reasonable long-term returns. Investors and traders who take greater risks should aim for higher returns, in the 15 percent range or more per year, as compensation for the intellectual work and emotional energy expended in owning and managing stocks. By rejecting crowd timing and tactics, such a rate can be attained, although mutual fund managers producing it on a sustained average basis are nearly cult figures. In many ways, however, individuals have certain advantages over money managers handling billions.

THE RULE OF 72

Most investors are familiar with the "Rule of 72," which is an easy way to determine how long it takes to double a sum of money at annual compounded rates (see Table 12–1). It is not 100 percent precise, but it is operationally realistic. For example, 7.2 percent for 10 years, compounded annually, produces $2,004.22 from an original $1,000 investment. There are three formulations of the Rule of 72:

- Years times rate equals 72.
- 72 divided by rate equals number of years required for doubling a sum.
- 72 divided by available years equals required rate of return to double a sum.

The table is truncated at 14 years because the returns implied by the rule at that point decline to below the certificate of deposit (CD) or medium-term Treasury bond rates, a level considered very unacceptable for investors assuming the risks of equity ownership.

---

[1] Roger Ibbotson and Rex Sinquefield, *Stocks, Bonds, Bills, and Inflation: the Past (1926–1976) and the Future (1977–2000)*. Charlottesville, VA: Financial Analyst Research Foundation, 1977.

T A B L E 12–1

The Rule of 72

Years	Rule-Implied Rate in %	Multiple of Starting Sum	Actual Rate to Double (%)
3	24	1.907	26
4	18	1.939	18.9
5	14.4	1.959	14.9
6	12	1.974	12.25
7	10.3	1.986	10.4
8	9	1.993	9.05
9	8	1.999	8
10	7.2	2.006	7.2
11	6.5	1.999	6.5
12	6	2.012	5.95
13	5.5	2.006	5.5
14	5.1	2.006	5.1

THE 9.2 PERCENT LONG-TERM RATE

The Ibbotson and Sinquefield study defined 9.2 percent as the long-term annual rate for equities. And 9.2 percent is close enough to the "9 percent/8 years" convention of the Rule of 72, so eight years can be used as a reasonable investment horizon for doubling money in stocks, low though that may sound after investors' giddy experience in the 1990 to 1996 period. In fact, the 9.2 percent rate compounded annually for eight years produces $2,021.99 for each $1,000 invested up front, implying accuracy within 1.1 percent over eight years.

Suppose an investor has conservative expectations and is willing to settle for the long-term norm of 9.2 percent per annum. Look back at Table 12–1 and see what happens when a stock that has been held goes nowhere. If it is held for one year with no gain, the average annual compounded return that is now required to catch up to the schedule of doubling in eight years becomes 10.4 percent over the remaining seven years (moving up the first column to a shorter time period to determine the newly required return in the fourth column).

This is not too dramatic. But if this stock goes nowhere for two years, then our required catch-up return rate for the remaining six years jumps to 12.25 percent, which is 35 percent more than the 9 percent required originally to double the investor's money and 33 percent more than the long-term mean rate discovered by Ibbotson and Sinquefield—a significant overperformance that must be achieved over the next six years. This is an indication of the performance required of a stock

TABLE 12–2

Loss of Capital

Percent Lost at Beginning	Years Until Loss Taken	Required Compound Return in Years Left, to Double in 8 years
10	1	12.1%/yr for 7 years
	2	14.2 for 6
	3	17.3 for 5
	4	22.1 for 4
20	1	14.0%/yr for 7 years
	2	16.5 for 6
	3	20.1 for 5
	4	25.7 for 4
25	1	15.0%/yr for 7 years
	2	17.8 for 6
	3	21.7 for 5
	4	27.8 for 4
33.33	1	17.0%/yr for 7 years
	2	20.1 for 6
	3	24.6 for 5
	4	31.7 for 4
50	1	21.9%/yr for 7 years
	2	26.0 for 6
	3	32.0 for 5
	4	41.4 for 4

that is going nowhere when it is patiently—and erroneously—held by a stubborn, fearful, unrealistic, or psychologically paralyzed investor.

Now consider the major damage that occurs when a stock's performance falls below breakeven. Watch (in Table 12–2) what happens when there is an initial loss of capital and when an investor dawdles before accepting that loss and moving on to better vehicles for recovery. Assuming for illustrative purposes a 9.2 percent long-term rate on equities to double capital over eight years, the required catch-up rates become greatly higher, obviously, as a function of both the severity of the starting loss and the amount of time consumed.

As Table 12–2 shows, taking any but a small and brief loss in the beginning requires that heroic returns be achieved to catch up to a doubling schedule in eight years. If a higher expectation such as a positive 15 percent average return is imposed, the required catch-up paces become breathtaking very quickly, even for fairly moderate losses.

For example, the 15 percent rate triples money (3.059 times) in eight years. Once the investor starts out with a lazy 20 percent loss in the first 24 months, to recover to 15 percent returns per year for the eight years, she needs to attain a little more than 25 percent compounded for the final six years. These rates entail higher risk, so the endeavor becomes self-defeating for all but the most successful investors. (See Figure 12–1.)

To put that 25 percent in context, the legendary Fidelity Magellan Fund achieved a return of 22.4 percent per annum from bear-market bottom in summer 1982 through the end of calendar 1995. That enviable performance over an extended period was achieved by a team of well-paid professional investors (led by individual stars) and only with the help of a rising market that may not continue at a comparable pace over the long term.

Two other statistics are germane to this example. Suppose that at age 25 an investor invests $1,000 for retirement at age 65, and the long-term 9.2 percent rate is achieved. If the money lies dormant for only the first year instead of being invested to achieve the 9.2 percent return rate, the retirement kitty is depleted by $2,847. Worse yet, if our young capitalist takes just a $200 loss (20 percent) in the first year and then gets the fund onto a 9.2 percent return track, the final retirement fund is short by $6,759—or nearly 34 times the modest initial loss.

When you as an investor play the equities game seriously for the greater potential it offers, remember that when returns are not helping they are definitely hurting you—even when stocks do no worse than stand still. Therefore, unless one is actually allowing profits to run, patience in investing is no virtue. Keep this sense of urgency in mind whenever hold/sell inertia sets in.

WHY AVOIDING LOSSES IS SO CRUCIAL

A corollary of money's time value, and a sadly neglected topic, is the importance of avoiding losses. The central objective of equity market participation is to keep making profits over time on balance, much like the effect of compound interest on a sum deposited in the bank. Expect ups and downs, but look for the main trend to be upward. Your goal in stocks (or equity mutual funds) should be to increase capital more rapidly than is possible in risk-free investments such as the bank or T-bills. The key to making big money in the stock market lies not in making the big gain. Rather the secret is not losing money. To use a baseball analogy, four singles are better than a home run and three strike-outs.

The overriding importance of not losing money is illustrated in the old saw about the two rules for successful investing:

Rule #1: Never lose money.
Rule #2: Always follow Rule #1.

The closer and more constant attention an investor pays to not losing money, the more disciplined is his or her approach to selling, by very necessity. To make

Sample Catch-Up Pace

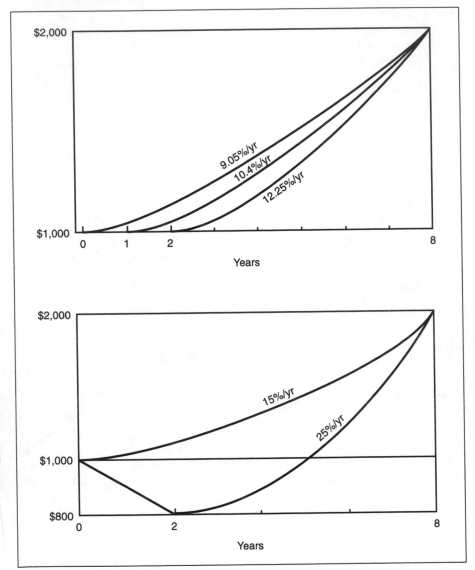

good returns in the stock market (or in other investment media, for that matter), investors must both buy right *and sell right*. Once a stock is owned, the entire focus of attention and effort must shift to the only remaining relevant challenge: executing a close-out of the position with a successful sale.

A successful sale is not defined by the resulting gain or loss reported for tax purposes; more important are the subsequent trends of the stock sold and the action of other available investments. If the sold stock goes down or sideways in price, or even if it goes up less than the general market (adjusted for beta) or less than your return bogey, the sale is a well-executed decision.

To succeed at not losing money, an investor must focus on and deal with objective realities and must sort out and discard to whatever extent possible the emotional, the irrelevant, and the misleading. If a stock is in a declining trend, rallies in price or good fundamental news items that do not reverse that trend serve only to create false hope. These developments encourage an owner to hold on because they renew his or her belief and hope that prosperity is just around the corner.

But as indicated earlier (Chapter 5), an optimistic mind-set rejuvenated by short-term, contratrend positive feedback can be a serious impediment to achieving capital gains. The reason: false hope tends to forestall a decision to sell just at those times when cool logic alone would dictate an opportunistically timed (i.e., well-priced) sell order. Simple and obvious as it may seem, the way to make maximum profits is to buy near bottoms of declines and to sell near tops of rallies. The losses to be avoided consist not only of actual sales below cost; missed opportunities to capture better prices often available on rallies in the interim count just as much!

There are several dimensions to the admonition of our first rule. First, in an ideal and perfect world, which does not exist, one would buy stocks that do not go down. Failing the ability to bat a thousand in that fantasy/perfectionist game, an investor must operate effectively at the next-best alternatives. Her capital at all times consists of the value of assets minus liabilities. In the stock market, some days capital goes up and other days it goes down. Each day—in fact, even from moment to moment—she experiences gains and losses as the prices of stocks rise and fall.

ANATOMY OF A LOSS

If an investor buys a stock at 20, watches it go to 30, and then holds on while it falls back to 22, he has suffered just as great a dollar loss as if he had bought it at 20 and watched in horror as it shriveled to 12. That paper loss of eight points is every bit as real in the 20/30/22 case as in the 20/12 disaster scenario. Our hypothetical investor probably does not feel quite as bad about that retreat to 22 because he still has a profit, but he ought to. Even though it is impossible to catch the exact tops and bottoms and although we cannot expect a profit on every position, that loss from 30 to 22 is a very real one in terms of opportunity. Our struggling trader missed out on an opportunity to cash in at 30 and do whatever he wanted with all the cash he would receive at that price. Now he has only 22 left. So in addition to actual losses that get recorded on Form 1040 Schedule D, we need to avoid these opportunity losses.

There is another, even more subtle, kind of opportunity loss related to the time value of money. The investor is stung when a stock goes from 20 to 12. He feels unlucky when it goes 20/30/22 but feels that is not quite as bad. Chances are that he does not feel bad at all when the stock just holds steady at 20—or more realistically, when the price fluctuates around 20 for a prolonged period of time. Unless he is collecting a good current income in the form of solid dividend payments or is successfully writing out-of-the-money options against his flat-priced stock, he is losing money.

Again, this is not a loss he can deduct for taxes. And it does not get perceived as a painful loss. It might become acute if the general market is zooming north and all his friends are gloating about their big winners. Among the three kinds of losses described here, a dead-money one, predictably, is the least painful and therefore the most insidious.

A stock going nowhere, although not as damaging as a stock shrinking in price, is still a source of opportunity loss and therefore is producing a real loss. First, the money could be in the bank, T-bills, or short-term municipals, earning some interest and not at risk in the market.

Second, with the cost of living generally on the rise, a dollar tomorrow is worth less than a dollar today in purchasing power. Third, our unfortunate inertia-laden holder is losing the one nonrenewable resource he owns in life: time. While this stock meanders back and forth around the familiar 20 level, this investor is missing any chance to make money in other stocks.

And finally, our investor is suffering a psychic loss: he is becoming frustrated with the market and/or is losing confidence in his own market-playing abilities. This negative feedback is doing damage, even if only subtly, to his ability to make future (and other current) investment decisions coolly and smartly.

So, setting aside the psychic cost, there are three kinds of money losses caused by underperformance in the market: actual Schedule D losses, those losses in the form of profits not taken and then "given back" on paper, and finally the serious implications of lost time value when a stock sits at the same price.

In the real world, stock prices continue to fluctuate. The investor's job is to take advantage of the ebb and flow of prices. One sees a stock that is undervalued and buys. But in order to cash in and realize our rewards for buying cheap, we must also sell dear to capture the difference. You can always buy that same stock back later. Buying and selling does not make us a trader, a short termer, or in any way a bad person. Once we buy, we must sell or become a passive collector with a full cupboard. Such investors will be frozen out of the action until they find more money—or until they change stripes and start learning to sell.

Suppose that for some combination of reasons an investor is relatively comfortable with the fundamental prospects of a company whose stock has an overall flat price over the long term. If she is extremely foresightful and a little lucky too, she could divine the annual tops and bottoms in the stock and buy in and sell out near those levels a number of times over the years.

In that way, she would make much more money than by holding because, in the long term, the price seems to come back to its old level. In fact, this approach is the only way she will make money in such a stock (beyond dividends or option premiums). Buying it at 20 and never selling it, or many years later finally selling it in frustration at 20, involves a tremendous opportunity loss compared with taking advantage of periodic fluctuations as they occur. (This concept of capturing periodic rises and falls around fair value, rather than holding on faithfully forever, is explored in great detail in Chapter 13.)

Investors should never be frustrated if they cannot capture *all* of a particular price swing. Take what seems reasonable, what is in agreement with past patterns. If the stock that stuck around 20 periodically swings between 15 and 25, an investor certainly is doing a creditable job by buying around 17 and passing it along to someone else at 23. Therefore, do not be afraid to pay a broker a little for the opportunity to nail down profits; moving out will prevent expensive opportunity losses, which are just as real as any other kind of loss. Think in your Wall Street dealings as you do in your professional business life: time is all you have!

One very useful way of visualizing money's time value in the stock market is provided by the National Association of Investors Corporation (NAIC), an educational umbrella group for investment clubs (see the Appendix for its address and telephone). The NAIC created a Stock Selection Guide for investors' use primarily in setting disciplined policy for buying. The guide can also be used for timing sales well; a price plotted well above the future expected-value line indicates likelihood of below-acceptable returns over the balance of the forecast period. (The NAIC suggests its members purchase stocks they honestly believe can double in three to five years, implying returns of 14 percent or more under the Rule of 72.)

13

Rethink That Old Buy-and-Hold Religion

KEYS TO INVESTMENT SUCCESS

- Understand that Fundamentals Change, Drive Value
- But Recognize that Investor Psychology Drives Prices
- Realize Why Selling Is Important
- Think of Advanced Price as Advanced Risk

A large army of investment advisors and commentators preaches the gospel of buy and hold. Prominent among them, perhaps not surprisingly, are mutual fund management companies, which benefit most if shareholders deposit their money for a permanent ride. Just buy great stocks and hold them for the long term, they counsel. This chapter takes the heretical position that following the old-time buy-and-hold religion will lead an investor to essentially average performance. Growing capital faster than merely average is probably the main reason investment books are purchased and studied, why analysts pursue their craft, and why advisory services and investment managers exist. Those who would settle for average performance over the long term should abandon direct ownership of individual stocks (which carries risks of adverse selection and lack of diversification); index funds with low expense ratios are designed for such investors. The next several pages will develop a contrary proposition, namely, that buying *and selling* has valuable benefits, can result in outperforming the averages, and actually reduces risk.

One reason the buy-and-hold admonition has gained prominence lately has been a recent run of extraordinary market circumstances. Since the depths of summer 1982, U.S. stock prices have risen without any lengthy interruption, driven mainly by declining interest rates reflecting lessening inflation. The current generation of market pundits and, disturbingly, young portfolio managers, has not known a bear market: as of 1997 the most recent declines lasting two calendar years were in 1977–78 and 1973–74. Thus, the "evidence" supporting a faithful buy-and-hold approach is skewed when viewed in longer history as a more valid context. Investing is not as easy as the period starting in 1982 would make it appear.

High on the list of buy-and-holders' arguments is the assertion that one cannot time the market. It is true that many computer simulations and models have been created and tested, with most failing to outperform the averages when they attempt to implement market-timing rules. Results of those tests do not conclusively prove the theory. Rather, such failures should be attributed to one of two possibilities: first, that the models (constructed by experimenters with an anti-timing bias) used bad rules and second, that markets that constantly change obviously cannot by mastered by any set of rigid or unchanging rules. Investing is an art and not a science!

While prices for individual securities and major overall market averages swing from overoptimism to the depths of despair and back again, the sizes of successive movements cannot be predicted with great accuracy. Mechanistic models that base predictions of one cycle on the size and length of its predecessor (or on prior averages) are doomed to failure. But human beings, by observing psychological conditions in the market, can successfully identify *areas* of temporary extreme valuation, both high and low (See Table 13–1.) That is the essence of contrarian investing. No pretense is made here that exact tops will be identified and sold nor precise bottoms bought. But reasonably intelligent investors, observing market moods and press headlines and keeping an eye on price charts, can usually tell a pure academician when the market is frothy and when it is afraid. Those areas are near tops and near bottoms. Those are times when market psychology and fundamentals have diverged significantly. Such areas cannot be predicted accurately in advance, but they are quite readily identifiable in real time. Taking action in the opposite direc-

T A B L E 13–1

Four Identifiers of Trends Primed for Reversal

Above-average longevity

Extremely steep slope of price movement

Acceleration of price velocity on high volume

Virtual unanimity of opinion; downplaying of risks (at tops) or opportunity (at bottoms)

tion of an extreme trend will not guarantee selling at an exact top or buying at a precise bottom. But selling above trend when markets are buoyant will produce returns above those from selling "on average" at the long-term trendline. (Buying well, namely when fear pervades, gives another advantage to the so-called timers.)

FUNDAMENTALS, WHICH CHANGE, DRIVE VALUE

Undeniably, fundamentals drive stock values over the long term. Earnings, dividends, and cash flows form the numerator of the value equation while inflation rates drive the required rate of return (interest or discount rate) that makes up the denominator. A company whose earnings and dividends grow at an average rate of 10 percent annually will see its stock price rise, over the very long term, at that same pace *on average*. The long-term buy-and-hold camp makes some key assumptions. First, they assume that a company that has historically grown will continue to do so. Second, they assume that its growth rate will be constant. And third, they assume an economy with little or no fluctuation in interest rates and without periodic recessions, implying only minor wiggles in price on the long upward climb. These are brave suppositions indeed!

This mechanistic mind-set of the modelers is again where the buy-and-hold theory breaks down. Companies do not continue growing just because a least-squares trendline of prior earnings points ever upward. They continue to prosper only because of excellent management, improving technology, and superior marketing skills. They continue to lead only if some other company does not come along and do the job better. And, in case those theoreticians missed it, capitalist economies go through expansions and then recessions in which very few companies feel no effects on their growth and profitability. The great buy-and-hold model is based on an assumed average growth rate of all companies, calculated based on perfect 20/20 hindsight. In the real world, investors buy individual stocks rather than averages, and those companies and their stocks stray from that smooth mathematical average as they navigate into an unknown future. Again, those who want to settle for the average should buy an index fund and save any further effort at excelling in their investment lives.

Table 13–2 lists twelve companies viewed as great growth vehicles and industry leaders—in their respective heydays. They were accorded elite status on Wall Street and were presumed to be destined for continued prosperity and market leadership. Interestingly, all provide or provided consumer goods and services, a characteristic statistically associated with lower risk than the heavy industrial and transportation sectors. And yet, somehow, their fundamental trendlines stopped projecting ever upward. Who can say that any one or several of today's revered leaders might not suffer similar fates? Arguably the most important industry of the 1980s was computer technology. Of the seven largest U.S. computer firms of 1984, only one (IBM) remains intact in its prior form and even it has gone through a

T A B L E 13–2

Companies Once Known as Growth Blue Chips

Apple Computer	L. A. Gear
Borden, Inc.	Levitz Furniture
Equity Funding	New Process
Four Seasons Nursing Homes	Polaroid
Franklin Mint	Tucson Electric
Kmart	Winnebago

wrenching transition and suffered at one point more than a 75 percent drop in share price. Burroughs and Sperry merged as Unisys, which struggles for marginal profitability. NCR was bought by AT&T and is now being largely written off. Digital Equipment has suffered major reversals and changed to a network solutions company. Honeywell's computer business was sold to France's Compagnie des Machines Bull, which has downsized ever since. Control Data has changed name and survives as only a minor factor.

The United States now has become transformed into primarily a service economy, as contrasted with its smokestack industrial nature of 50 or 75 years ago. The Dow Jones Rail Average has substituted several truckers and airlines and become the Transportation Average. Half of the 30 components of the broadly followed Dow Jones Industrial Average have been replaced since 1961. Fundamental trends do not continue undisturbed, much as we investors might wish for such a simple landscape. Thus, the advice to buy and hold long term begs a critical question: *buy and hold what?* (And, amusingly, if the answer is that one should buy and hold a good growth mutual fund, it should be observed that many of these engage in 50 percent to 100 percent or faster annual turnover (rather than buying and holding!) in their efforts to stay atop the best holdings!) Bottom line: fundamentals are not a given that can be assumed.

INVESTOR PSYCHOLOGY DRIVES PRICES

While fundamentals drive value over the long term, the path of value is neither smooth nor forever necessarily sloped upward. But even if it were, stock prices do not inch along with the regularity of interest compounding in a bank CD. Stock prices fluctuate sharply in response to significant swings in investor psychology. Prices reflect changing collective moods of optimism and pessimism. Bull and bear markets wind around the long-term upward slope of national output and personal income. Intermediate price swings punctuate those bull and bear markets. Daily and weekly fluctuations provide ripples around those swings.

Calendar 1995 provided an interesting, if upward-biased, illustration of how widely prices move. Excluding shares priced below $5 at year's end and excluding closed-end funds, the average NYSE-listed stock traced a price range of 60 percent from low to high during the year. Earnings per share rose about 10.5 percent, coincidentally equal to the long-term average rate of return on common stocks as noted lately by Ibbotson Associates. Major market averages showed gains exceeding 30% for the year. Thus, 1995 represented a time in which a bull market in prices was strongly outrunning stocks' underlying fundamentals, while, as usual, individual stocks also were fluctuating much more widely than the overall net price change itself. Those passively holding for the long term in 1996 were assuming that corporate earnings would catch up with the recent 30 percent-plus price gains, believed interest rates would move permanently lower, or were setting themselves up for the inevitable fall. Markets rise and fall; they do not proceed smoothly on a path of long-term mathematical average growth.

WHY SELLING IS IMPORTANT

Buying and holding for the long term assumes that one is willing to settle for whatever long-term average results. Buying and holding for the long term also assumes that one can successfully select a stock, or group of stocks, whose fundamentals will continue intact. Technology is moving ever more rapidly, and for most companies the relevant competitive context has become worldwide, whether or not they wish it were so. These facts imply that selections of companies may not remain valid for as long as they did in the past. The price of investment success is constant vigilance.

A logical, although disturbing, question to the long-term buy-and-hold advocates would be this: assuming you are not willing to abide a possible 100 percent loss of investment in case your selected company suffers a fundamental and permanent loss of stature, when do you plan to sell out in the event of such a failure? Presumably, the long-term holder has resolved to passively ignore market rises and falls and so, rejecting that alleged canard called market timing, would not be a seller above the long-term trend during a frothy market or late in an economic expansion. Logically, then, that holder would take considerable time to observe and admit that fundamentals have deteriorated *permanently* and that this formerly leading stock should be sold. Our long-term holders, if indeed they ever abandon their faith and do sell, would be doomed to sell *below* the slope of the formerly healthy average fundamental projection. Their sales would come late, well after many more nimble investors have perceived trouble and exited. Our long-term holders will sell below the former trend and thus will actually achieve *below-average* (and below their theoretical) returns. They will let their successful positions run to an eventually average result but will realize below-average net results, possibly including significant actual losses, on their less fortunate selections.

The opposite of holding is selling. Buying *and selling* allows an investor flexibility that buy-and-holders deny themselves. Those willing to sell are capable of capturing excessive returns as market cycles develop, rather than settling for (at best) long-term average results. Logically, an investor either should surrender the battle of active stock market participation and buy a low-cost index fund or should adopt buy-and-*sell* as his or her modus operandi. Those who retreat to buy-and-hold as a credo either assume they cannot beat the average and/or accept it as given that they would sell badly if they tried to sell. Selling well is the subject of this book, and, admittedly, is one receiving little attention. Buying badly and selling badly are symptoms of succumbing to crowd psychology. Buying well and selling well reflect independence of mind and action. Buying and selling, as contrasted with holding long term, is a mind-set designed to capture profit opportunities that markets provide periodically. Selling above the central (average) trendline captures abnormal profits.

Figure 13–1 presents a stylized version of major market swings, powered by emotions, driving prices successively to considerably below and then well above value as defined by fundamentals. (For simplicity, fundamentals here are assumed to improve smoothly and dependably over time.) Those pursuing a buy-and-hold approach accept two risks to their capital when markets are in an above-trend area near point A. First, they are exposing their capital to some subsequent decline into a depressed region near point D and requiring that they will neither panic at the worst

FIGURE 13–1

Market Timing versus Holding Long Term

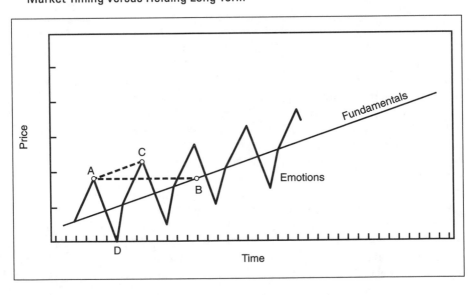

of times nor need their funds at a very unfortunate point in the cycle for such uses as education, housing, medical emergencies, etc. Second, they are allowing their capital a lazy period from the time of A to the time of B, when fundamentals will presumably catch up with the temporarily excessive price levels that prevailed around time A. By holding resolutely for the long term despite the interim favorable selling opportunity near A, the investor is accepting a remaining long-term average return slightly flatter than the slope of the presumed fundamentals, namely, a return from the A area to the right-hand endpoint of the fundamentals line. That point might represent retirement or death, which are the logical ends of long term. The only way a long-term holder who eschews the benefits of selling near A can capture a return equal to the fundamentals' slope is to convert from buy-and-hold to buy-and-sell near area C or one of its later cyclical equivalents.

Opportunities for capturing excessive profits are not, however, limited to selling near major cyclical tops such as were represented in Figure 13–1 by area A. In Figure 13–2, the fad-driven trend or cyclical advance is the major slope that is rising away from a longer term, fundamentals-justified price level. This fad-driven trend here is a blow-up of the latter half of an advance from a low area like D to a high area like C in the original plot. Not only is the cyclical or fad-driven move generating a major medium-term divergence above value, but ripples up to areas near point X provide multiple short-term opportunities to sell and capture excess prices. In this second graph, areas near points E, F, G, and H represent short-term

F I G U R E   13–2

Ways of Viewing Risk

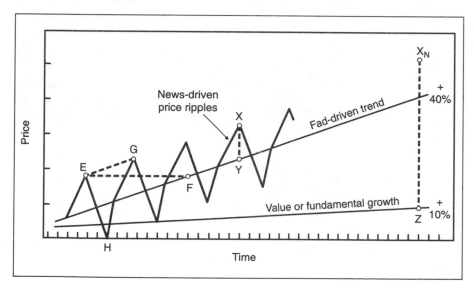

situations analogous to the longer term ones posed by A, B, C, and D in the longer
context of the earlier graph.

THINK OF ADVANCED PRICE AS ADVANCED RISK

Focus now on a time period in which a bull market is pushing the price level cumu-
latively farther above true fundamental value. Here, in Figure 13–3, vertical distance between the long-term fundamental line of value at the bottom and a point on
the cyclical trend such as Y or Z can be thought of as not just advanced price but
also extended risk. For this reason, the scale on this graph has been relabeled as
"Risk" rather than "Price." Given that prices will fluctuate, high price is also high
risk. On this graph, areas near points E, G, and X represent doubly risky times
when short-term rallies in a bull market push prices (and thus risks of giving back
gains) temporarily above the bull trend, which itself is increasingly far above value.
     The virtue of selling well is even greater when one considers Figure 13–4.
Underlying our measures of perceived risk in the three prior graphs was an *assumption* that fundamental value could be accurately assumed. But the world is not that
simple. It is possible that your company might develop an important new technology or that tax-law changes might raise the value of corporate earnings or that
interest rates might permanently shift downward, thus fundamentally raising a company's value. But, of course, equally important and opposite changes can also

FIGURE 13-3

Deflate Trend for Change in Value; Change in Price Is Change in Risk

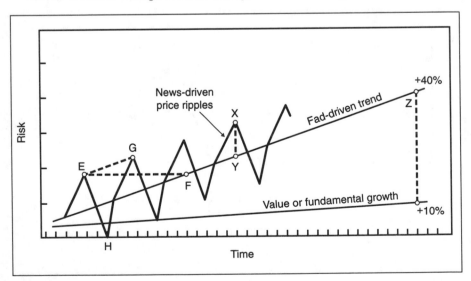

F I G U R E   13–4

Fundamentals and Discounting Rate Determine Value

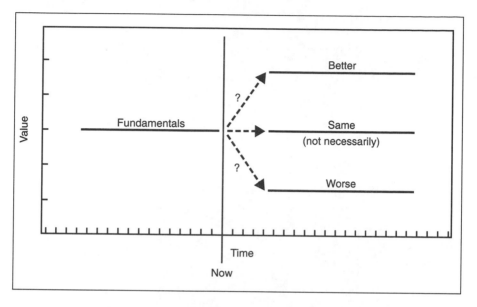

occur. A court could set a precedent holding tobacco companies liable for product effects; corporate tax rates might rise; some new Middle East cartel success might drive sharp inflation; a new competitor may leapfrog a former industry leader's product position. Any such shock can radically shift the position of that "fundamentals" line. If that shift is to a lower position, the risk as previously measured will prove to have been a vast underestimate. Thus, advanced price poses hidden risk in an unmeasurable amount—a difference that means that the vertical distance between fundamentals and point Y or Z on the prior graph was an understatement of exposure to capital loss.

With the significantly increased amount of institutional domination in the market and the faddish chasing of high earnings and price momentum, even a single earnings disappointment (which may have no special long-term significance) can suddenly shift the position or slope of the perceived fundamentals line. An extremely unpleasant and immediate loss of capital can result. This is illustrated by the accompanying price chart (Figure 13–5) of Department 56: its quarterly earnings grew a mere 31 percent in the December 1995 quarter, representing a vast disappointment (to greedy trend chasers) after the 42 percent growth in the prior quarter. A $38 stock became a $22 stock in one day! Viewed in this context, selling in areas above trend and above value is a form of risk reduction at the same time it captures abnormal profits. What a pleasant double bonus for the good seller,

FIGURE 13–5

Sudden Revision of Expectations

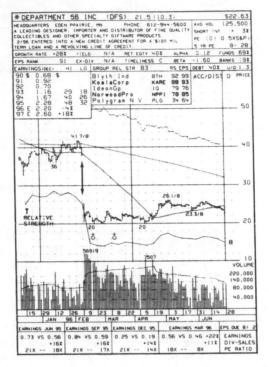

providing all the more support for buying and selling rather than passively holding long term!

Successful selling requires an investor to manage his or her own emotions in a disciplined manner at exactly those times when most other investors are letting psychology ruin them. While this chapter's major thrust has been selling versus holding as related to fluctuating trends against values, selling has another advantage over holding: it relates to one's mind-set regarding taxes.

All too many investors have frozen themselves into never selling stocks that have treated them well because their large long-term gains represent huge tax liabilities. Selling periodically along the way, paying the resulting tax, and then buying another stock or the same stock on a dip rids one of psychological lock-in from taxes. That lock-in can skew decisions in harmful ways. IBM is a classic example of this problem. For decades its stock had been a great performer; it was a core holding for most institutions. Earnings began faltering in 1985. The shares traded above $160 in both 1986 and 1987. Thousands of investors had locked themselves in with perhaps tenfold gains over many years. At $160 they "couldn't sell because of the taxes to be paid." Likewise at $120 in 1990–1991 or at $90 in 1992. Taxes on their long-term gains were locking them in, they felt. Perhaps when the stock fell below $40 in 1993 that problem had been cured. Only then, with earnings at a deficit and after two dividend cuts, was the threat of taxes on their gains small enough to allow them to sell (at the bottom). Being emotionally and intellectually prepared to sell any holding at any time will free investors from the tyranny of tax lock-in.

To summarize, this chapter has challenged, in prototypical contrarian's thinking manner, the generally espoused merits of long-term buy-and-hold orthodoxy. We have noted significant questions about that approach's underlying assumptions. We have come to view advanced price as a measure of risk. We have started to focus on the emotional condition of the market as one that can be accurately perceived, and certainly as one that can be graphically observed in the form of price charts. We have seen that the difficult art of active market timing is not the only possible alternative to passive holding, that taking advantage of periodic positive and negative emotional excesses when presented can be of great advantage and a means of reducing risk, even though the timing of such events cannot be predicted. The long-term holder's problem of psychological tax lock-in was also exposed. If the reader still harbors any tendency to hold passively, the prior chapter has challenged that from another important vantage point: money's time value. Again, passive holding (the opposite of occasional opportunistic selling) is proven suboptimal.

14

Calibrate Decision Making to Personal Emotions

KEYS TO INVESTMENT SUCCESS

- Recognize the General Warning Signs
- Know Your Personal Warning Signs

The worry threshold can be avoided in most investments by limiting buying size and selling when emotional concern rises. Most investors fail because they sell from worry when a market bottom occurs—not at market tops when their bouyant emotions *should* act as a signal to worry.

For example, the presence of gloating and smugness should signal concern about pending buy decisions that most likely are inappropriate. Gloating can consist of such behaviors as uncharacteristic celebrations, self-congratulation, bragging, or an unscheduled counting of the chips—all of which propel unwary investors into putting more cash into the market just when they should be selling.

To be successful, you must *lean against the wind of market emotions, observing and thinking as a contrarian.* The harder the winds are blowing, the more firm must be your resolve—at just the time when temptation to join the crowd is greatest. Recall that, by definition, a major bottom occurs in an atmosphere of fear and gloom, sometimes panic. Major tops form when investors are at their most euphoric; when all the newer buyers have already come in and all the older players have exhausted their buying power, the balance literally must shift to the downside because there are no more buyers' dollars to create further net buying.

This point of overoptimism defines a top. When the euphoria gets to him, the investor must do exactly the opposite of what his emotions support: he must sell. Once that critical psychological signal that a top is at hand is received, he must not rationalize inaction, tell himself he can get one more eighth of a point, chase just one more hot story or current fad, or get swept away by the excitement of his peers.

RECOGNIZING THE GENERAL WARNING SIGNS

Each investor tends to have his or her own pattern of emotional reactions as a top arrives. Because such responses are predictably recurring and serve as the single most telling personal indicator of the need for action, it is worthwhile to describe them carefully here in order to identify and catalog the most common personal signals. Some of those may include:

- *Self-congratulation*—usually occurs gradually when an investor has a single huge winner over time (or several large winners) and no offsetting losers. These occurrences should signal taking profits because the market has performed well for a lengthy period and is nearing a high.

- *Smugness*—can occur when there is a spectacular success in the portfolio or a run of several consecutive heady gains. Psychologists would call this a feeling of grandiosity, meaning belief in one's superiority or indestructibility. When an investor starts to feel he has learned the secret formula for winning that cannot miss, it is an urgent signal to sell.

- *Strong confidence*—even the quiet, self-contained person is not out of the woods emotionally when, secretly savoring her success, she notes that things really have been going extremely well lately. The contained person usually does not recognize her feeling as a danger (sell) signal because it is so moderate—but it is nevertheless important despite its moderation. If, by nature, you are a person of moderate emotional swings, you should not expect to experience total euphoria before the market tops out.

Smugness and related emotions are danger signals because ultimately they produce two behavioral problems for the investor, and, paradoxically, they are opposites: one is hyperactive play (driven by overconfidence in a frenzied market atmosphere); the other is inaction resulting from complacency (precisely because everything is going so well).

An example of excessive or hyperactive play is the investor who, after a major advance has finally created a comfort zone, drains his savings for the big plunge. The suddenly massive flow of money into equity mutual funds in January through May 1996 may prove to be a classic collective example, following as it did a 35 percent market advance in 1995. Other patterns of excess late-bull activity are people who open their first margin account and use this new buying power to the maximum or speculate in situations that have an uncharacteristic high-risk/high-reward profile compared with past personal patterns. Multiply this unnaturally aggressive behavior by tens of thousands of investors and a classic overheated market is created. Hindsight calls that market period a *top*.

Such aggressive trading behavior requires that the investor have a feeling of overconfidence, which is most often experienced only following highly successful recent history. Some investors increase the number of positions they hold, open added brokerage accounts (for wider exposure to hot IPOs or more expected good tips), raise their frequency level of trading activity, take on higher-than-typical risks, or become so satisfied and happy with their success that they raise their targets and hold their stocks stubbornly for imagined further gains. In each of these instances, the investor is doing the wrong thing: either buying or holding just when selling is the right course of action. Therefore, take the first sign of any of these impulses as a strong warning sign, and do some selling.

For many investors, feelings or hunches alone are not a sufficient signal that the time to sell has come; for them, overt action is the key indicator to watch for. Investors who try to control and override their own feelings must examine past and current actions in relation to the stock market as a gauge to help them discover what works as a true signal.

It is unlikely that any investor exhibits all of the symptomatic behaviors of overconfidence; no one behavior is by nature more right or wrong or more valid a signal than another. The key is to identify which ones apply to you and then take selling action when those behaviors crop up.

This process of definition and discovery can lead to a second-level problem—an intensified need to become alert and ready to act (i.e., to sell stocks) as one watches oneself in self-observation. This is because once an investor becomes aware of what personal triggers signal trouble, he or she begins to block or suppress those actions when greed kicks in. The desire to deny that the game is about to end creates irrational behaviors. When reaching this stage of awareness, one must use a more sensitive screen by beginning to interpret the mere impulse to act, even if it is overridden eventually, as a strong signal.

KNOWING YOUR PERSONAL WARNING SIGNS

Common actions that should act as danger signals range from cautious to bold; whatever your personally relevant signals, you must remain aware of them and not become judgmental or self-righteous in comparing your self with others. Seven actions are typical key indicators:

- Quietly confiding investment successes to others.
- Spending increased time in market study.
- Openly bragging about winners or a hot streak.
- Celebrating in unaccustomed ways.

- Counting the chips more frequently than usual.
- Adding more money (including use of margin).
- Playing the new-issues game.

These signals are listed in qualitative order of increasing severity. If these behaviors are absent from an investor's reaction repertoire, he should not necessarily take comfort in noting their absence; most people practice some variation on one or more of these themes.

In crossing the dividing line between feeling responses and taking actions, probably the most restrained behavior is the quiet confession of successes. This is, of course, not a case of bursting into a colleague's office and announcing that XYZ stock just jumped six points for a 50 percent profit. It merely means letting others know "how it's going" in the market. It may be an unpretentious comment when someone else mentions his own success or frustration with a recent trade or investment or an opportunity missed in a roaring rally. It may be as innocent or intimate as mentioning how well it is going if that is not something the investor usually divulges. The point is, for any investor not regularly in the habit of sharing personal financial affairs (or other confidential matters) with others, breaking of that usual taboo is noteworthy and should be considered a signal.

Spending an increased amount of time studying the market, devising systems, surfing financial databases and chat rooms on the Internet, researching companies, or reading advisory reports also can be a signal. Although serious study is good, uncharacteristic attention to trading signals that the investor is excited; this occurs only when the market has run up quite a distance already, not when markets are dull or depressed. Collectively, advisory services reach subscription peaks at or just after market tops. So does trading volume. So does the number of people deciding on a career in brokerage or in professional money management.

An investor paying much more attention than usual should watch out. It may be time to direct that energy toward stocks that should be cashed in rather than toward new buys. But beware: brokers are very unlikely to comment disparagingly about new-found investor interest. More frequent calls to a broker can lead to more trading, usually in the form of buying.

More toward the overt end of the reaction scale is active bragging about trading successes. This usually means going out of one's way to inform others about remarkable investment conquests or airing financial affairs in the presence of outsiders. When the investor behaves uncharacteristically in this way, it is a selling signal. Remember that bragging in any form occurs not after failure, loss, or price decline but after one or (usually) more successes. And contrary opinion predicts a reversal after a series of rises. The fact that a series of investments performed beyond normal expectation suggests that a bull market has been running for a while. Therefore, assume that a top is much closer than a bottom.

Bernard Baruch is reputed to have avoided the October 1929 bloodbath because he used the too-much-talking signal on the part of others as his indicator to sell in the summer and early autumn that year. Why? He noted that even cab drivers and newspaper vendors were talking about their market conquests and dispensing advice. (Will the 1996 publication of a stock market advice book by a teenaged "whiz kid" prove a similar red flag?) Baruch accurately concluded that there was too much good feeling about the market for it to remain in an upward trend much longer. This was a classic contrarian observation of the tendency of tops to develop when the market is a frequent front-page story in the national media and even local nonfinancial media.

An even more overt behavior is celebrating market success uncharacteristically. Although most everyone goes out to dinner to celebrate a raise or a promotion, it is the *change* in typical celebratory behavior that should be considered significant enough to take action on. One example is taking the whole office out to lunch instead of a just your spouse or best friend. When the impulse to make a grandiose, sweeping celebratory gesture occurs, cash in some of the chips without further delay.

When the game has become so pleasant and profitable that an investor wants to total up her holdings, an intermediate or final top can be directly at hand. Naturally, the impulse to take an inventory is absent when the market and personal fortunes have declined or when a listless period of sideways action has occurred. But let the market roar for an extended period or let an investor make several consecutive great trades, and that desire to stroke the ego is stirred.

This is not to imply that investors should fail to track how they are doing. Take a regular inventory in the form of both historical tables and graphs. One very easy way to do this is by keeping securities in street name so that the monthly brokerage statement includes a computerized valuation. Be sure to note all cash infusions and withdrawals promptly so that the tally is kept on a fair basis.

The key point is to heed *excessive* chip counting because such counting is never done at market bottoms. Valuation normally should occur every three to six months. In fact, some investors use even a conscious curiosity or semiserious intention to count their chips too frequently as red flags. Calibrate your own typical pattern: if you usually count monthly and now start looking weekly, that is your signal.

Another and even more dangerous indicator of a market top based on internal response patterns is the decision or serious temptation to add capital to one's equity account (or mutual funds portfolio) after a significant market rise. This takes place because the investor erroneously decides that the bullish trend is well established and, therefore, that it is foolish not to increase exposure. Or he may perceive an excess of attractive new ideas and—anticipating that price strength will continue—will not want to sell any existing holdings to fund new purchases. In effect, he is acting like the proverbial child in a candy store: he wants one of everything. The predictable result will be an adult-sized bellyache when the feeding frenzy is over.

A variation of the adding-money warning is the substitute practice of selling in order to buy. This pattern occurs in cases where the market already has risen substantially, increasing the investor's excitement and storehouse of allegedly attractive ideas, especially when there is no more available cash to add to the account. Therefore, to satisfy the urge to buy into the new ideas, an investor liquidates one or more existing positions, not on their own merits, but to raise money to pay for greater excitement.

This substitute behavior is a good example of how the failure to exercise a specific red-flag behavior should not be excused. If the investor seriously *considers* adding to her stake after a long rise but instead ends up merely selling in order to buy, the danger signal is just as validly in effect.

Ideally, and as discussed in more detail in Chapter 17, each sale should be timed and made on its own merit. Over time as a market's cycle matures, a diversified portfolio should gradually be liquidated as an increasing number of stocks reach or exceed reasonable or targeted price levels. Unless the investor has identified truly countercyclical issues to buy at that time, the multiple sales she makes should act as a signal of topping out rather than as a ready source of funding for new buys.

A wary investor should also be suspicious if there is the urge to sell existing positions to move funds into recent new issues or actual initial public offerings. Even if one eschews the IPO games, moving to more risky (e.g., high price-to-earnings ratio, high-technology) stocks late in a rise is a similar symptomatic signal. It is very likely he has become psychologically bullied by an overheated market environment, seeing so many stocks doing well and hearing so many friends bragging of their successes.

Typically, investors will be getting virtually no encouragement from brokers to sell at a time like this. Brokers, too, are enjoying the ride and are in a very positive frame of mind. Their training, dependence on trading commissions, and refusal to rain on client parades by suggesting that even bull markets come to an end all point to no talk about selling. This means that investors will need to lean against the tide and feel lonely in order to sell in a timely manner. Just as at such times you will be getting a lot of unsolicited broker suggestions about new ideas to play, so the temptation to put more chips onto the table will feel overwhelming.

Any or all of these phenomena should suggest an extended or overheated market that threatens to top out soon. Heed such signals and sell. Selling at the time can be a lonely exercise, but the reward comes from quiet knowledge that the crowd is usually wrong and the contrarian usually correct at turning points. So, when tempted to add money or when the list of "I oughtta buy"s is getting long, sell instead.

There *are* some conscientious brokers who have the moral fortitude not to pander to a client's overexcitement when they personally believe it is time to sell. Get help from this kind of broker by asking one to give a loud warning as soon as any overconfident behavior arises. Not just incidentally, if your broker refuses to participate in such an arrangement, says conditions are "different this time" than in the past, or tells you it is unnecessary because the market is in no danger, consider that a strong, even an urgent, signal to sell (and to change brokers). Brokers are human beings, and you can watch their behaviors, in addition to your own, for emotional signals of the time becoming ripe for selling.

15

Adjust Sale Targets Rationally

KEYS TO INVESTMENT SUCCESS

- Have a Price Objective with Three Key Elements
- Make Reasonable Downward Modifications to Expectations

Most investors inevitably wonder if the market plays fair; this chapter demonstrates that stocks go where they want to despite what investors think is justified and despite what they wish would happen. For example, the price objective that seems valid to an investor when first established, that is, the price he wants, tends to be biased toward what he privately concludes is initially attainable. But what any single investor *wants* is irrelevant, so it is important to avoid developing a concrete mind-set about price objectives.

Be prepared as well to let go of original price opinions, if or when events warrant a change. Remain flexible and realistic rather than unreasonably optimistic and/or obstinate. An investor unable or unwilling to change—to become right in a world that itself does change—is doomed to lose.

There are two primary ways that investors get into trouble when setting price objectives:

- The initial idea, including the selling-price objective, may have been wrong from the start.
- Although right at first, the original idea can become outdated and, therefore, inaccurate as subsequent events transpire.

In both cases, original thinking can be either overly optimistic or unnecessarily pessimistic. It is important to reexamine the market environment constantly in search of inputs that warrant adjusting the scenario on proper valuation. When analyzing the environment, exercise extreme care not to be selective—not to credit only those factors that support the starting thesis. An approach that merely seeks to validate original thinking is worse than valueless because it misleads one by neglecting to prompt valid cautions. It strokes the ego (with either validation or consolation) while allowing the brain to run at idle speed.

A PRICE OBJECTIVE WITH THREE KEY ELEMENTS

Price objectives, both when set initially and when reconsidered later, should have three elements. Failure to include them indicates a purchase or a holding decision not well thought out. Such holdings will become permanent relics through the mental back door. Absence of the three realistic assumptions signals probable rationalization.

When a stock is purchased, it should be with a sale target in mind. Buying merely because a stock is acting well or represents a great company is the beginning of trouble since those mind-sets imply no clear exit path, no sell discipline. A proper sale target includes a combination of three parts: a *price,* based on a *story,* and in a *time frame.* This can easily be remembered conveniently as PST, like the whispered voice of reminder or conscience. Such a script or scenario for a stock purchase might say, for example, that XYZ shares should trade at $39 because a certain new product (or expanding market or improved margins or cost cutting, etc.) will produce earnings per share of $2.60, and a justifiable price/earnings ratio is 15; those earnings should occur in 15 months, so the stock should sell at $39 at that time.

If any element is missing, the story is too loosely conceived, and the holding will become open ended, resulting in financial drift and wishful thinking and probably leading to a loss. If there is no story, or driver, the idea is probably nothing more than the chasing of current momentum. If there seems to be a story (e.g., "a great research and development program") but it has no clear date or goal for accomplishment, the true story may amount to no more than admiration of reputation. A biotechnology company should have a specific drug due for approval by a predictable date. If not, you are buying merely on vague hope or general corporate aura. If there is a clear story with a related time frame, it still must be quantifiable. Just generally seeing the market as being excited over that new drug approval or an expected granting of a key patent is not enough. Current (buy) price may already discount that expected future excitement.

One must be able to project a future climate in believable numerical terms: the earnings will be X and the P/E reasonably will be Y, or analysts will then project a market of Z dollars and say the company should sell at so-many-times sales, which represents its realistic attainable market target. Failure to have a concrete price goal allows you to fall into the trap of celebrating good news while having no disciplined intention of asking whether a resulting price jump is high enough to justify sale.

Successful investing requires correctly anticipating change. Projecting merely an extension of the present is lazy thinking, and a changing world is likely to prove such soft scenarios off base. The market, meaning the crowd, has now paid (in today's price) for what it can already see! Your buying, and your price target, should be based on a specific something additional or different.

When reconsidering a price objective, be careful not to become greedy and turn into a cheerleader for the stock. Only new and positive information that previously was unanticipated should prompt an increase in your price target. If good news—a new product, a contract won, strong EPS, a higher dividend, or even a takeover proposal—is in line with earlier reasons for buying the stock, note merely that a part of the projected scenario (i.e., your story) is coming to pass and that the stock may begin to achieve the price objective. Do not double count such positives.

If good news does occur, it then becomes important to remain calm; excitement over the good news should not overwhelm judgment just because everything is going so well. The investor who counts positive factors twice is engaging in self-delusion. There are both positive and negative factors that legitimately prompt a reassessment of price objectives and they should be studied in light of two strong caveats: (1) as noted in Chapter 8, your price paid does not matter, and (2) while realistic reasons may arise that lead to cutting the price objective once a stock is held, do not allow those changes to prompt lowering a stop-loss order.

Except to protect against possible panics in heavily weighted institutionally owned stocks, it is generally not a good idea to use stop-loss orders. This heretical position is expounded in Chapter 23. But if entered, stops must not be pulled or lowered, or they become useless. They may actually become worse than useless because they provide false comfort if later disallowed.

When examining a potential equity investment, an investor makes a number of assumptions, any of which can be unconscious or wrong. Some of those buying assumptions are as follows.

- Information sources are accurate and disinterested.
- Some specific good thing actually will happen fundamentally.
- That event will be big enough to move price meaningfully.
- That event is not already anticipated in the price.
- Interest rates will be at a certain level and moving in a favorable direction, supporting the general level of future stock prices.
- The psychology of the market, irrespective of fundamentals such as earnings and interest rates, will be in a certain state.

- The projected price is not out of line with demonstrably reasonable valuation standards such as yield or P/E ratio.
- Major developments in the industry or in relevant sectors of the economy will create or allow the expected price climate to exist.
- Political and/or geopolitical factors will be as expected.
- The projected scenario can happen in the time window used.
- The investor is not oblivious to important factors that, if known, would temper his enthusiasm or make him think the stock is not undervalued.
- He has not been misled deliberately.
- The world will go on as it is now.
- There will not be positive or negative wild cards in play.

MODIFICATIONS TO EXPECTATIONS

As indicated earlier, each, or at least very many, of these factors should be in place when the buying decision is made, but they cannot be expected to remain stable. Therefore, set a reasonable selling target for the stock at the outset, but understand that any target becomes subject to immediate and ongoing modification because the world does not stand still. Assume that change *will* occur; to do otherwise is operating on a fantasy designed to justify your mental inertia.

Suppose, for example, that an investor is attracted to a certain company, perhaps a drug firm that has a good record of increasing earnings and that occupies a leading position in prescription preparations for diseases of the elderly, a growing population sector. Stocks in general have been soft lately, so, as a contrarian, she senses an opportunity to buy a fundamentally attractive stock at a good price.

She checks several sources of earnings estimates and projects that, at an historically realistic relative P/E ratio, the stock could sell at $38 in 18 months, despite a current $28 quote. She then buys, setting $38 as the objective. (Actually, she should be prepared to sell out below that objective so that a 100 percent perfect analysis is not required to generate acceptable locked-in profits.)

Each of the factors in that extensive list given above is subject to sudden or gradual change, so our investor must always be ready to adjust the price objective for cashing in. Here are just some things that could go wrong:

- Product tampering on an over-the-counter medicine could hurt the company or cast a psychological pall over the whole group; in another industry scenario, an airplane crash could raise safety concerns about all small or discount airlines.
- Management could signal upcoming fluctuations in earnings due to product testing and R&D costs, whereas smooth earnings had earlier been the general expectation.

- Analysts and portfolio managers could become considerably less tolerant of even minor changes in sales growth or earnings trends, particularly in high-technology or high-P/E groups.
- The value of the dollar could fluctuate, changing translations of foreign costs or earnings.
- A strike may disrupt production or supplies of materials.
- Federal deficit-reduction pressure could intensify, putting a tighter squeeze on medical reimbursements and/or raising interest rates.
- A competing firm could come out with an exciting new product or technology.
- Generic equivalents could gain market penetration faster than earlier expected.
- Tax or antitrust legislation could dampen takeover appeal across the board, causing an industry's stocks to lose attraction.
- The company could be sued by a competitor for patent infringement, by the government for poor testing procedures, or by the industry for antitrust violations.
- The market could become speculative, abandoning traditional growth stocks in favor of short-term concept plays; it could change emphasis from cyclical to growth stocks or vice versa. Preferences between small- and large-cap stocks could flip.
- Tax laws or merely the aging of the investing population could make dividends more attractive than growth.
- Margin regulations could be tightened (although this has not happened for many years).
- Fund managers could decide that other industries are more interesting.
- On further reading, the investor could discover that some of the good things projected were already predicted by a major brokerage analyst, implying that the remaining upside is smaller than thought since those ideas are already in the price.
- Wild-card trouble of some sort could develop.

Here are some unexpected good things that could happen, thereby raising a target:

- Management could announce an unexpected but promising new drug (or other new product type in a different industry).
- Major magazines could feature this stock as one of the top 10 to buy for the next year or as some star portfolio guru's favorite, raising awareness and price.

- Tax laws more favorable to R&D or to offshore manufacturing could be proposed or enacted.
- Economic forecasts could shift positively, implying that stocks are due for a more extended rise than had earlier been thought reasonable.
- Mild recession talk could develop, cutting interest rates and moving investors toward defensive industry groups such as drugs, foods, supermarkets, and utilities.
- A change in control of the White House or Congress could occur, implying more spending on health or reduced regulation.
- An existing company drug could be discovered to have positive side effects in the treatment of a second major disease.
- The company could have a breakthrough in research on a hot drug type for treating AIDS or cancer.
- The company could announce a restructuring plan designed to enhance shareholder value.
- A well-known corporate raider could take a position in your stock or in another one within its industry.
- An actual takeover or share buyback could be announced.
- Earnings could rise above estimates for sustainable reasons.
- Favorable foreign exchange fluctuations could occur.
- Positive wild cards could develop.

Tactically, only the introduction of dramatic new factors should serve to override previously established estimates of reasonable value. A near-term jump of two points on good quarterly earnings is not a reason to raise a long-term target by $2. If truly important new information arises, expectations must be adjusted up or down. Suppose that, in the preceding example, the initial judgment of fair value is $38 and the target for cashing in is $35. Suppose time has elapsed and other factors have not changed (unlikely), or there have been offsetting pluses and minuses that leave the target unchanged.

The investor has been lucky, and the price is now at $33.50 due, primarily, to a rising overall market. Suddenly, a bid is made for another drug company by a major European or Japanese conglomerate. This opens a new round of potentials on the upside. The valuation numbers may get historically full, but the market senses that a phase of bidding up is just starting. The holder might suspend temporarily her resolve to sell at $35 because the sights for all drug stocks are going to be raised.

Suppose instead that a hostile bid comes in for the company. The bid is $40 and the stock goes to $41 in hopes that another shoe will drop. The investor thinks $40 is fundamentally excessive, and she may well be right. But if management, normally circumspect and credible, advises shareholders not to act hurriedly and to anticipate a possible company response that could raise prices further, our holder should very temporarily suspend that standard of reasonableness by a few points and sell on the next concrete positive news. One must remain fluid but totally logical, reacting realistically to major new items in the picture but yet not getting carried away with enthusiasm. The question, "Would I buy it now?" is always a highly useful focuser of one's thinking.

Now look at a few negative jolts. A major externality, as the economists call it, such as a regional war or a new worldwide oil embargo threatens to disrupt the economic expansion or to boost inflation sharply. Bonds and stocks will fall across the board, regardless of the attractiveness of specific companies, their newest exciting products, or their present relative undervaluations. Re-visit Figure 13–4.

In this suddenly changed scenario, P/E ratios, driven by rising yields, generally will fall, forcing the investor's relative P/E-derived target lower. The stock remains undervalued, but at a lower price and with a lowered future target. And the time frame for a possible realization of one's original scenario is considerably lengthened because inflation takes a long time to quiet down. The target must be lowered and very likely the stock sold immediately regardless of the existing paper gain or loss. The old target literally has become an irrelevant relic of a past time.

CASE STUDIES

Other major factors, not even related directly to the company, can force a lowering of targets. For example, companies in other high-technology or growth industries such as computers and software (does this sound like early 1996?) start reporting disappointing earnings. As a result, the bloom comes off the rose for many growth stocks with traditionally high multiples, even though their specific fundamentals may be unchanged.

Therefore, analysts cut EPS estimates. Investors trim their levels of tolerable risk. On seeing signs that a major shift is occurring among institutional investors, you must assume that—right or wrong—this new opinion or perception trend will take some time to play out; it will end with prices lower and attitudes less favorable toward the growth drug company (or whatever else is the case) than they are today.

In this scenario, one's earnings forecast may still prove entirely correct, but the expected actual or relative P/E ratio has been rendered too high for the time frame originally established for cashing in. The psychological damage may take a long time to repair. On a multicompany scale, our investor is looking at the longer term or bigger picture equivalent of a company announcing good news on a day when the market is down 90 points on heavy volume. The positive fundamentals are swept away by the negative psychological tide of the time. Thus, expectations must be adjusted downward to account for the emotional damage sustained or one will in fact be holding the stock to reach a now-unrealistic goal.

Here is an actual case illustrating the need to modify targets. An investor in late 1989 purchased Long Island Lighting Company (LILCo) in the $17 to $18 range. Under an agreement with the state of New York, LILCo scrapped its costly Shoreham nuclear plant in exchange for needed rate hikes for several years. It then publicly committed to dividend rates of $1.00, $1.50, and $2.00 for the years 1989, 1990, and 1991. The original downside scenario for late 1991 was that, even if no more dividend hikes were in prospect, the stock could sell on an 8 percent current-yield basis, or at $25, which implied a very attractive total return over 24 months from a buy price in the $17 to $18 range.

Although dividends grew less sharply than originally desired, only the temporary surprise of the Gulf War kept interest rates from declining faster than earlier hoped. By late 1991, with a dividend rate of $1.70 in place, a reasonable discounting yield was down to 6.5 percent rather than the projected 8 percent, allowing an increase in the investor's target, to $26.25. The stock actually moved to above $29 in 1993.

But during that year (1993), directors sharply decelerated dividend growth, raising the payout from $1.70 to just $1.78. Having been given a gift in the form of unexpectedly low interest rates, and therefore raising his target, the investor would be foolish to ignore a second negative dividend signal and should have been happy to accept $26.25 (a modified target) on unexpectedly low interest rates. That the stock overshot by three points was not to be regretted since a second negative fundamental red flag had been raised. Had one not been out at the target price (through placing an above-market order well in advance), the dividend slowdown would have been a sell-at-market signal in 1993, in effect representing a sharply reduced price expectation. This situation involved both an upward revision (due to lower-than-hoped interest rates) and a downward revision of sale targets (due to negative dividend-growth signals).

A high-tech example of changing targets also comes to mind. Lotus Development Corporation suffered an earnings downturn in 1993 due to product development costs with *Lotus Notes*. Its earnings quickly rebounded, with estimates of $2.20 per share for 1994. If one had estimated a reasonable P/E of 20 times, based on growth for a software company, the price target would have been $44. However, as soon as IBM was rumored to be interested in acquiring Lotus, the target would have been suspended. IBM's decision would have been the sell trigger either way: if Big Blue walked away, figuring it did not want to pay a premium above $44, what investor should have doubted its judgment? A sale would be in order at market. When IBM decided to pay $66 in a preemptive strike, that also became an immediate sale signal well above the original $44 target. Why wait around for any possible trouble like a not-inconceivable Justice Department inquiry, perhaps a disappointing earnings quarter to make IBM rethink its decision, or anything else? Take the gift!

Curiously, another IBM decision stands as an example of a reason for changing price targets: the decision not to acquire Apple Computer. Apple had lost its founding chief, Steve Jobs. Its penetration had begun slowing, and its market share was slipping. Price objectives were dropping until both Sun Microsystems and IBM were named as suitors. As events had it, both passed on the opportunity. In such a high-technology industry, when two leaders demur on acquiring a company, the revised target should immediately become "sell at market." Apple stock has since been sliced in half, from $40 to $20.

Sale-price targets must be set from the start, or there is no focus and no discipline. But those targets must be written in pencil because circumstances in the real world will almost always change. And one must work hard to keep the ego firmly under control so that changing an original price target is not a psychological problem. The mind should remain fluid, looking for important factors to add to the equation as plus or minus adjustments to that original price objective.

It is critical, although by no means easy, to sort out in real time the truly important from the passing and trivial. It is crucial to resist emotional tides and take action only after the mood of the crowd has abated. The market moves to manic tops as well as to panic bottoms, so the investor must adjust targets and risk tolerances for such extremes. And at all times, she must be mindful of the need to remain dispassionate by resisting the temptation to become a holder turned loyalist or cheerleader. Again, the critical question should be asked: "If I did not own this stock already, would I buy it today, knowing what I (and the market) do now, at the current price?" If the honest answer is not affirmative, it is time to cash in and move on.

There is no need to be loyal to any stock; it is an inanimate object without feelings to be hurt. You can change your mind and sell. If you are wrong, you can always buy back. The lower your commissions expenses, the less it will cost to buy a little distance and risk insurance, even if you later do change your mind and buy back. Keep your price targets fluid and realistic. The market will always have its own way, without regard to what your old opinion was. No need to lock in on that opinion forever!

16

A Suggested Exercise in Self-Discipline

KEYS TO INVESTMENT SUCCESS

- Let an Options Trade Teach Discipline
- Take the Tutorial for Options Novices

It is said that there is no substitute for experience. In the real world (of investments and otherwise) where decisions are required in an on-line, real-time mode, experience picks up and fills in where theory ends. In making decisions to hold or to sell stocks, reality is a great teacher and disciplinarian. In fact, all too commonly the decision to hold a stock is not, generally, conscious; usually it is an inaction by default. The purpose of the nondecision to hold is to spare the investor the tension of making a decision to sell and of actually executing that decision.

LETTING AN OPTIONS TRADE TEACH DISCIPLINE

This chapter presents an exercise that helps investors learn the discipline necessary to make the selling decision consciously. In this exercise, your author suggests that investors buy options—worse yet, short-term options. This experience, carefully chosen and timed as outlined here, has a great deal of educational and psychological value that does not exist in any paper experiment. An imaginary scenario theoretically involving options cannot teach the lessons of urgency and discipline that are required for real market trading because there is no money involved in a fantasy, and no emotions are involved—including the pitfalls of and tactics to use against greed, fear, pain, and elation. Fantasy paper profits are not real, so they are not exciting enough to cause mistakes.

In a similar way, there is no means to artificially create true-time urgency. One of the aspects of selling that subtly but so often strongly leads investors to fail is the lack of any forced closure point: the market opens up again tomorrow, so the game continues if an investor does not take action today to stop it. It will continue until he takes such action. If he never takes the action, the game will go on in spite of him (and because of him); he has become a collector rather than an investor.

Options have a unique characteristic that makes them ideal for teaching discipline: they have a finite life. There is an absolute end to each option's life: the Friday afternoon before the third Saturday of the month. Thus, calling a time-out is impossible. Option holders must sell or exercise, or lose whatever value remains. (Some brokerage firms exercise *for* the option holder if he fails to respond to expiration notices and if there is enough value to cover round-turn commissions.)

Although this exercise entails probable cost (there is a way to minimize the cost), consider that expense worth the opportunity to learn how to make a decision to sell in a real-world environment.

Assume that the options are calls because people usually think in bullish terms and because understanding value in these contracts is easier than with puts, if the investor is an options novice.

To limit the possible net cost of this exercise, buy options that have a very short period of time remaining to expiration—about two weeks is a good period for this purpose. Further, choose a stock whose trading price is at, or slightly above or below, a multiple of $5.00, which is the multiple of striking prices on listed options. Finally, select a stock that is relatively stable or nonvolatile and that provides a good dividend yield. All three of the suggested criteria—short remaining life, proximity to strike price, and underlying stock price stability—will contribute to a low exposure in terms of dollars.

A good example is a telephone or electric utility stock. Choose a company with a record of ongoing annual dividend increases to avoid falling into a snake pit by accident. Also, be sure that the stock does not go ex-dividend during the remaining option life. And do not purchase in the month the company reports quarterly earnings (i.e, the month after the quarter ends).

For illustration, assume that on or about September 1, 10 calls on XYZ Electric Service are bought with a strike price of $25 and expiration of September 16. Suppose the stock is trading at $25.25 at the time and that $3/8$ is paid on a limit order for those options, plus commission.

For 10 calls, which gives the right to buy 1,000 shares, $375 plus commission has been put on the line. Thus, a game is created that must be played actively. The first goal is to make money. The fall-back position is to minimize any loss. In either case, learning while playing is most important. Consider the clock an enemy—and a helpful goad.

A TUTORIAL FOR OPTIONS NOVICES

For options novices, the following is a description of the purchase: a call option is a contract that allows its owner the right to buy 100 shares of the related underlying common stock at a specified price (called a strike price) up to and including a specific date or expiration.

In this case, each call entitles an investor to buy 100 shares of XYZ Electric at $25 per share up to market close on September 16. After that moment, the option will have expired with zero value if it is not exercised. It can be sold at any time before it expires, thereby transferring the right (and the time pressure) to a new buyer. With the stock trading above the strike price, namely at $25\frac{1}{4}$ per share, the option has intrinsic value: it can be exercised now and the stock would be worth above the $25 paid on exercise. The option is inherently worth the difference, or $\frac{1}{4}$ point. But the option trades above that intrinsic value because it has some remaining life. It has a time value, although in this example there is only minimal speculative value to that time. Therefore, $\frac{3}{8}$ as a total price is realistic.

Sometime between purchase date and expiration date, the time-value premium of $\frac{1}{8}$ essentially disappears, and the option trades at intrinsic value alone. But this disappearance of premium for time happens late in the game—so late that the slight premium should be paid in order to buy a remaining game that will take enough time to be a useful teacher.

The object is to come out of this trading experience with as much money as possible and with a newfound sense of urgency and decisiveness about all choices of whether to hold or sell. As noted earlier, nothing forces an equity investor to make a decision about selling. If he holds today, he can think about it again tomorrow. If he holds tomorrow, there always is another trading day after that. With a stock, there is no imperative closure, no deadline.

Option rules are, however, critically different. There is no escaping that expiration date on your calendar; a decision must be made. Playing this option-trading game greatly intensifies, on a daily basis, all those feelings normally experienced when one owns a stock; a sense of urgency is overlaid because of the approach of expiration. (See Figure 16–1.)

If an investor buys a two-week contract, 10 percent of his possible-profit window disappears the first day. With just four days left, 25 percent of the remaining time horizon evaporates the next day. With two days left, it is 50 percent. You must decide to act today or accept tomorrow's verdict, which will be final.

Normally when an investor owns a stock, he feels good when it rises; he wants more and fears giving back the paper gains. When it goes down, he resents the loss and fears the price may evaporate further, causing more loss. But because it is a stock, he can stretch out his time horizon and let the stock and the general market do what they will. He is under no requirement to sell at any time. The option, by

F I G U R E 16–1

Option Market Value: Intrinsic and Time Components

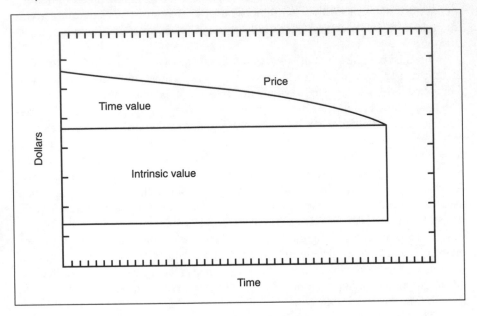

contrast, dies at a known time. Therefore, choices are defined within a very specific time window.

This tension is unpleasant. Often, passing time generates such pressure that an option holder makes a mistake in sale timing that she would not make ordinarily if she were selling a stock. By actually doing this exercise, an investor learns that she can pull the sell trigger and that doing so is not as frightening or as unpleasant as imagined. She then owns the experience of having done it, so selling will be familiar and less difficult the next time. But most of all, the pressure of time forces her to make a decision rather than postpone it.

Each day the stock may fluctuate by a fraction. Unless something surprising happens to the overall market (perhaps caused by interest rate expectations), expect the stock to wiggle only a little. This relative stability helps backhandedly: because of its low volatility, the stock is unlikely to move much on any day or two. Therefore, with just a few days left until expiration, the investor realizes that further movement is likely to be minor. That should help tilt the decision between holding and selling. If the stock starts by going up, there is little reason to let greed take over: this is a stock with narrow moves so, to be realistic, do not expect much more in just two weeks.

Even if the company is strong, the overall market could go down tomorrow or the next day for some reason, taking away the gain swiftly with only an even shorter opportunity left for possible recovery before expiration. If the stock instead begins by going down, our investor lacks the luxury of being a trader-turned-collector: the game will end on the appointed expiration date, and her job is to salvage what she can.

The point is to try to get the best execution in the remaining days. Early in the game, there is a time premium that can be sold to someone else. But later on, you will have consumed that premium as a payment for having stayed in the game.

Note that the emotional effect of each fluctuation is intensified. For example, a mere $1/4$-point rise in the stock's price virtually doubles the option quote. An investor might start thinking that if it would go up just a dollar he could make several hundred percent. The press of time should, however, curb such wild imaginings.

What if the rally reverses and he starts giving back what he earned? He must be tighter on the trigger than if he owned the stock, which he could keep holding for months or even years, in hope or in stubbornness. If he owned the stock, a $1/4$-point rise would cheer him little if at all because he would know the stock is typically stable and might give it back in a week just in normal fluctuation. And by owning the stock rather than the option, he is signaling a possible long-term relationship that he does not intend to terminate for a mere quarter point.

But with the option, he is in a damage-control mode in which he must pay a second commission to get the best price in two weeks' time. Should he hold and take another eighth's risk or cash in now? What if he cashes in to end the risk and tension and the stock runs to 26 but corrects back to $25 1/4$ a week later? How will he feel then?

No matter whether the stock rises, falls, or holds steady in the first week or so, if he is still holding the options he will have completely forgotten the meaning of the phrase "Thank goodness it's Friday." The Friday deadline will be a sword of Damocles hanging over his head, forcing him to make a decision. If he holds, each day of no change or fractional loss leaves him less time for potential gain or for recouping losses. He starts looking at each eighth or quarter in fluctuation as a big percentage against his stake—and it is. The time constraint allows him no chance to relax though, because all could be lost with one wrong decision to hold too long. The option could go to $1/16$, or it could be $1/16$ offered, no bid, so he must decide not to allow himself to forfeit everything he has put on the table.

Expect that the decision will not be perfect. Unless it is sold extremely late into the two-week period, the stock and the option will probably have time to tick up above the exit level at some point before the final bell tolls. That's just the way the market is and always will be. Therefore, learn to accept that result as virtually inevitable. Do not expect to beat the market for all the profit it offers—for the proverbial or literal final fraction. Learn to live with your choice, and move on to the next situation. This exercise in decisiveness may cost a few hundred dollars. Consider it tuition well spent. You will own dozens of stocks in the future, and a little extra learned decisiveness could save you thousands. You *must* learn to sell, to commit that act of accepting closure in the face of uncertainty. A little options trading could be a valuable teacher of that reality!

17

Separate Selling from New Buying

KEYS TO INVESTMENT SUCCESS

- Expect Rotational Group Leadership
- Beware of the Simultaneous Switch
- Keep A Seller's Checklist

There are several reasons investors should not sell one stock to raise funds for buying another. A stock sale transacted solely to fund a new purchase frequently turns out to be a double mistake: the sale can be badly timed, and the purchase can be badly chosen or poorly timed. Based on a matrix of relative post-switch performance, the odds (unweighted by frequency of occurrence) are more than two-to-one against a successful transaction. (See Figure 17–1.)

In general, the odds are more favorable if an investor is buying but not selling or selling but not buying at any given time, rather than doing both at the same time. The exceptions to this guideline require having pinpoint accuracy in detecting rotational group leadership in the general market or knowing something that borders on inside information or just plain blind luck. Smart investors dismiss blind luck. Luck is something to accept when it happens but not something to count on, which leaves rotational group leadership to consider.

F I G U R E   17–1

Relative Post-Switch Performance Results

| | | **Action of Replacement Bought** | | | | |
		Up More	Equal Move	Down More or Up Less	Flat	Down
Action of Old Stock Sold	Up	Good	Out commission's cost	Bad	Bad	Bad
	Flat	Good	Out commission's cost	Bad	Out commission's cost	Bad
	Down	Good	Out commission's cost	Bad	Good	Out commission's cost

ROTATIONAL GROUP LEADERSHIP

Significant stock market movements tend to carry the majority of stocks with them in one overall direction—either up or down. In fact, market historians and technicians use a tool called a "diffusion index" (see in Chapter 18) as an indicator to detect the end of an advance. By definition, a top occurs when a majority of stocks are no longer moving up within the time frame studied.

Because the majority of stocks move in the same direction most of the time, mathematically the odds do not favor the investor or trader who buys one stock and sells another at the same time, unless it is done because the sold stock has fundamental or technical problems or has reached a technical price target. If the market is in a period of broad advance, raw random odds indicate that both the stock currently held as well as the proposed buy candidate would be advancing. Conversely, if a declining period is to follow the switching action, the odds favor both the stock currently held and its proposed replacement moving lower at the same time.

Naturally there are exceptions, as in any case in which mathematical probabilities are operating. But the odds exist as described earlier, and, over time, an investor fares better by playing on the side of the odds rather than against them. Most expert advice consists of steering investors away from situations in which their success odds are negative and toward seizing opportunities where probabilities of winning are higher.

As previously described, the single exception to not selling and buying at the same time involves successful timing of group rotation. During a period of market advance, not all stocks rally at the same pace. While the overall bias for a majority of issues is generally upward in a bull market, some individual stocks or entire industry groups push ahead for a while even as others seem to lag behind and rest. Then a rotation of leadership takes place; prior laggards come to the front of the pack while recent leaders rest.

At the bottom of a major market cycle, those investors who have the courage to buy at all tend to concentrate in blue-chip stocks. At the top, when optimism reigns supreme for weeks or months, speculative fever takes hold and lower quality or smaller capitalization issues provide most of the action and the leadership for the rally. This is a very broad, or macro, description of rotational leadership. Industry-oriented rotations take place as well. The group that leads at any given time depends to some extent on what industry has been lagging lately and so becomes more attractive. This pattern has become even more apparent in recent years as money managers use computers to monitor market movements more closely and comprehensively and more in real time than was the case through the mid-1980s.

Another factor that affects rotational leadership is the national (or even world) news environment. Depending on what news dominates the media at a given time, certain industry groups lead and others lag. For example, if inflation is quiet, the expectation of lower interest rates is likely to develop. Interest-sensitive industry groups then get an upside play, including banks, savings and loans, insurance firms, and utilities. Housing and automobile manufacturing stocks may move up in this phase in the expectation that lower interest rates will encourage consumer purchases.

If the dollar is low or falling in international value, the idea of a boom in basic industry stocks, supported by favorable changes in export/import trends, can take hold. Steel, machinery, and chemicals issues do well in this phase. The point is that in a sustained advance, one group leads for weeks or months only to be supplanted by another.

In this scenario, simultaneously buying one stock and selling another makes statistical sense only if the investor presumes to identify the rotational leadership changes and to time such changes accurately. This is very difficult to do; unless she can do that successfully, the statistical odds of her winning in a simultaneous buy-and-sale are low. The likeliest probability is that both stocks will move up or both will move down.

Thus, except for the possibility of a much greater percentage move in one stock versus the other, there usually is insufficient justification for a sale-purchase switch. To recap, if most issues are dropping or seem poised to decline, sell and postpone reinvesting the proceeds. (One makes invisible profits by standing aside and not buying too high; these are not as exciting but add every bit as much to capital as the visible gain that comes after a successful purchase.) When stocks are generally running or seem about to rise, it is better not to sell at the time of another purchase. Buying is more profitably accomplished with added funds or even through using margin. Such choices should come only in a contrarian mode.

BEWARE OF THE SIMULTANEOUS SWITCH

There is a dangerous psychology in the sell-to-buy of a simultaneous switch. If an investor is buying a stock and is already fully invested, it is probable that he has begun to indulge a prevailing bullish frame of mind to overrule logic. Presumably if he is already so fully invested that a sale is required before he can make a purchase (to generate funds), the market itself might be well into an advance. One is typically not invested fully at the bottom because of fear.

As the market moves higher, particularly for a stretch of a few years or at least many months, investors begin to see more success stories and to feel some strongly performing stocks are passing them by. The game seems to be easier, the odds more in one's favor.

When this scenario develops, it seems a time for the investor to retain what she already owns. Although she also wants to grab for a little more gusto and ride the bull full tilt, she should consider it a warning signal if she feels herself getting into this frame of mind: falling prey late in the game to prevailing psychology instead of leaning against the trend.

Elsewhere in this book is the suggestion to keep a notebook in which to record market movements, stock actions, personal emotions about the market, personal gain/loss performance, and focus of personal attention. If these notations are correlated with past market action over a period of time, such a personal notebook can serve as a useful way to calibrate one's habits and patterns against the emotions of the marketplace. The object, of course, is to discern when a good feeling is too good and when a depressed or scared feeling signals that a bottom is close. One easy way to track market phases is to write in red ink on down days and green on up; use blue or black for sideways.

It is a natural human tendency to study the market and individual stock opportunities more intensely as an advance becomes broad and mature. That spreading of enthusiasm is why bull markets occur on rising trading volume over time. So, if an investor is caught up in the predominant optimism of the cycle, he is studying possible purchases. Being focused on this intense study of buy candidates when already fully invested signals a problem.

In the mid- to late stages of an advance, the investor should ideally be examining each of his positions to identify which stocks should be retained and which need to be sold. If he is fully invested and has not identified sale candidates, he has been devoting insufficient attention to the selling side of the equation. If he is fully invested and is still spending mental energy looking for new stocks to buy, that is also neglecting sale discipline. Fully committed investors who think about additional buys literally are working on the wrong problem! Therefore, develop an innate sense of contrarianism to serve as a warning signal against the seemingly natural, easy thing to do.

Thus, selling a stock as a forced activity driven by the need to raise funds for a new purchase reflects an ill-timed or overly optimistic purchase. A surefire way to detect this investment pothole is to note frame of mind and very recent short-term trend action. Is there real excitement about the new buying idea? Does it look more like a sure thing than any other that has come around in a while? Does your fear focus on missing a major chance by not getting on board right now, rather than on any possible risk of loss? (Fear of missing a profit is greed. Buys made without some accompanying true fear, i.e., of loss, usually prove to have been done late, in a high market.)

If your answer to any two of the preceding questions is yes, then back off and postpone buying because it is too late in the current game. In this kind of environment, the buy side of the simultaneous sell-to-buy is poorly timed. It is time to sell but too early to reuse your funds. The time to redeploy funds will come later; best buying times occur in the *absence* of excitement—when there are doubts about the market's ability to pick up and rally again. Lean against the tide. Do what feels uncomfortable.

Turning now to the mechanics and psychology of the sell side of this proposed simultaneous sale/purchase, how or why is the sell side likely to be a mistake? As stated earlier, if an investor is focused on the buy side, sale questions are getting short shrift, so she needs to refocus on selling, giving it at least equal thinking time. Forced sales probably are not well chosen because they are likely to be done in haste. Each sale should be done on its own independent merit and timing.

Visualize here the random walker's favorite cartoon caricature: a blindfolded investor throwing a dart at the quotation tables and buying whatever stock she hits. In a similar way, a sale forced by a proposed purchase is equally foolish. In effect, our selling investor is throwing a dart—not at the price page but at the calendar. She sets up the sale-timing randomly, without due consideration for the reasons behind sale or for current price. She is forcing herself to sell not to benefit from the performance or revised prospects of an owned stock but for a completely unrelated factor: a need for capital to make a proposed purchase. It is possible, even probable, that a sale made to raise cash on an emergency basis for funding a purchase is a sale poorly chosen among the available alternatives. A quick decision might be dominated by boredom or recent short-term frustration rather than by more sensible considerations such as fundamental value or near-term price movement potentials.

Whether a stock is trending upward, downward, or sideways in a channel, the best time for its sale is when price reaches one of its periodic high points along the continuum of fluctuation. If an investor chooses a stock to sell from frustration or boredom, it is likely that the stock has not been acting in a positive way lately. Therefore, it probably is nearer a bottom than an interim top of its price channel. A frustration sale may then turn out to be a disadvantageous transaction.

A SELLER'S CHECKLIST

If an investor needs to sell to fund a buy, he should acknowledge that he may be revealing a serious problem, and he should step back to impose self-discipline (some analysts will disagree with this assessment, unless the investor already has a large portfolio). An exercise of general value at any time will also serve here: make a thorough and logical inventory of all stocks currently held, writing down for each stock the answers to such questions as the following:

- What is a realistic price target and over what time period (and what is the implied return per annum from today if that projection is correct)?
- Is the stock now undervalued, fairly valued, or getting full?
- How does the stock fit against today's market tastes and group leadership patterns?
- Is this a volatile or a stable stock, and what does that imply if the market should correct and move lower?
- If stocks literally could be reviewed for three months, how high in the comfort sequence for continued "blind" holding would this one be?
- Does this stock overrepresent in the portfolio one sector of the economy or one industry?
- Would this stock be purchased again today? If yes, why?

A comparison of the answers across one's current holdings will usually reveal which are the best candidates for current pruning and which still have most merit for retention. This is one of many instances where the self-imposed discipline of standing back, taking a mental deep breath, and committing some unbiased factual items to paper will serve any investor well.

18

Use the Personal Diffusion Index

KEYS TO INVESTMENT SUCCESS

- Understand Advance/Decline Indicators
- Utilize a Market Diffusion Indicator

This chapter presents quantitative indicators to use as actual selling signals. It introduces as a useful indicator a "personal diffusion index," which falls under the broad category of technical indicators and, specifically, overbought/oversold timing oscillators. The first few pages describe such indicators generally; the subsequent material reveals how to personalize this kind of analysis.

ADVANCE/DECLINE INDICATORS

The simplest overbought/oversold indicator is an easy, 10-day total of net advances less declines. This market statistic is tracked by subtracting daily declines from advances (usually on one exchange such as the New York Stock Exchange) to arrive at a net figure for the day. Then the last 10 days' daily figures are added, resulting in a number that generally ranges from a few thousand positive to several thousand negative. While precise buy-and-sell signal ranges vary over time depending on the emotion level of the market, following this indicator over a period of months is a useful way to time sales (and purchases) to short-term swings within about two days. One can readily see where the high and low ranges are.

The overbought/oversold indicator is a short-term measurement and is useful only for limited purposes. So is the weekly net advance-decline measurement used by some market analysts. In contrast, many market technicians consider a measurement called the "cumulative advance/decline line" to be one of the more powerful indicators of changing intermediate-term direction in the market. This line is calculated in very much the same way as the 10-day line, except that a cumulative total (rather than one for 10 days) is kept from the time one starts the project. The current plot of any investor's indicator has exactly the same shape, no matter the data-collecting start date, but the net total for each differs (by the same net amount) ad infinitum into the future. The absolute total does not matter; relative movement over time is the key to watch.

Technicians use cumulative advance/decline figures to detect divergences in market behavior. They plot this indicator graphically against a popular market measure such as the Dow Jones Industrial Average and look for differences in the shapes of the lines. Because the cumulative advance/decline total is much broader (encompassing all stocks on the exchange(s) studied), it is considered a more valid signal of market direction than is a narrower index such as a 30-stock average.

What technicians look for are points in time when the two lines move in different directions. As a selling signal, they watch for the cumulative advance/decline line to move sideways or even downward while the market "average" is still moving up—or for the advance/decline indicator to move down while the Dow moves sideways, as occurred in rather classic form in late 1989, prior to that October's mini-crash. The theory behind divergence readings is that a longer list of stocks tells more truth than the mathematical average of a few, which can be skewed by only one or two individual performances among its components. For example, within the Dow 30, a few high-priced oils, or a high-priced IBM or 3M, can carry the others that are collectively no longer advancing.

THE MARKET DIFFUSION INDICATOR

Another useful indicator based on advance and decline data, which has even longer term implications, is the market diffusion indicator. This is constructed somewhat differently; because of its difference, it tends to reflect more profound changes. Surprisingly, it seems not to be tracked by major charting services these days, probably because of the methods by which computers have been programmed to store data.

Most chart services focus on very short-term data, programming their computers to plot closing prices (and maybe highs, lows, and volume); many compile lists of stocks showing the largest day-to-day percentage price changes or the largest weekly net changes. Market diffusion indexes look at a much longer period than a day or week and, therefore, give big-picture signals.

In the 1960s and 1970s, a Boston-based advisory firm (which is no longer in business) published a weekly stock market advisory service called the "Spear Market and Group Trend Letter." Its editors performed extensive research on industry

FIGURE 18–1

More Stocks Join the Party

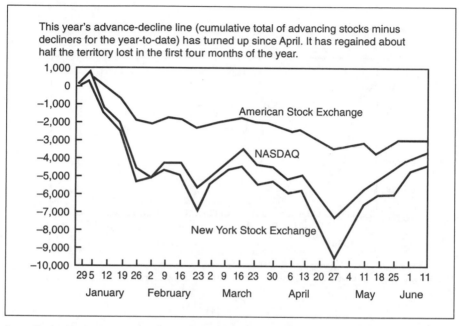

This year's advance-decline line (cumulative total of advancing stocks minus decliners for the year-to-date) has turned up since April. It has regained about half the territory lost in the first four months of the year.

price movements and also on major technical indicators. The service was conservative and longer-term oriented. The few indicators it used were designed to identify significant long-term market trends, not to wiggle every week or every day. After backtesting decades of data, the Spear editors found that the most meaningful basis on which to plot a long-term market diffusion index was a nine-month window.

The index took time to compile, but the work was less mathematically intense than the research supporting advance/decline indicators as described earlier. The analyst simply compared each stock within the defined universe with itself as of a fixed earlier time (adjustments were made for stock splits). October 10 was compared with January 10, October 17 with January 17, and so on. The number of stocks up in price, net, over that period was plotted as a percentage with no adding or accumulation. Each period's calculation was a snapshot.

Market diffusion indices, when plotted, tend to be shaped somewhat like the mathematical first derivative of a simple plot of the overall market level. Well before the market makes its top in a major cycle, the diffusion index tops out and heads down. The diffusion index falls through the all-important 50 percent level

FIGURE 18–2

Fewer Gainers

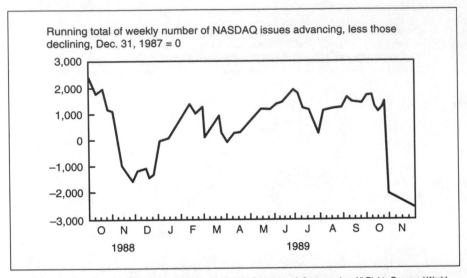

Running total of weekly number of NASDAQ issues advancing, less those declining, Dec. 31, 1987 = 0

quite close to the time when the overall market makes its top as recorded by major "averages." (A fall to near the 0 percent level indicates exhaustion on the downside and signals that selling is too late because a bottom is near.)

What any long-term diffusion index records is the tendency of a market's leadership to narrow as a bull market matures. Fewer stocks continue to make new highs over a period of months. More seem to be consolidating (but hindsight will show they were actually forming distribution tops). (See Table 18–1.)

If the percentage of net advancing stocks is dropping in the later stages of a bull-market advance, it follows that the odds of making profits on the long side, or even of achieving increased profits on positions already held, are falling before overall market averages hit their final cyclical peaks.

This is a very important observation to understand when you are considering holding versus selling. The urgency of diffusion data and the importance of heeding its warnings are all the more critical for another reason: it is precisely during those late stages of a major advance that excitement builds and the temptation to jump in (or to commit more cash, or even to use margin) is greatest. That is exactly when the odds are starting to swing against holding and toward cashing in because, while some issues make spectacular advances, fewer stocks still are going up overall. A diffusion index tells that tale.

Unfortunately, it appears that none of the popular hard-copy chart services currently track this indicator. The explosion of on-line technical analysis packages makes such a statement in that realm risky, however, so some exploration may prove worthwhile. But an investor can follow diffusion data relatively easily if he or she is willing to invest the time. Use a chart service such as Daily Graphs by William O'Neil & Co. (see the reference list at the end of the book), or use the *Monthly Stock Guide* handbook by Standard & Poor's in the local library (perhaps your broker may be willing to supply a used copy). Or follow the prices in *Barron's* or *The Wall Street Journal* and post them in a tracking ledger, perhaps a spreadsheet program.

The chart-inspection method is a faster because it requires only quick visual comparisons. Only a few stocks trade so close to nine-month-ago levels that an investor needs to look closely. Select a universe (e.g., of perhaps 50 or 100 major companies covering a full sample of industries), and track them each month, comparing the latest price against the nine-month-earlier price (adjusted for splits). Plot the percentage of total issues up. Purists might want to take unchanged issues at a $^1/_2$ value and add these, if any, into the total; whatever method is used, be consistent so that your graph remains meaningful over time.

Some market students reduce the workload required to use a diffusion indicator by narrowing their universe further. To do that, follow the 30 Dow Jones Industrials. This list changes pretty infrequently (just 15 substitutions in the 35 years through 1996, so it holds consistent over time. Tally the total of "up" components and divide by 30. Plot the result.

Because the difference created by one Dow Jones stock equals 3.33 percent in the result, be sure to score unchanged stocks as $^1/_2$ each to refine the reading a bit. Once your tally reaches extremely high percentages, the process of a rounding top will begin, with progressively fewer stocks moving ahead. The key change in momentum and the all-out sell indicator occur when the index reading declines below 50 percent from a high of 90 percent or more.

Another way to do the same exercise without subscribing to charts is to keep a list of diverse stocks (it should be consistent over time, with changes due only to acquisitions or leveraged buyouts or the like). Tally these once a month in a vertical column. Compare the price at the latest date with the price nine months earlier, and score one for each up stock. Divide the total ups by the size of the universe, and plot the percentage result on graph paper. A good way of capturing an unbiased and broad sample across the market would be to track a number of the Fidelity Select (sector) funds as if they were individual stocks. One caveat: adjustments must be made in October when annual capital gains distributions arbitrarily reduce per-share net asset values of the funds.

Another handy source for this kind of tracking exercise is your local Sunday newspaper. If such a weekly source is used, go back approximately 39 weeks or take the Friday prices closest to the end of the calendar month. The manual posting

TABLE 18-1

Diffusion Index on DJIA through Mid-1996

	Mar 95	Apr	May	Jun	Jul	Aug	Sep	Oct	Nov	Dec	Jan 96	Feb	Mar	Apr	May	Jun 96
AA	41.50	44.88	46.50	50.13	57.00	57.13	52.88	51.00	58.50	52.88	55.50	56.88	62.63	62.38	61.63	57.38
ALD	39.25	39.63	40.38	44.50	46.75	44.38	44.13	42.50	47.38	47.50	49.88	55.63	59.13	58.00	54.75	57.13
Example for ALD: Up/even/down vs. 9 months earlier:										+	+	+	+	+	+	+
AXP	34.88	34.75	35.50	35.25	38.50	40.38	44.38	40.63	42.50	41.38	46.00	45.88	49.38	48.50	45.75	44.63
T	51.75	50.75	50.75	53.00	52.75	56.63	65.75	64.00	65.88	64.75	66.88	63.63	61.13	61.25	62.38	62.00
BA	53.75	55.00	58.88	62.63	67.00	63.75	68.25	65.50	72.88	78.38	77.50	81.13	86.63	82.13	85.25	87.13
BS	16.13	14.13	14.75	16.25	15.75	14.63	14.13	13.13	14.00	13.88	15.13	13.75	13.13	13.63	12.75	11.88
Example for BS: Up/even/down vs. 9 months earlier:										-	+	+	+	+	+	-
CAT	55.50	58.50	60.25	64.25	70.38	67.13	56.88	56.75	61.38	58.75	64.38	66.75	68.00	64.13	65.63	67.75
CHV	48.00	47.38	49.13	46.38	49.38	48.38	48.75	46.75	49.38	52.38	51.88	55.63	56.13	58.00	59.75	59.00
KO	28.19	29.06	30.81	31.88	32.81	32.13	34.50	35.94	37.88	37.13	37.69	40.38	41.38	40.75	46.00	49.00
DIS	53.50	55.38	55.50	55.50	58.63	56.25	57.38	57.63	60.13	58.88	64.25	65.50	63.88	62.00	60.75	62.88
DD	60.50	65.88	67.88	68.75	67.00	65.38	68.75	62.38	66.50	69.88	76.75	76.50	83.00	80.25	79.75	79.13
EK	53.25	57.50	60.38	60.63	57.63	57.75	59.25	62.63	68.25	67.00	73.38	71.50	71.00	76.50	74.38	77.75
XON	66.63	69.50	71.38	70.63	72.50	68.75	72.25	76.38	77.38	80.50	80.25	79.50	81.50	85.00	84.75	86.88
GE	54.00	56.00	58.00	56.38	59.00	58.88	63.75	63.25	67.13	72.00	76.75	75.50	77.88	77.25	82.75	86.75
GM	44.00	45.13	48.00	46.88	48.75	47.13	46.88	43.75	48.50	52.88	52.63	51.25	53.25	54.25	55.13	52.38
GT	36.75	38.00	42.13	41.13	43.38	40.00	39.38	38.00	42.38	45.38	47.88	47.38	51.00	52.13	50.50	48.00

IBM	82.13	94.63	93.00	96.00	108.88	103.38	94.50	97.25	96.63	91.38	108.50	122.63	111.25	107.75	106.75	99.00
IP	37.50	38.50	39.31	42.88	42.25	40.94	42.00	37.00	38.25	37.88	40.75	35.75	39.50	39.88	39.88	36.88
JPM	61.00	65.63	70.88	70.13	73.25	72.88	77.38	77.13	78.50	80.25	81.25	81.88	83.00	84.13	86.88	84.63
MCD	34.13	35.00	37.75	39.13	38.63	36.50	38.25	41.00	44.63	45.13	50.25	50.00	48.00	47.88	48.13	46.75
MRK	42.63	42.88	47.00	49.13	51.63	49.88	56.00	57.25	61.88	65.63	70.13	66.25	62.25	60.50	64.63	64.63
MMM	58.13	59.63	60.00	57.38	56.63	54.63	56.38	56.88	65.38	66.38	64.50	65.13	64.63	65.75	68.25	69.00
MO	65.38	67.75	72.88	74.38	71.63	74.63	83.50	84.25	87.75	90.25	92.75	99.00	87.75	90.13	99.38	104.00
PG	66.25	69.88	71.88	71.88	68.88	69.38	77.00	81.00	86.50	83.00	84.00	82.00	84.75	84.50	87.88	90.63
S	26.91	27.35	28.49	30.00	32.63	32.38	36.88	34.00	39.38	39.00	41.50	45.38	48.75	50.00	50.88	48.63
TX	66.63	68.38	68.50	65.63	66.38	64.75	64.50	68.13	73.88	78.50	80.88	79.75	85.75	85.50	83.75	83.88
UK	30.63	32.13	29.13	33.50	34.75	35.50	39.75	37.88	39.63	37.50	42.13	45.00	49.63	45.50	43.13	39.75
UTX	69.13	73.13	75.88	78.13	84.00	83.38	88.38	88.75	93.75	94.88	102.63	107.38	112.25	110.50	109.38	115.00
WX	14.13	15.00	14.50	14.63	13.63	13.63	15.00	14.13	16.88	16.38	20.75	18.50	19.38	18.88	18.38	18.88
Z	18.50	16.00	15.38	15.13	15.63	13.38	15.75	14.63	15.00	13.00	11.25	12.00	15.63	19.13	20.50	22.50
Diffusion index: percent up vs. 9 earlier:										93	97	90	93	87	90	87

and comparison method takes longer than chart inspection, so be careful to adjust for stock splits when major drops in price appear from month to month.

The signals that a market diffusion index provides are as follows:

- Move the 90 percent, early selling warning: do no more buying, and start to weed out stocks and build cash.
- Decline from more than 90 percent to 50 percent: immediate final sell signal—this is the market top. Act without delay or excuses.
- Less than 10 percent: do no selling because it is already too late. A major panic-type bottom is forming. (Consider buys despite your fear!)

Note that the market diffusion method is much better as a selling indicator than as a buying tool because tops in the overall market form gradually even though individual stocks may display exhaustion peaks; bottoms are violent. At bottoms, an oscillator-type index such as an advance/decline or diffusion index can appear numerically oversold, but the final and usually most violent decline can take a few days or a couple more weeks and still result in severely lower prices. Therefore, as a buying indicator, a diffusion index is an imprecise tool—as are most other technical indicators when severe panic psychology is running the market.

Creating a diffusion index can be a highly personalized exercise. Investors not only can choose a universe to follow to customize the diffusion indicator, but they can and should keep a tally on those stocks they actually own. As an indicator per se, this is more crude and is subject to statistical imperfection because the sample size is small and the list itself is subject to revision over time as one's portfolio changes. However, it is a useful exercise if done in the following manner. (See Table 18–2.)

Keep a looseleaf sheet in a notebook on which to log the periodic closing price of each stock held. For personal diffusion-index purposes, use the last Friday of each month or the one closest to month-end rather than the actual last day of the month. This lets weekends conveniently allow more chance for real-time data recording and for prompt study. Record each stock's current quotation, and compare it with a past period's price.

With a personal portfolio list, use a three-month rather than a nine-month window. There are two reasons: (1) portfolio turnover, overlaid on a nine-month window, reduces the number of stocks in the sample at any time quite significantly, and (2) the shorter window is more sensitive. The indicator should be designed to say something soon, when a significant market move has occurred.

Also consider this guideline: when a personal list shows all winners over a three-month period, do some selling. Such a reading means that the market has been strong and/or the investor has been hot (probably aided by the overall trend), and this probably will not last for long. Because the market makes just a few mean-

T A B L E   18–2

Personal Diffusion Index on a Five-Stock Portfolio

Stock (Cost)	Dec 95	Jan 96	Feb	Mar	Apr	May	Jun 96
AXP (45)	41.38	46.00	45.88	49.38	48.50	45.75	44.63
up/down	–	+	+	+	+	+	–
IBM (105)	91.38	108.50	122.63	111.25	107.75	106.75	99.00
up/down	–	+	+	+	+	+	–
KO (35)	37.13	37.69	40.38	41.38	40.75	46.00	49.00
up/down	+	+	+	+	+	+	+
XON (82)	80.50	80.25	79.50	81.50	85.00	84.75	86.88
up/down	–	–	–	+	+	+	+
Z (15)	13.00	11.25	12.00	15.63	19.13	20.50	22.50
up/down	–	–	–	+	+	+	+
Total up	1	3	3	4	5	5	3
Percent up	20	60	60	80	100	100	60

Personal start-selling signal occurred April 30, 1996, at 100%

ingful wavelike swings per year on average, a three-month window is likely to help catch roughly a full wave.

Note also the need to make mental adjustments about one or two stocks in the list. For example, one stock in a list of 10 took a bad tumble several months ago, but the investor held it. If there are problems with this company and the investor remains stubborn, he effectively must forgive the index for including the stock because realistically he cannot hope for a 100 percent (the usual signal for selling) reading while this laggard remains on the short list.

One final caveat: be sure to look at price performance over a fixed time interval for all current stocks, not net price performance since the dates they were bought. It is obvious that a hugely successful, long-term growth holding would always give a plus reading on the latter basis, providing no guidance. Therefore, track changing intermediate-term momentum, and use a three-month comparison window.

Again, not only should some stocks be sold when there are all winners (because momentum cannot get stronger), also use a fall through the 50-percent level as the trigger for serious selling. This means that either the market itself has rolled over and lost momentum or that your individual feel or judgment about stock performance and prospects has lost contact with current market tastes. Always consider contrariness as a virtue in investing. When an investor feels the most confident, that is exactly a time to lean the other way deliberately and sell. A diffusion index is a powerful mathematical guide to use when contrary selling should be implemented. A personal diffusion index, as described in this chapter, both tailors the signal to personal holdings and provides an excellent disciplinary tool for portfolio reviews.

19

Overcome Greed: Stop Chasing the Last Eighth

KEYS TO INVESTMENT SUCCESS

- Learn to Walk Away
- Beware of Rush Sales
- Know That Hurried Thinking Breeds Hurried Sales

Investors, and particularly traders, all too often succumb to the temptation to seek what is virtually impossible: the legendary "extra eighth" of a price point, both in a literal (micro) and in a figurative (big picture) market sense.

In the literal sense, logical investors realize that the odds against selling a stock at *the* highest price—on a short-term swing or in a major bull market move—are overwhelming. For example, a reasonably seasoned blue chip, exchange-traded, low-beta common stock might trade in a range between, say, $30 and $50 over a 12-month period. Examples of such stocks are Goodyear, JC Penney, and Union Carbide.

Elementary mathematics indicates that a 20-point price range includes 161 eighths (with the extra eighth), so the random odds are 160:1 against selling at the top price. From the technician's viewpoint, volume peaks before prices in a bull market; therefore, on a volume-traded basis, the odds are that fewer shares will trade at the top eighth than at prices several points lower. So those stated 160:1 odds against are actually too low.

Even if an investor watches a quotation machine all day long with an uncanny, intuitive sense of technical action, he still needs terrific luck to catch the top eighth. What kinds of things can go wrong even if he is that smart?

His timing, indeed, may be perfect, but his broker may be on the other line and cannot get back to him until several minutes later. Or, with the stock trading at its absolute high for the day and the year, he enters a market sell order and it is executed down an eighth at the bid, while someone else's buy order at market is transacted at the offer, coming in perhaps just a few seconds later.

Contrast the two traders' feelings: one buys at the exact top and the other's worst failing is to sell just a mere eighth lower! Or say a seller somehow catches the top of the day. But overnight the dollar is up against the yen and the Federal Reserve Chairman makes a speech that Wall Street likes. Program trading opens the market ahead 40 DJIA points, and yesterday's high eighth is now eclipsed. Clearly, by any objective standard, the chance of getting out at the exact high is slim.

Despite these odds, a surprising number of investors and traders get trapped into trying for the last eighth by ego, fantasies of wealth, and an unbridled need to "win." These people literally want to go for it all. But going for the last eighth can be very costly. Or, all too often, it can be an excuse not to act at all.

LEARN TO WALK AWAY

The expression "the last eighth" is misleading and too literal. In the industry it means the attempt to squeeze out just a little bit more, or it can mean staying around too long. Either way, the meaning is reduced to the notion of getting greedy when reason, near-term timing logic, or one's predetermined target price says now is the time to sell.

When that time to sell arrives, it takes tough mental and emotional discipline to pick up the telephone and call a broker with the instruction to sell (do not wait for your broker to call unless you are fortunate enough to have a nearly unique relationship with an excellent, old-school stockbroker). Even when having the discipline and good sense to dial the call promptly, an investor can confound her own good sell decisions with poor tactical execution. Any number of factual inputs, hunches, or emotional reactions can induce her to enter a limit order just a little above the market. Target limits should have been entered long ago and well above then-current prices, not now when one is feeling giddy and greedy.

She may muse that, after all, the stock has been strong enough to land on the 52-week high list, so why not let nature take its course and let the momentum give her a couple of extra fractional up-ticks just for being a little more patient? Surely sometime today or tomorrow the stock's current strength and natural fluctuation volatility will net just a little more rise.

Such thinking is overly optimistic; selling a stock near its top is a difficult exercise that requires tremendous discipline, a contrarian's mentality, an updated feel of the tone in the particular stock and the overall market, and a strong dash of luck as well.

When the stock has exceeded an investor's objective or especially when new market/industry/company developments prompt a reduction in price objective, the most prudent course is to enter a market sell order. An even more judicious action, which would avert the entire emotion-laden situation that will crop up at a later time, is to enter a good-til-canceled (GTC) order at the target price when the stock is originally purchased. Recall PST in Chapter 15.

Knowing that he is out on a market order, he can move on to some other selling or buying idea without the distraction of waiting or worrying. He can feel less exposed to a possible drop in the overall market because he will have lightened up his position.

When a stock is peaking, an investor runs a very serious risk of missing the top area altogether by trying to stretch winnings too far. Once a stock stops rising and starts declining, the difficulty of selling it becomes even greater. Giving up points that have already melted away is more painful than imagining giving up points of paper profit that have not yet been created. As veteran observers will all attest, it is easier to sell on the way up than on the way down.

Usually, an investor's tendency is to remember each high in a successful stock rally. Each further advance to a new price peak then establishes a new psychological high ground from which perspective operates. He begins to view that level as an entitlement and believes that height is attainable again.

If, in fact, the real lasting high has already been reached (a fact the investor will not know for some time, and then only with useless hindsight), his efforts and hopes for "just a little more" already are doomed from the beginning. His mental state heads south with the stock's price, weakening his decision-making abilities. Thus, when a predetermined price objective is reached, the best policy is to sell at market and walk away (or better, to have been taken out on a GTC order).

When an investor has made the decision and has actually walked away by selling out, he should just keep walking: unless there is a specific reason to continue watching the sold stock, don't look at the quotes for awhile once the stock is sold. Count on *not* getting that final eighth, or point, or two points. Move on without regrets and without looking back. If your stock reached its sale target, those who bought it higher—even if they now have a small profit—are among the greater fools and just do not realize it yet. Do not worry about them getting the extra point because it was not obvious in real time that the stock would go any higher; this type of self-second-guessing is not only useless but self-defeating.

BEWARE OF RUSH SALES

Ironically, the flip side of the error in holding on for the proverbial extra eighth of a point is overstaying when it is smartest to cash in. The exit is needlessly hurried once the sale decision has been made. This is not the macro-level problem of failing to let profits run; it is the micro-tactical tendency of many investors simply to throw in a market sale order and depart in haste. Psychologically, having endured the stress of coming to a sell decision, one wants to ensure closure since only closure will end the experience with certainty.

When a trade is to be closed in a generally stable or rising market environ- ment, bypassing a market order and making other reasonable efforts over the short term might net a better execution without unnecessarily exposing the holder to a nasty downside erosion. The objective here, at the margin, is to increase the profit (through good micro tactics) from many positions as they are sold out. The way to do this, in defined circumstances, is to slow down and take what the market allows instead of insisting on the immediate gratification (hooray, look at my nice profit!) and relief (gosh, am I glad that's taken care of!) afforded by a hasty sale.

This advice applies best when the sale is made in response to achievement of a fundamental target rather than as a technically driven action designed to avoid danger. It must be emphasized, however, that if a stock's sale is being made for more urgent tactical reasons, say, to avoid declining prices caused by important bad news or a failing general market, slowing down is not the right action. But if an in- vestor is selling a stock because it has reached her objective on a fundamental basis, why should she be in a hurry? Suppose her studies indicate that a stock is likely to be fully priced when it reaches 120 percent of the market's P/E multiple, two times book value, eight times cash flow per share, or a dividend yield of two percent.

Those specific targets are not likely to be shared universally by other holders. So there probably will be no sudden huge rush of sell orders entered (or even a large cluster on the specialist's book) when the stock hits our hypothetical seller's particular fundamental target.

Nor is she a market guru like Gabelli, Zweig, or Garzarelli, whose publicized targets and known actions create headlines and move stocks. Bear in mind that just as the market does not pause to note an individual's purchase, it takes no special notice of an individual's fundamental target prices.

If your sale is being made based on fundamental measures, barring the bad luck of sudden bad news or a slumping overall market, be in no special hurry to get out. Do not let ego rule your exit tactics. Take a little more if the market will allow it, but never expect perfection. Always recall that the odds of selling at the very top price (for the year, for the move, or even just for the near-term future) are very low. A perfect exit is nearly impossible to execute, so do not bedevil your mind by seek- ing one or by missing one.

HURRIED THINKING, HURRIED SALES

There are several subtle sources of emotional baggage carried by investors who jump quickly and get bad executions in what should be no-rush sales. Not all past sales closed out profits, and some closing trades later were regretted (whereas all buying decisions are made in an upbeat frame of mind).

The tendency to "get it over with" when selling is supported by one or more of the following six excuses to hurry:

- Selling to raise funds for a new purchase (note the warnings given in Chapter 17).
- Wanting to end an unsatisfactory experience.
- Selling mainly based on frustration or boredom.
- Being accustomed to instant gratification.
- Wanting relief from uncertainty or stress.
- False (externally imposed) urgency over shifting market expectations.

When an investor decides it is time to sell, earlier patterns and experiences pop up from the conscious or unconscious; they define the way he or she feels about present sales and influence current actions unless consciously recognized and controlled. This is important to remember for fundamentally driven, non-urgent sales, especially presuming your sale proceeds are not being recommitted the same day.

On the other hand, some fundamentally driven stock sales—even though they are not urgent—are caused by reassessing prospects and lowering expectations:

- The company has not been reaching the accelerated sales pace you had projected.
- Interest rates have risen sooner or more than you expected.
- The general market feels like it is topping, which implies some need to prune over the near term.
- Group rotation seems to be moving away from this stock, indicating that your hoped-for P/E is not to be achieved.

Often, a revision of expectations, although not a sudden disaster, carries disappointment when compared with original hopes for the stock position. Thus, investors rush to sell this mildly underperforming investment (to push away the disappointment) when actually there is no solid reason for hurrying.

Selling a stock out of frustration or boredom has similar results. For example, an investor may hang in with Dullsville, Inc. stock when it has not lived up to expectations instead of riding Whiz-Bang Spiffycorp. Belatedly, he now awakens to the fact that he has wasted the time value of his money and that his snoozing position is going nowhere fast.

But this late dawning of the light does not mean that the smartest way out is an immediate market-sell order. If there is no reason to suspect the stock will crack over the short term, at least one can try to do better on the exit than he did on the entry. The best action is to control the desire to move impulsively away from the frustration; to proceed more slowly toward a good execution.

A subtle reason for making foolish sales when it is unnecessary is the nature of America in the twentieth century. This is an age of instant gratification and computer speed. In just the past 15 years, the concept of speed has changed radically. Computers churned on big problems for minutes in the mid-1970s; if spreadsheets take more than seconds to recompute, we now become annoyed and impatient. With this mind-set shaped by so many experiences in daily life, Americans are subconsciously programmed to reach for an instant sale confirmation when it is time to sell. But if there is no valid fundamental or technical reason to rush, they pay in lost dollars for irrational, habit-driven impatience.

When an investor finally decides to sell a stock, the conditioning created by uncomfortable past experiences with uncertainty comes into play. She feels, even if perhaps only subconsciously, that she can at least take control in one aspect of trading by selling immediately. She may jump instinctively for the market order without any really good reason. By becoming aware of this unconscious, ingrained tendency, one can take conscious steps to control it and then usually can get more profitable results on the margin.

All an investor has to do in these circumstances is slow down. Stocks have a natural tendency to fluctuate—over a week, day to day, and intra day. If there is no immediate deterioration in fundamentals or in overall market psychology, on average a seller can presume to do moderately better than the randomly priced last trade or the current bid by exercising patience and entering a smart order on a limit instead of a market-sell order.

Distributions of returns, and therefore of micro changes, are statistically shown to vary with the square root of time. Thus, for example, an exchange-traded stock that typically fluctuates within three points in a week's span might be expected to wiggle by a bit more than 40 percent that much, or $1.25 on a daily basis,

or $\left[3 \times \dfrac{1}{\sqrt{5 \text{ days}}} \right]$. Starting from a randomly selected price such as yesterday's

close or the morning opening, one might thus project fluctuations as much as $5/8$ of a point higher (and lower) during today for such a stock. That makes entering an immediate market order seem a bit shortsighted, assuming a sideways market.

Note that over the market's long history, prices average a small net gain per day—not a small loss. Thus, on average, waiting can gain a fraction if there is no bad news in immediate prospect and if one is not palpably in a bear market. Learn to take advantage of natural random fluctuations instead of ignoring them. Be satisfied with a quarter, half, or point's improvement over randomly determined current market. In many instances, improved exit tactics can at least pay for one's commission cost.

CHAPTER 20

Sell When It Just Feels So Good

KEYS TO INVESTMENT SUCCESS

- Evaluate How Fast the Stock Can Rise; and for How Long
- Ask Yourself What Further Good Things Could Happen to the Stock
- Know What to Do if Good News Does Not Move the Stock

Every stock has its own peculiar behavior patterns. These can be triggered by news, by psychological or technical conditions in the general market, by the passing enthusiasms or phobias of momentum-chasing institutional investors, or by the movements of other stocks in the same industry group. And, fortunately for investors, sometimes the ways in which stocks behave actually provide signals to exit.

This chapter focuses on how fast a stock can reasonably be expected to rise and for how long. Such information should discipline investor thinking regarding successful positions that are so good that a temptation develops to fall in love with the stock and marry it for the long haul.

Because nearly all good things do come to an end—or at least simmer down—the tactically most successful investors are those able to step off before it becomes obvious to the majority that the market's direction has become overdone and due for reversal.

HOW FAST CAN THE STOCK RISE; FOR HOW LONG?

When a stock starts acting heroically, that in itself is a sell signal. Acquire a set of charts, either daily basis or long term in format. Again, technical analysis is not the purpose; simply study wavelike movements in broad terms.

Take, for example, a growth stock such as PepsiCo, McDonald's, Colgate Palmolive, or foodservice distributor Sysco. Over the very long term, such persistently successful companies achieve growth in earnings of perhaps 15 percent per year. Over the long term, of course, a stock's price cannot be expected to move faster than in proportion to earnings and dividend growth. To ask for more requires a secular increase in P/E ratios, but such changes tend to reverse when interest rates rebound or during recessions and bear markets. All a long-term, buy-and-hold investor can reasonably hope for is price growth in line with long-term earnings trends.

But stocks—even those of the established growth company machines—do not climb a steady, slight incline from day to day or from month to month. (A $50 growth stock with a 13 percent growth rate should advance, net, by $6.50 per year, which works out to just $1/8$ point per week; yet virtually any stock moves much more widely than that within such a narrow track.) Prices gyrate up and down in waves at percentage rates well in excess of the fundamental growth rate of the underlying company. In the process, a stock swings from being "ahead of itself" or overpriced to being oversold. If only an investor had perfect foresight, he or she theoretically could catch each top and bottom and thereby become wealthy rapidly.

Reality demands that we not attempt to catch tops and bottoms of each swing perfectly because failure in that endeavor is certain; aiming or hoping for 100 percent perfect execution will only create self-defeating frustration and tactical second-guessing. However, it is readily possible to track the multiple wavelike movements that stock prices exhibit while swinging around their long-term growth slopes, as in Chapter 13. Within these movements, and well short of their extremes, lie opportunities for above-trend returns as well as for investment education.

Look at the accompanying price charts of Colgate Palmolive and Sysco (Figure 20–1) for instance. While the earnings momentum of these two companies is fairly steady at about 15 percent per year (and, therefore their stocks tend to mirror that net pace over the long term), there are both large and small wavelike up movements at a much more rapid pace (interspersed with corrections). Even in a 12-month period when the stock might rise by its net theoretical average of 15 percent, one can easily spot three or four quick price moves of 10 percent to 15 percent each, taking only several weeks to accomplish. Those moves present up slopes that are fundamentally unsustainable over the longer term, but they provide very profitable opportunities for the nimble investor. The trader tries to catch most of the move over the short term. But the longer-term-oriented investor should also see such moves as unsustainable and use them as timing opportunities to cash in; one

FIGURE 20–1

Colgate Palmolive and Sysco Price Charts

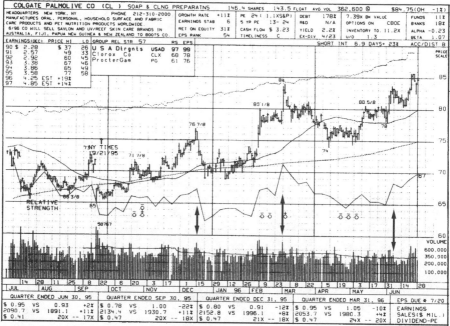

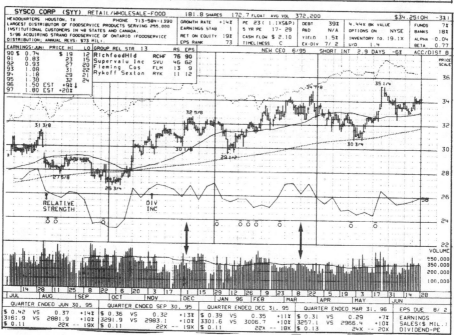

Courtesy of *Daily Graphs and Long Term Values;* P.O. Box 66919; Los Angeles, California 90066–0919.

FIGURE 20-2

McDonald's Price Chart

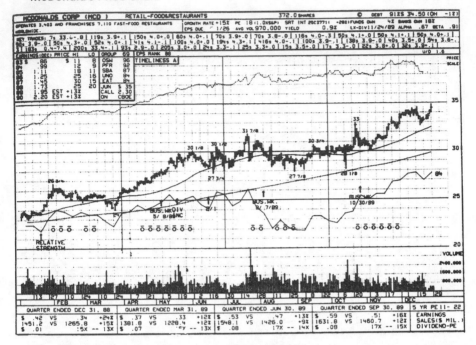

Courtesy of *Daily Graphs and Long Term Values;* P.O. Box 66919; Los Angeles, California 90066–0919.

can always re-enter later. (See Figure 20–2.) Recall that Chapter 13 laid out the mathematical and psychological reasons for cashing in frequently (higher net returns and lowered risk), while Chapter 10 warned of the heightened risk of giving away pleasant paper profits when institutions suddenly abandon a stock! Both of those factors are reasons one should capture unsustainably sharp, brief runups rather than just let the capital ride for the predictable correction or lengthy pause.

Because this is not a study on technical analysis, there is no attempt to quantify the number of moves per year per stock or the average percentage slope that can be expected. Such parameters differ for each stock, and they may well change over time for any one issue. The phenomenon of unsustainable upward movement is described here, however, because it offers an opportunity for well-timed sales. In fact, some of the best selling opportunities occur when it seemingly just can't get much better. (See Figure 20–3.)

After a very strong short-term advance, one is quite likely to be virtually in love with the company, fundamentally for its presumed long-term virtues. But sup-

FIGURE 20–3

Unsustainably Rapid Upward Moves

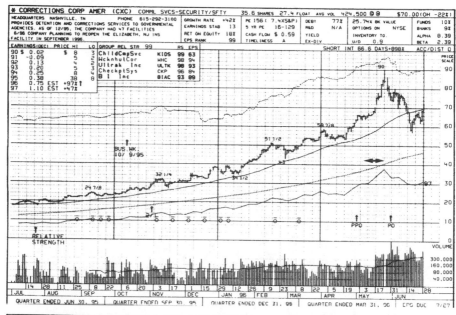

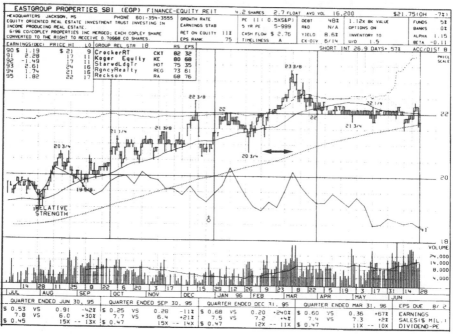

FIGURE 20–3 (continued)

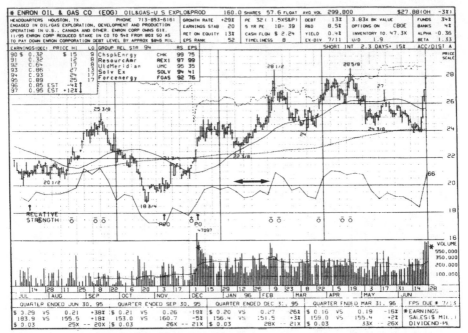

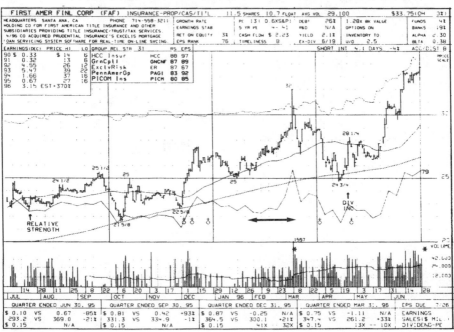

F I G U R E 20–3 (continued)

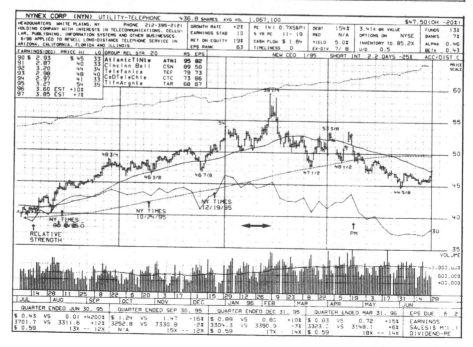

FIGURE 20–3 (concluded)

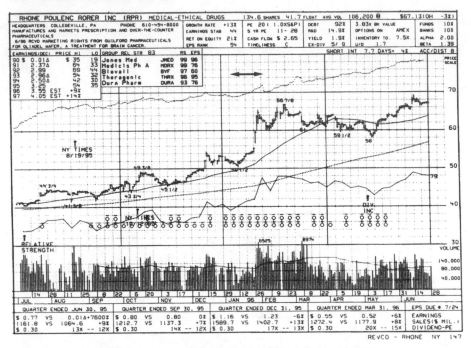

Courtesy of *Daily Graphs and Long Term Values;* P.O. Box 66919; Los Angeles, California 90066–0919.

pose that just now an analyst's recommendation envisions a 25 percent increase in stock price over a 12-month period, driven by good fundamentals and rising appreciation of the company's strengths. If your broker calls after the stock has just risen 15 percent in perhaps less than a month, tell that broker to stop chasing strength. You should resist that temptation to buy what feels most obvious and comfortable (look at how well it's been acting!). Instead, the proper course is to place a below-market GTC limit order to buy lower on the next reaction. This requires patience and guts for both broker and investor, but it pays handsomely in the longer run.

The same principle applies when your already-owned stock is running ahead sharply. Omitting the occasional spectacular move on rumored takeover offers, when a stock moves several percent in a week, exciting but unrealistic annualized capital growth rates begin to dance in your head like sugar plums. Just 3 percent per week is 156 percent per year! But each stock and its moves are unique. And the tone of the general market affects each stock differently on each movement. Thus, there is no universal formula or meaningful average measure that can be applied. One way of deciding in the short term that enough is already enough is this: if your stock has moved a full year's worth percentagewise (its fundamental sustainable growth rate) in a month or two, give it a rest. Viewed in realistic perspective from a non-owner's distance, such a stock has done more than its share of rising for the short term and should be logically avoided for awhile until it cools off.

In an orderly market, each stock—particularly a stock that is traded heavily by institutions—tends to form its own patterns. Some technical traders notice these patterns and assume they will repeat. Their buying and selling tends to make such expectations somewhat self-fulfilling, but exact percentages and point moves are unequal each time.

Therefore, look at each individual stock chart and see what the stock's past moves were. For example, use rules of thumb such as these: in a McDonald's or a Colgate Palmolive, be a seller rather than a buyer after a rapid (two week or less) 10 percent price move, or after a 15 percent move in two to three months. In a slower but still dependable grower like General Electric, 5 percent to 7 percent in a week is a major move that should be sold into. Discover the typical patterns in each stock you own, and lean against the happy tide when such fast moves occur.

The charts in the preceding few pages illustrate climactic but unsustainable rallies. This pleasant experience is somewhat different from the several-a-year undulating trading rally described earlier. The pattern here is a sustained gradual rise followed by a curve seemingly accelerating almost straight skyward. Such culminations of moves usually occur on high volume and, in fact, with such frenzied trading that it cannot be maintained for long. Sometimes short sellers are being squeezed, adding to the obvious buy-side pressure.

Often such a pattern occurs after a concept has been prominent in the news for some time and after virtually everyone finally becomes convinced. Examples here include prison privatization, the Internet/telecommunications frenzy, pharmaceutical merger fever, and a purported resurgence of oil-price inflation.

It is usually impossible to predict an exact top in such emotionally charged phases, just as one cannot tell precisely how deep a panic sell-off will go before reversing. Two clues are usually helpful, however: (1) a decline of trading volume on a rising-price day, and (2) a general market upset (perhaps economic data drive fears of Federal Reserve Board tightening) that is likely to find portfolio managers scrambling to nail down profits in their most recent and hottest winners. When a stock has taken you for a giddy ride, the temptation to get greedy is extremely strong. At the first sign of hearing yourself say, "just one more day," or "just so many more points," sell out immediately.

On rare occasions, the market provides a true textbook example of how to know when (but not at what level) a price rise will end. Figure 20–4, charting Green Tree Financial and Humana, illustrates this. Both issues were added to the Standard & Poor's 500 Index: Humana on December 1, 1995, and Green Tree in March 1996. Hundreds of billions of dollars are invested in index funds by individual investors and especially by institutions that have given up trying to beat the market. When a new component enters the S&P 500, all such mutual funds literally must

FIGURE 20-4

Stocks Entering the S&P 500 Index

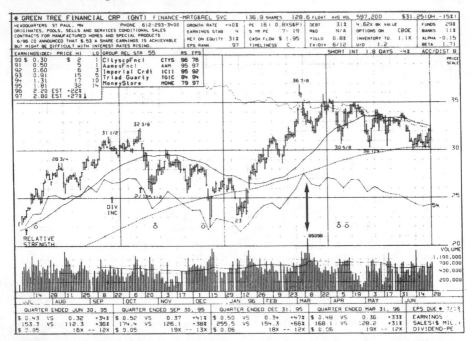

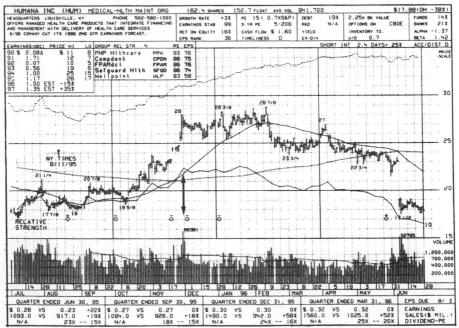

buy it. Technically, they should buy it at the close of trading the night before it becomes a component.

The resulting cluster of buy orders is monumental, and its timing is precisely known a few days in advance since S&P discloses such changes in news releases. In both of the cases cited, volume topped 8 million shares on the appointed day. The charts indicate that at least temporary important price tops coincided exactly with those volume explosions. Why this type of event created a top is literally answered by asking what could possibly create a greater concentration of buying orders; answer, nothing short of a surprise takeover announcement. The only logical action in such cases is a sell-on-close order or a sale at the next morning's opening. Actually experiencing the positive reinforcement of timing a sale perfectly in such a case (regardless of the exact dollar profit nailed down) is of benefit to one's future confidence in pulling that sometimes-rusty sale trigger!

WHAT FURTHER GOOD THINGS COULD HAPPEN TO THE STOCK?

Once a stock stops rising briskly, it almost never levels off calmly at its new higher level. Get out of the way rather than risk exposing your capital and your mental well-being to the negative emotions and darker imaginings that take hold once a price pullback gets under way.

Another important cue for assessing how much better it can get lies in fundamental developments. In the same way that a stock can get so technically strong that there is no encore possible, company news can line up at the ceiling. When that happens, it is a signal at least to become extremely cautious; at most, it acts as a direct signal to cash in. This observation is more than an extension of the old admonition to buy on rumor and sell on news. At issue is fundamental exhaustion on the upside. Sometimes there simply is nothing left that has not already gone right. At some point, investors collectively expect everything to continue positively, so there can then no longer be any further price impact from good news. All the good news has already been anticipated, and "everyone" interested is already on board. There literally are no buyers or buying reasons left untapped; the stock can only retreat.

Once again, this measurement is more an art than a science. Point values cannot be assigned to dividend increases, stock splits, contracts awarded, earnings gains, important new technology, clustered analyst recommendations, or patents. Simply observe a number of situations and from them develop a sense of how good it gets. From that rough measure, project approximately when the party will wind down.

It is extremely dangerous to try to sell at the very top during an emotionally charged market period; be resigned beforehand to the certainty of missing tops in a spike-shaped move by quite a bit. Be content to come out a decent winner and to learn a little each time from the micro experience in which you participated in making your exit.

The following is the story of one stock that illustrates the boundaries of the possible on the upside and what good news can and cannot do for a stock. A microcap electronics company in the southwestern United States had good products and a smart management team that kept overhead expense low. Quarterly revenues fluctuated noticeably as big orders came and went, so the stock moved in a wide range.

Soon it appeared that big developments were afoot: the company was developing highly significant new markets for its product line and started hooking some very impressive prospective customers. The selling cycle was predictably long on these deals because they involved major corporate decisions by the buyers. But the array of pending and rumored deals, across a number of new customer industries, was exciting.

The stock was trading at below $2.00 per share. When management hinted briefly in quarterly reports about important orders, the stock perked up to more than $3.00 per share. Pending deals involved a first-echelon bank, two major oil companies, a major foreign government agency, a leading retail organization, and a top-name regional bank.

Two of the potential orders (likely, units times price) each exceeded the company's highest previous total annual revenue. The prestige of capturing industry leaders as customers would have spillover effects on sales. Predictably, brokers and investors started asking one analyst following this little stock how high it should be expected to go. The reply was that market conditions would dictate that at the time announcements were made. Given a decent overall market climate, each of the two most important awards, when and if actually received, would be good for a point in the stock almost overnight. The scenario was to wait for the number of anticipated contracts to be won and announced and then exit with good profits.

Some brokers, appropriately trained to think in terms of fundamentals, asked what the company's earnings stream would look like and what P/E would be appropriate. The analyst's response, to their surprise, was that it did not matter. Once the company was actually delivering on the orders, the peak of excitement would have passed. The hottest news would already be past. The critical task was to identify when the sizzle was so hot that it could not get much hotter. The prospect was for blockbuster contracts compared with the company's previous contract history. The earnings probably would follow, but mere actual future quarterly EPS releases could in no way top the impact of a string of contract announcements for excitement. The revenues would be nonrecurring, as in the past. Therefore, the market would not assign a high P/E when the actual earnings would become known. It literally was a classic illustration of "just how good can this get?"

An investor, like that analyst, who thinks ahead in scenarios harbors no illusions about divining the peak of excitement in such a stock. But after a nice string of positive announcements, she does feel confident that the news can hardly get more exciting; at that point, prices probably will have reached a point when staying for more is greedy. It is, therefore, impossible to quote a price objective or a time frame in advance. (In this actual case, the stock moved to $8.00 before the game was over.)

Without knowing what is really going on at a company, investors can create mental scenarios about what is realistic; they can make up a wish list. When a few of those wishes come true, especially over a short period in a generally uptrending market, investors then must ask themselves what more could realistically go right. Because at that point, *any* of those playouts of the company's plot is a signal to sell. The psychology becomes incapable of further improvement.

Remember, too, that it takes rising volume to take stocks to higher price highs, which requires increasing doses of fundamental news, investor excitement, and (especially) sponsorship. An investor may not know exactly what the upper limit will prove to be, but she can develop a good intuitive feel of approximately when "enough is enough" by observing a number of these situations carefully.

Once again, take written notes and record personal feelings in real time. Keep a chart of the stock and date the observations, keying them to price history on the chart. This helps you develop a documented record that is useful as a model for parallel future games. Also track major concept stories in unowned stocks that are in the news. See how long they take to play out. Never expect things to be exactly the same twice; do look for clusters of events or for general patterns.

WHAT IF GOOD NEWS DOES NOT MOVE THE STOCK?

Now what happens if good news does not move the stock? This requires only brief treatment: the bottom-line answer is that selling without delay is in order. One of the definitions of a bear market is a time when investors just do not care about good news. Applying this logic to individual stocks, if good news fails to elicit positive stock price action (in a reasonably hospitable market climate), there is no longer enough unsatisfied buying interest in that stock to push it higher.

Here, the excitement has passed its peak, volume will be unable to build to new highs, and the price must erode. A sophisticated market observer can use this insight as a signal to cash in, while others less savvy use the latest good news as reason to buy the stock. Unfortunately, they fail to realize that they are buying into distribution and are starting to play much too late to be able to win in this game. Again a question of comfort arises: when it become obvious that fundamentals are wonderful, the big move (or perhaps the entire move) will already have been seen. Buyers are paid for investing while uncertain; sellers win by providing stock to the innocents who come late in the move and pay up for whatever is already grossly obvious.

What causes a stock to fail to react to good news (nonroutine news such as big contracts, new technology or patents, or a good acquisition—not just positive quarterly earnings)? First, the general market tone may have turned so cautious that not enough investors are willing to buy to move the stock. Second, the news itself may have been anticipated, so the item that looks like news is actually already priced into the stock.

Or the news may be less exciting than previous news, implying that the best is no longer yet to come. The stock already could have been sponsored heavily by brokerage recommendations and pushed ahead by institutional buying, so there is little untapped buying available. It is, in reality, an old story. In any of these cases, project lower prices for the stock. The game has already been played out past its peak of excitement.

It is important to exit a stock promptly when expectations are wrong. Holding a stock—dead sure the market is wrong not to be excited *and* after there has been a good upside move already—is a mistake, which means that the investor has gotten too enamored of the stock, has become greedy, or has misgauged how good it really can get. It is imperative to close out such a position to protect profits and to insulate oneself from second guessing and regret.

21

Sell into Price/Volume Cresendos and into Long Runs

KEYS TO INVESTMENT SUCCESS

- Gauge the Momentum
- Know The Odds in Runs

An absolutely central tenet underlying technical analysis of stock-price behavior is its attempt to identify, measure, and act upon changing relationships of supply and demand. Whether the specific technical approach is point-and-figure charting, the study of trends and channels, the identification of resistance and support levels, or the price-volume methods popularized by several authors, its core is supply and demand.

Most of the time, stock prices move in a primary direction—up or down—on heavier trading volume than they experience when making countertrend or sideways movements.

Because the way to make above-average profits is to sell when stocks are up rather than when they are at average prices or at temporarily depressed levels, this chapter focuses on two interesting short-term upside phenomena: crescendos and multiple-day runs. This emphasis helps identify and define high-volume tops and unsustainable rallies as they occur.

GAUGING THE MOMENTUM

Our first focus in identifying upside crescendos is based on the observation that volume tends to build when prices move in their primary direction; it tends to fall during the countertrend, during corrections, or during pauses in a stock's move.

One of the major tenets underlying technical analysis of volume-price behavior is that a continuing price advance requires successively higher trading volume over time. Many technicians base their analyses and decision making on this important relationship. When they see a stock continuing to rise to new highs without ongoing strong trading volume, they refer to the price move—even if it is to new highs—as a weak advance.

The term "weak advance" has nothing directly to do with the increment of rise (e.g., in the sense of $1/_8$ being weaker, or smaller than, $7/_8$). It refers to the cause, or the driving force, behind the price rise. As long as bulls who have been pushing the price higher continue to have strong conviction and remain unsatisfied in large numbers, they will still be active buyers and trading volume will remain heavy.

However, if interest shifts to other stocks in the same industry or if the market as a whole continues a strong advance but with other industry groups in the lead, the stock under study may simply keep rising in sympathy with the trend. Because it has done well, there are many happy holders and few sellers; such a stock can still rise briefly on lower volume.

This situation is inherently unstable and self-terminating. At some point in a price advance, more and more owners will view the stock as getting high in price or ahead of itself and will want to sell. If there is no longer urgent or large buying power left to be satisfied, the sellers will begin to overwhelm the few remaining buyers, and the momentum and price will crack.

The speculative bulls, seeing that the excitement has at least temporarily halted, will pull back and wait for confirmation from other buyers that there is still some upside play left. But if upside volume is broken, price cannot be long behind. Because of these supply/demand, volume/price dynamics, tops in stock prices tend to occur on high trading volume. In timing sales, you as a successful trader want to sell when they are hot, which is exactly when the trading volume is peaking on rising prices and in concert with general excitement about the stock.

Obviously, it is not always possible to know in real time exactly what day will be the height of volume or price. In general, however, there are two clues to watch. One is in the volume trend and the other is in price, and often they both apply. When they start to diverge, take it as an urgent sign to head for the exit door.

Volume tends to build toward a crescendo. The bar plots of consecutive daily volume resemble the shape of a mountain in which the slope becomes increasingly steep on the way to the pinnacle (some technicians refer to crescendos as parabolas). Not every single day falls perfectly in line, slightly higher than the day before and lower than the next. But the general shape is clear, and interruptions seldom exceed two days. Study the volume peaks on the charts shown in Figure 21–1.

Volume cannot rise indefinitely over a short time frame. As it shoots progressively higher, it is nearing exhaustion. A look at historical charts can be useful in identifying what the peak volume was when previous high points were reached. A look at a one-year daily chart, such as those supplied by the Daily Graphs service of William O'Neil & Co., quickly shows what the rough order of magnitude of the individual high-volume days has been over the past 12 months (about 250 trading days).

These previous volume heights should be used as serious warnings, but do not expect them to be matched exactly or necessarily to be exceeded before you accept current action as a valid signal of a peak. When current volumes of daily trading reach into the *general neighborhood* of old highs, be ready to sell without delay.

Price also provides a clue. While the broad market averages very seldom reach a final high on a pattern of sharp acceleration called a "spike," often individual stocks do, as was illustrated in some of the charts in Chapter 20. This apparent anomaly is explained by the fact that averages are exactly that: they combine individual elements that sometimes diverge from day to day, so they smooth the results. Not all stocks make their individual highs (or lows) on the same day or even in the same month. But when viewed individually, many do make highs on successive spike-like rallies accompanied by frenzied volume.

What is happening in these stocks, and what causes them to change? For a while, successive price rises generate interest in a stock. Price starts to accelerate, meaning that it starts to rise by larger increments each day or each week. But trends don't last indefinitely: at some point, traders begin to get cautious about owning, let alone still buying, this stock that has recently gone up so quickly.

In effect, the acceleration itself begins to discourage new players. And the most nimble owners sell their shares, causing the price first to decelerate, then to halt its rise, and finally to start falling. Remember, too, that each day's trading includes equal amounts of buying and selling, but the personality of the players shifts as this scenario plays out. As price has risen sharply, more holders become nervous or satisfied by the newfound price levels, so selling volume is building. (And more owners are recent short-term buyers, often referred to as hot money; these are unstable holders ready to move out as soon as the action cools.)

When the urgent speculative buyers finally are satisfied or go away, some sellers remain who have been waiting for one more good day or one more point. Thus, when the price does stop rising, it falls sharply from its peak as those latest satisfied owners or nervous sellers fail to find enough interested buyers; volume, therefore, falls off. Note again that stocks can fall of their own weight, but it takes buying pressure to boost them up.

Of course, it is usually not possible in real time to identify with certainty the

FIGURE 21–1

Price Tops Coincide with Volume Crescendos

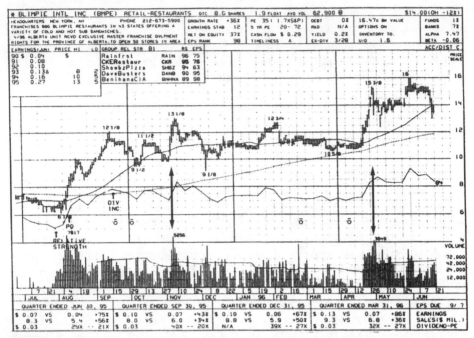

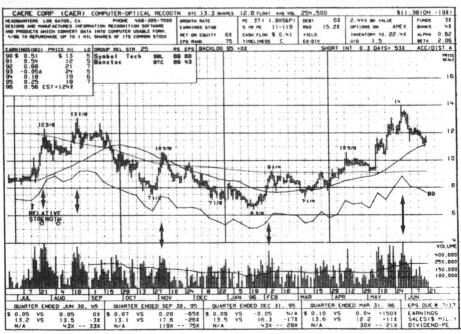

F I G U R E   21–1 (continued)

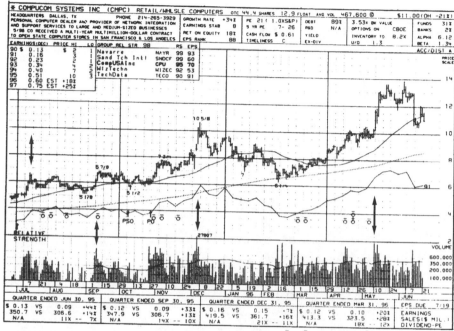

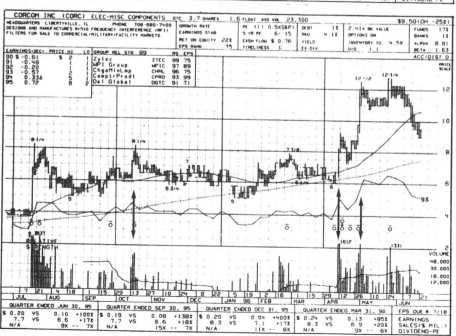

FIGURE 21–1 (concluded)

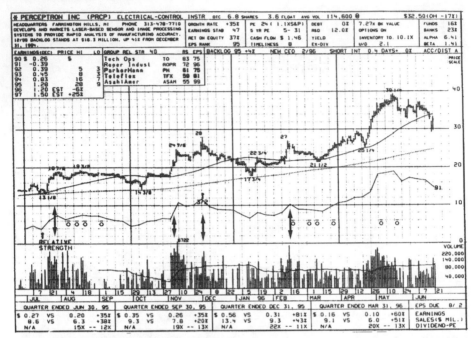

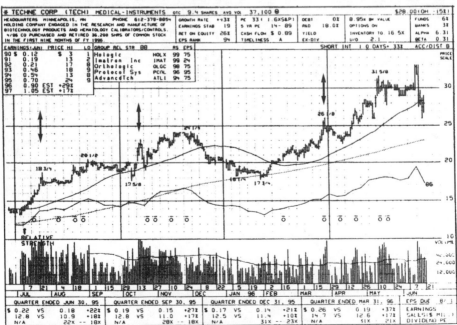

Courtesy of *Daily Graphs and Long Term Values;* P.O. Box 66919; Los Angeles, California 90066–0919.

exact high day in price or volume. A careful study of past patterns can, however, define an intertwined pair of yardsticks—price and volume—with which to assess when a stock is close enough to make a sell decision wise.

There is something in human nature that makes it difficult to execute this maneuver. One unscientific, but still effective, approach is self-monitoring. To calibrate yourself, you as an investor need to own a given stock and watch it closely on a daily basis. Record in a notebook how many consecutive days the stock has risen, and also whether a strong run in the major market averages is helping it. (Doing this exercise on paper while not owning the stock might prove somewhat interesting but would be sterile because of an absence of emotions.)

As the stock crescendos in price and volume, note personal daily reactions like the interplays among fear and greed and excitement; record these observations on a page, keyed with a letter, and mark that letter at the appropriate day on a price chart for future reference. When a sale is made during this flagpole runup, take note afterward whether the decision came prematurely or late—and, if so, by how many days the actual peak was miscalculated.

Note also what the best hunch was at the time the sell order was given. In effect, that is calibrating your own personal pressure gauge. Photocopy the daily price chart a week later, and attach it to your notes. Then, next time, incorporate the latest results into an operating plan. Naturally this is an imprecise art rather than a science, and your perhaps alternating or overcompensating (later/sooner) approaches may feel awkward. But after a few experiences, you will find that an improved sense of touch develops. Again, this exercise works only in real trading in the presence of risk and tension as real dollars and your self-esteem are on the line. It is also most effective if several observations can be made in a fairly concentrated period of time, at most a couple of months. Otherwise, even with written notes, recall is not very accurate because of lack of intensity.

One of the key points to remember in a rapid price runup is not to expect to achieve a perfect exit. The stock's action will be very volatile from hour to hour; if an investor is typically busy at work, she probably has only one decision time per day with a broker, perhaps two at most. The advent of large numbers of on-line quotation systems that allow bypassing a broker conversation when only monitoring the current action is desired serves as an increasing help.

Therefore, do not expect to get the highest eighth. Any investor able even to hit the best day, let alone the top price, is doing very well indeed: partly clever and partly lucky. Taking action within no more than one day on either side is still quite accurate. So keep a cool perspective: if a stock makes three high-volume price peaks a year, being within a day of the top when selling means picking one of the nine best trading days out of 250 in a year. That is besting odds of more than 25:1. Congratulations!

Both buying good stocks and selling them well are required for making profits. To trade successfully in up markets, one must sell into strong price and volume crescendos, that is, selling just as the buying crowd reaches its fever pitch rather than becoming part of that crowd. Do not worry about catching the top perfectly, and enter sell instructions in this circumstance at market rather than getting greedy. Even if there is more frequent (more than once-daily) contact, decide to make only one choice (selling or holding) per day. That construct will impose a degree of structure on your sell decisions. Resist wanting to think more about it or to wait for just a little more (technical) information. Come to closure.

Once having sold, walk away. Be content to look back again at the stock no sooner than a week or two later: if it was sold anywhere near the height of a mountain of trading volume, more than likely you will see that its price has fallen back and that the sale was a good one. Your exit will not have been perfect, but you will have the great satisfaction of knowing how much better it is to have gotten out near that top than still to be in and be further away from it!

In summary, there are two aspects of selling on high volume to remember:

- Realize that volume will crescendo only so high, and use stock-specific past history as a guide to its reasonably likely upper limits.
- If volume starts to trail off after a buildup but price keeps going up, this is the weak, later portion of the price rise and time is running out fast. Figure 21–2 illustrates the failure of volume build-ups to support further price advances.

KNOWING THE ODDS IN RUNS

A second interesting and potentially very profitable upside phenomenon is the run of consecutive daily advances. Often, although not always, such a run is accompanied by rising volume. Moves into new high ground or moves to close a prior downside gap do not always need higher volume. Putting aside the issue of trading volume, one can isolate on examining the price run in terms of the odds of continuing or faltering. In the same way that the emotions and momentum chasing described earlier will cause a crescendo to reverse itself once the price rise stops, the end of a long run of daily advances will be followed by price reversal as both short-term traders and observant, tactically nimble holders cash in. You should be aware of how the odds work and should take selling action accordingly.

Our study of runs applies both to individual stocks and to the broad market as measured by widely watched averages. Tracking runs in major averages is helpful because it aids in timing one's sales of individual stocks. While not every stock rises or falls on the same day as a major average, the general tone or trend of the market does influence single stocks' prices. During a run, market participants become increasingly confident and happy, regarding the whole experience of investing or trading as more and more pleasant. Once the string of positive daily reinforcements (rises) is broken, a return to reality (this is, after all, a two-way street) sets in.

FIGURE 21–2

Lower Volume Defines Weak Advances

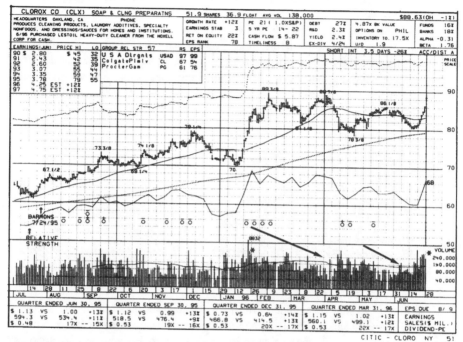

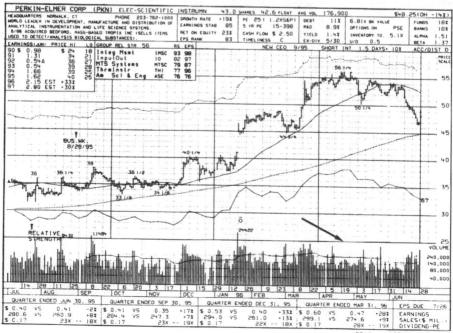

Courtesy of *Daily Graphs and Long Term Values;* P.O. Box 66919; Los Angeles, California 90066–0919.

Precisely because collective human emotions are involved, runs rather than random movement characterize stock price patterns. Emotions switch from overly optimistic to cautious and then to overly fearful and pessimistic; stocks rise for a time and then fall back.

If advances and declines actually were random events, and if the possibility of unchanged days were conveniently not a complicating factor, one might imagine constructing probability tables for predicting the frequencies of given price runs. For example, imagining that there were no unchanged days and that advances and declines were equal in number over the long term (like the two sides of a fair coin), the following would be the pure statistical odds of various upside runs:

Days in a Row	Odds	Times per Year
One or more	0.5	126
Two or more	0.25	63
Three or more	0.125	31
Four or more	0.0625	16
Five or more	0.03125	8
Six or more	0.015625	4
Seven or more	0.0078125	2
Eight or more	0.00391625	1
Nine or more	0.001958125	0.49
Ten or more	0.0009790625	0.24

Thus, assuming all that was stated earlier, in a typical trading year of 252 sessions one might expect to see four times when an advance ran to six consecutive days or longer; an eight-day or longer upside run would come once a year. An advance extending to 10 or more consecutive days should be seen only about once in four years.

Thinking in terms of weeks, on a purely statistical basis, one might expect runs of at least the following:

Weeks in a Row	Odds	Times Per Year
One or more	0.5	26
Two or more	0.25	13
Three or more	0.125	6 or 7
Four or more	0.0625	3
Five or more	0.03125	1 or 2
Six or more	0.015625	0.8
Seven or more	0.0078125	0.4
Eight or more	0.00391625	0.2
Nine or more	0.001958125	0.1
Ten or more	0.009790625	0.05

In early 1996, the market as measured by the Dow Jones Industrial Average at one point rose for 10 consecutive weeks. Historians dug back and noted that this had last occurred in 1965, some 30 years earlier. The table of odds places the frequency of this unusually persistent kind of a rally at 1 every 20 years.

The stock market is a marketplace defined by human reality rather than one operating on pure statistical odds. News and emotions tend to get in the way of neat mathematically determined odds working out as perfectly as they can be stated on paper. A week usually consists of five trading days; it is possible for the market to pause in midweek for a correction and then burst on ahead, showing a net plus for the week when perhaps three days showed losses. Similarly, the day consists of hours and minutes; the net movement for the day might be determined in the final 30 minutes. News events drive reactions by people. While government agencies release key economic statistics on a predictable cycle, a Kobe earthquake or a political assassination or a major corporate bankruptcy could occur at any time; such events could interrupt advances or prolong declines.

The preceding tables are based on a random 50 percent of days being "up" days. In actual fact, the stock market over the long run goes up more days than down, so the actual odds of a single daily advance are about 52.4 percent rather than just half. The tables also ignore the potential for unchanged days, which can serve as regrouping pauses that may actually extend advances (or declines). Obviously, in bull markets the odds of a rising day are higher, while in bear markets the odds of declining days exceed 50 percent.

Because these and other real-world effects confound the theoretical mathematical odds, actual experience is a bit different from that in the tables. Actual observation is that for extended runs of consecutive daily advances (say, four days or longer), the real odds are about half those in the table. Thus, for example, a seven-day rally seems to actually happen about once a year and an eight-day upside run only about once every couple of years. Actual incidence of downside runs is a little more frequent than that of equally long rallies; logically this should be so since fear is a stronger emotion than greed.

All of this is potentially quite useful in a practical sense when an investor is considering selling a stock on a nonurgent basis. Suppose his stock has roughly reached its fundamental price goal and he is ready to sell, but there is no immediate news that inclines him to want to jump out immediately. If the market gets into a run of consecutive days, that upside momentum and bullish state of mind will help move most stocks, including his sell candidate, higher. As an informed and savvy seller, he now knows roughly what the odds are of a run of consecutive days continuing once it reaches perhaps five days or more. He can use this background information to help determine when to make a graceful exit.

Paying attention to such signals is important, for two reasons. First, as the advance gets going progressively longer, it is fun and an investor falls more deeply in love with his stock and with his own self-perceived brilliance in picking it. The natural temptation is to promise to sell after just one more day or just one more point, rather like a Las Vegas gambler on a supposed hit streak who plans to quit after doubling down just once more. The second reason that knowing these rough odds is useful is that remorse and stubbornness set in after a stock starts declining; there is a tendency to hold on for a return to the high, and our investor then does not sell at all, giving back all of the recent advance (and the time value of money) as a result. Knowing how long the odds are against a further advance, when the investor has already enjoyed a good run, should help give him the added contrarian's discipline to sell while things look most rosy.

In the cases of both price/volume crescendos and extended daily runs, there is no exact formula for precisely when to sell. However, this chapter has provided guidance on the signs to look for in attempting to time sales on the upside very well, even if not perfectly. Being mostly right but less than perfect (selling near the top) is a lot better than being wrong and holding on into the next decline.

SELLING TACTICS

22

Differentiate Market Stock and Loner Stock Characteristics

KEYS TO INVESTMENT SUCCESS

- Know the Portrait of a Market Stock
- Contrast the Portrait of a Loner Stock

When considering whether to hold or sell, one of the determining factors is whether the stock is what is termed a "market stock." This is an important consideration because it can tilt investor judgment at the margin: if there is a forceful trend in the overall market (either up or down), this can affect the stock's performance in the short term, or it may not, depending on its nature. The opposite kind of issue is characterized here as a "loner stock."

The following two lists differentiate characteristics for these two categories of stocks. Note that a stock need not fit all of the descriptors in either list.

Market Stocks

- Held primarily by institutions.
- Consistently heavily traded and liquid.
- Big-capitalization issues.
- Stocks with high betas or betas near 1.00.

- Among the Dow Jones Industrials, or especially the S&P 100; sometimes in the trend-carrying or fad-leading industry.
- Stocks in which options volume is heavy.
- Nonfinancial and nonutility companies.
- Household names with average individual investors.
- Outstanding fundamental achievers in their industries.
- Not noticeably out of favor.
- Familiar and acceptable to non-U.S. investors.

Loner Stocks

- Not widely held by institutions.
- Small-capitalization companies.
- Medium-capitalization but not always heavily traded.
- Often listed on the AMEX or over-the-counter below the main NASDAQ list, with few market-makers.
- In interest-rate–sensitive groups.
- Unique-product concept or story stocks.
- High-technology, unseasoned companies in a market phase not dominated by technology groups.
- Low-priced issues.
- Stocks with betas below 0.50 or negative (including golds).
- High-yield situations.
- Not widely followed, if at all, by analysts.
- Recent new issues outside the currently dominant fad industry.
- Held primarily by insiders or parent companies.
- Countercyclical-industry members.
- Stocks that fall outside conventional industry descriptions (sometimes, conglomerates).
- Regional or local companies not widely known elsewhere.
- Regarded as fundamental laggards in their industries.

PORTRAIT OF A MARKET STOCK

What defines a market stock is a high coincidence of daily price moves parallel to the direction of the major market averages. Statistically that means perhaps 7 days in 10 because on days of clear market force, typically 60 percent of stocks move in the dominant direction. But such a high correlation of individual daily movement with the overall trend is not something that can be checked readily when the need for a real-time decision to hold or sell arises. The prepared investor must know in advance.

A recent run of 7 out of 10 days could be just a coincidence, or it could be driven by unusually sweeping and emotional trends in the overall market. Therefore, in testing whether an issue is a market stock, refer to the preceding lists of traits. The benefit of knowing these characteristics is that they can be reviewed at any time before the pressure of a sell/hold decision actually arises. Make a mental or written note about which characteristics of the stock apply when it is bought, or even before.

Knowing whether the issue is a market stock or an independent stock is important when making a hold/sell decision and also when it is time to cash in for a good sale in terms of micro tactics. Under these circumstances, with a market stock one depends more heavily on judging the short-term trend or the likely action of the general market. Table 22-1 lists a few contrasting examples of market stocks and loners.

This review is important because, statistically, a market stock is likely to perform in line with the overall list direction and may move by a meaningful percentage. In this case, the consideration should be the merit of selling at market versus an above-market limit (or, conceivably, a stop-loss order) in the context not only of the stock's action and chart position, but also in light of the overall market's dominant trend and probable daily action.

Take McDonald's, for example, which tends to move with the market on most days when there is a clear market trend. With the exception of being in a trend-carrying group (restaurants have not been trendy for most of the 1980s or 1990s), McDonald's fits the list of typical market stocks. If there is a broad market rally or a

T A B L E 22–1

Contrasts of Market and Loner Stocks

Market Stocks		Loners
McDonald's	but not	TCBY
Sears	but not	Service Merchandise
General Electric	but not	Westinghouse
Exxon	but not	Mesa
Intel	but not	National Semiconductor
AMR	but not	TWA
Goodyear	but not	Cooper Tire
Home Depot	but not	Payless Cashways
Safeway	but not	Hannaford Bros.
Hewlett-Packard	but not	Arrow Electronics

sharp sell-off in which major money moves the market, McDonald's is very likely to move in the dominant direction. This is because the stock is a leader in its group, a component of the major averages, subject to inclusion in program trading, and a big-capitalization name that institutional and individual investors (domestic and overseas) readily trade when they expect a sharp market move.

Except shortly after one of its periodic splits, McDonald's is usually highly priced enough that a change of a point or more is not unusual on a big-move day in the overall market. Thus, if a McDonald's investor has decided to cash in, she should pay more than the usual amount of attention to the general market's near-term direction.

Suppose McDonald's has had a pretty good run to the upside lately and an investor, therefore, thinks it is getting overextended. If the general list is moving up or is likely to react sharply to some favorable overnight economic or geopolitical news, our seller ought to give McDonald's a little more running room right now because it is a market stock. Instead of selling outright at market, she puts in a limit above market (unless the stock is running into serious resistance or unless some company-specific news is out).

However, if the stock, on its individual merit, is not thought to be an urgent sell but the dominant market trend seems sharply down and/or the current day's direction is a real "flusher," our informed investor should lean more heavily toward an immediate sale of McDonald's because of the market context. She assumes that the stock will move with the overall list because of its personality and because of the deep pockets who are likely to be trading in it.

In this case, the stock is unlikely to "fight the tape" of the general decline. Because of the nature of the stock and its holders, it probably will drop with the list despite its own merit. Our investor is better served to sell at market rather than to reach for an above-market limit. It is better not to miss the market and give back a fast point or more of paper gains.

PORTRAIT OF A LONER STOCK

In contrast is the typical non-market-influenced, or loner, issue. By any one or several of the listed characteristics, this stock simply is not in daily rhythm with the general list. Probably the most common keys to identifying these loner stocks are low daily trading volume, less than stellar fundamental performance within their industry, off-beat company natures, and regional rather than national or international stature.

These attributes make a stock somewhat unattractive to big players, which can cause holders disappointment on the upside. There is a consolation: except in crashes and temporary panics, nonmarket stocks probably hold well against a market downdraft lasting a day or two. The reason is that there is no hot money in them so they are not vulnerable to profit taking by active big players.

It is most important not to count on the strength and direction of the overall list when making a sell/hold tactical judgment about a loner stock that marches to its own separate drummer because it is too easy to become overly optimistic about the stock's short-term prospects in a strong market environment. Here, an investor often decides the overall market is so strong that the stock should get some benefit; he holds on in the belief that the rising tide will raise all boats.

If he is dealing with a stock that acts independently, his mistaken logic is likely to cause disappointment. He is probably allowing the market's action to provide a subtle rationalization for postponing a sale decision or is allowing greed or stubbornness to rule his thinking. Thus, it is important to know the differing personality patterns of market and independent stocks and to factor those traits into the hold/sell decision. On a short-term tactical basis, this added insight can often help investors realize better selling prices.

23

Use Above-Market Instead of Stop-Loss Orders

KEYS TO INVESTMENT SUCCESS

- See the Weaknesses of Stop-Loss Orders
- Use the Advantages of Above-Market Sell Orders

Those few brokers and investment books that do provide any guidance to clients regarding selling almost always advocate using stop-loss orders as a selling strategy. This chapter advocates, instead, the use of above-market sell orders (except in very limited circumstances), which tend to be more profitable. Above-market orders execute one's strategy by targeting a specific successful exit price and by selling temporarily above the fair-value range; stop-loss orders guarantee a lower price and are executed only if and after something fundamental or technical has obviously already gone wrong.

First, consider the old investment slogan: cut your losses and let your profits run. The theory is that investors and traders should be relatively intolerant of non-performing or weak positions and should resist the temptation to pocket a quick, small gain on successful buys, holding on instead for a hoped-for major, long-term payoff.

This prescription *sounds* simple and obvious, but it is difficult to execute tactically. Needless to say, one can hardly quarrel with an objective like avoiding losses or with honoring the time value of money since time will prove to be either a friend or a subtle enemy. Obviously there is no argument with letting big profits accumulate.

The trick is choosing between these two kinds of standing price orders in real time. When there is actual money on the line and when emotions are clouding the decision-making process, it is difficult to discern which current, small-loss stocks will hibernate at current quotes or go south even further and which others will turn into glorious successes.

WEAKNESSES OF STOP-LOSS ORDERS

Stop-loss orders should be used in very limited circumstances because their success depends upon being implemented with near-surgical skill. Their most common usage is often a cop-out on the part of the supporting writer, the broker, and the investor who implements the tactic.

Cop-Outs and Crutches

Brokers, as described in earlier chapters, are loathe to deal with money-losing positions. One convenient way for any broker to avoid the inconvenient bind of discussing losses is to advise clients to limit their exposure by placing stop-loss orders a moderate percentage away from the buy point (recall the critique of that entry-point-based tactic in Chapter 8). If an account shows a mixture of profits and losses and if the losses are never drastic, the broker and his firm are safe from charges of incompetence or inattention when using this strategy. Almost always, they will be able to point to at least one major loss avoided.

While stop-loss orders routinely placed closely below the buy level do limit the size of individual losses, their main function is to relieve the broker and the investor of making a decision—in real time, when money is on the line—about selling, holding, or doubling up on an underwater position. The market does it automatically for the broker and the client, or it does nothing. The automatic pilot gets the credit or blame.

Bad Placement

In addition to this shortcoming, routine stop-loss orders have two other weaknesses: they are usually not placed at a logical price level, and, even more importantly, they necessarily cause a sale based on weakness rather than on strength.

For example, many advocates of the routine stop-loss order advise its placement at a standard percentage-below-cost basis. The most commonly advocated allowable losses are 10 percent, 5 percent, and 15 percent. To all but the most timid market players, such losses are acceptable even though they obviously fall short of the originally intended result. There are three objections to the use of arbitrary percentages:

- The entry point (purchase price) is irrelevant to defining a good exit point, as detailed in Chapter 8.
- Routine use of a fixed-percentage-width cushion ignores the inherently varied volatilities/liquidities between different stocks.
- The stop-loss point should be set on the basis of support levels or trend lines, which may be closer or farther away than some standard percentage method would dictate.

The importance of the first point cannot be overemphasized: the level of your personal cost price has no impact on the overall market and therefore no relevance to the question of where to cut losses (or take a profit). Without solving the long-standing debate about the merit of technical analysis, any reasonably experienced market participant not even professing to be a chartist can look at a price-history chart and make reasonable judgments about the prices at which a given stock will have proven something (on the upside) and at which it will have shown fatal weakness (on the downside).

If a chart analyst is told by a stock's owner, "But I should have told you that my cost price is 44," the only logical response is, "So what?" The point is, if a stock breaks major support by breaking $43^{1}/_{2}$, that is a fact regardless of who the unlucky holders are and regardless of whether they paid 44, 21, or 65. A particular percentage down has no merit as a selling yardstick. If selling down 10 percent were always right, bargain hunting down 10 percent would always be wrong. And yet, buying lower always allows more upside profit than buying higher.

If this book described how to buy stocks, it would define how to buy to avoid the danger of being so close to the breakdown point. But here, our selling perspective emphasizes that cost basis is irrelevant to a sale decision. Therefore, attaching any specific percentage limit below the cost point is an irrelevant formula. It is about as logical as basing salary on a fixed multiple of age or height.

Setting aside the problem of using cost price as a starting point, the use of any fixed tolerance measure related to now-current price (e.g., X percent or Y points) is unrelated to the characteristics of the position. Stocks have inherent tendencies toward volatility, which may be defined roughly as percentage fluctuation within a day or week compared with the percentage fluctuation of a broad market index (students of market action and measurers of investment manager performance refer to this as beta).

There is no need to know whether the price volatility of a given stock is caused by price level, floating supply, player emotions, institutional participation, or other factors. Just observe that stocks fluctuate with their own amplitudes that generally tend to change only over long time periods. For one stock at $25.00, a daily range of plus or minus $0.125 is normal (check many utility shares as examples); for another $25.00 stock, a $1.00 or even wider daily range is typical (look at biotechnology, Internet, semiconductor, and computer-peripherals issues).

What is tolerable "in-the-noise" movement for one stock is a sign of significant change in the supply/demand balance for another because they have inherently different personalities. Because of these observable and very real differences, allowing only a single rigid percentage of breathing room on all stocks is nonsensical.

A well-placed stop-loss order at least ought to take into account the natural fluctuation tendency of the stock in question rather than assume that all are alike. A staid utility is reacting to a massive change in interest rates or major risk to its dividend by falling as much as 15 percent, so here a 15 percent stop is much too loose. A wide-swinging growth stock might gyrate 20 percent around its moving average several times annually without breaking its basic upside momentum, so here a commonly advocated 10 percent or 15 percent stop-loss range will prove self-defeating from the start.

Properly, a stop-loss should be at whatever level is dictated by trend lines or support levels rather than at some percentage subtraction from a level such as entry. Take as a theoretical example a stock in an established trading channel for several months between the prices of 40 and 46. If it is clear that $39\frac{7}{8}$ is a breakdown in support, then the proper stop-loss point is $39\frac{7}{8}$, which means that if an investor buys the stock at 41, the 5 percent, 10 percent, or 15 percent-down tolerances are too wide. And, if he buys above 44—in the upper half of the range, in the hope of a breakout—the 5 percent and 15 percent allowances are still naive in light of what the chart says. The 5 percent level would probably whipsaw the investor, getting him out below 42 just as the stock starts to find support in the lower end of the channel—from which it might rally again. The 15 percent allowance from 44 would be at below 38, well after the stock will have clearly broken down.

The accompanying chart of ITT Industries provides a real-life example of where stop-loss orders ought and ought not to be placed. (See Figure 23–1.) Notice the obvious recurring technical importance of the $24.50 to $24.75 area on the chart, first as a supply zone needing to be penetrated and, for the final five months, as a multiple bottom or support area. (This happens to illustrate that arbitrary round numbers such as $25 are not always ideal order points.) At the time of this chart's printing, a breakdown below $24.75 and absolutely one at $24.375 would spell significant trouble. Orders should now be placed at those levels. Previously, ITT Industries appeared to have begun an uptrend, neatly defined by a line connecting its bottom prices in December, January, and April. Each week a holder should have raised her protective stop to the gradually higher level of that line. By doing so, she would have been stopped out immediately as the stock broke down just below 27 in mid-June. As of two weeks later (at the very end of this chart), bargain hunters might buy at $25 but should allow no more than a half-point of downside risk, at the well-defined multiple support point. By trying to give the stock a little breathing

FIGURE 23-1

Key Support Levels

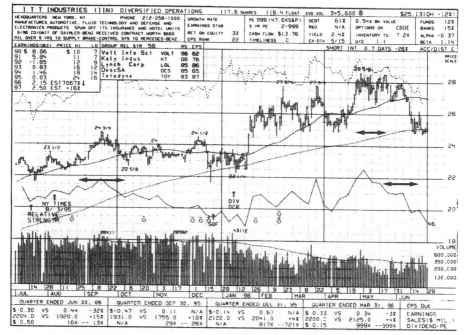

Courtesy of *Daily Graphs and Long Term Values;* P.O. Box 66919; Los Angeles, California 90066–0919.

room, say, in placing a stop at $23, one would certainly be stopped out at a doubly bad spot. First, an order at $23 would have wasted the first $1.50 below an obvious breakdown level; second, a stop at $23 would close the position just as the stock finds its next important support and prepares for a mild bounce-back rally.

The point is that the stop-loss order, if used at all, should be placed with some precision based on the market condition of the stock and not on a percentage formula. Also, it should be placed where its violation signals a significant negative move for the stock: not higher and not lower. This involves a precise analysis of the chart and should never be related to an investor's entry point.

Although having provided the preceding tutorial in stop-loss placement, this chapter actually takes the seldom-stated position that stop-loss orders should be used sparingly, if at all. Their placement should occur only after taking a close look at a stock and thus deciding—on merit and on the basis of the chart pattern—what price says bail out and what price indicates that the market is saying something unknown is going wrong. If an investor is in touch with the market on a daily basis and develops the mental discipline this book teaches, the psychological crutch of a stop will be unnecessary.

If an investor is in contact frequently with his broker (daily or more), he does not need an order on the specialist's book. If he has noted the critical level in advance and is disciplined, he will prefer to sell at market when it happens. However, if an investor travels or is inaccessible or finds he always has great difficulty in pulling the trigger under stress, then a stop-loss order should be used.

Harmful Market Influences

There are times when a technically well-placed stop-loss order is an error. For example, when general market weakness takes place on rumors or in response to massive program trading, price levels in individual stocks become meaningless as their usual liquidity disappears and as all buyers run for cover.

In this case, when the temporary but sharp overall market downdraft passes, many stop orders will have proven too tight, even if placed with good stock-specific logic beforehand. In 20-20 hindsight, it is easy to see that the investor was stopped out for market-driven rather than stock-specific reasons, and she will have cash rather than a full portfolio after the temporary panic bottom has passed and stocks (including the one now sold) have bounced back nicely.

Finally, it is important for the investor to fine tune the use of stops according to her broker relationship. If using a discount broker, she will need to lean more toward stops for any given situation. If using a full-service firm, she may get a warning call from the broker when a stock starts breaking down off its highs or when the news goes bad. In this way, she can sometimes get out at a higher price than if she waits for the stop to be exercised.

In essence, then, it is better to rely on broker assistance when it is being paid for than to use the mechanical stop-loss order. Some brokers occasionally accept discretion in placing an order if they cannot reach a client. If a broker agrees to operate on this basis, here is yet another good reason for not using stop-losses.

ADVANTAGES OF ABOVE-MARKET SELL ORDERS

Rather than using a stop below the market, which means that the sale, if any, will occur at a price below the available level at the time the order was first entered, it is preferable to use *targeted sell stops above the market.* When these orders above the market are executed, they give a better price than that price prevailing when the order was entered.

Like stop-loss orders, these orders also carry caveats and qualifiers. An above-market stop-sell order is not appropriate in all situations; sometimes a market sale is better. Any above-market stop-sell order must also be placed with precision and care.

To place a stop-sell accurately, first visualize what kind of overall market climate prevails and is likely to exist over the period of time the projected order will be in place. A stop-loss below market is there to provide protection against further loss, while an above-market stop-sell order should be used to exit a stock when the investor believes reasonable patience and the market's normal fluctuation working together can provide a better price. At any time, a reasonable expectation for upside potential is determined to some degree by the overall market trend and also by the stock's own price pattern.

Going back to the stock with a lengthy channel between 40 and 46, assume that a sale seems in order but is not extremely urgent. In a market moving sideways or moderately higher, an investor would be wise to set an above-market sell-stop order at $45\frac{1}{4}$ in this situation.

If the overall market is quite strong but the stock remains frustratingly trapped in its channel, he might have more aggressive expectations and put the order at $43\frac{5}{8}$ or $43\frac{3}{4}$. He certainly would not put in a sell at $46\frac{1}{4}$ or higher because that would be triggered exactly and only when the stock surprises him with an upside breakout. That level would give exactly the wrong sale timing by being at the wrong price.

On the other hand, in a moderately weak market, the owner might be happy with anything at all in the upper half of the channel; so he might set the stop-sell at $43\frac{1}{2}$ or 44, at most.

In a violent bear move, there would be no sense in setting an above-market sell level except when a fairly sharp interim selloff has just been completed: if the investor is not willing to hold this stock through the coming carnage, he should assume the damage will continue and should, therefore, sell now at market rather than wait for a rally.

On a short-term basis, also observe the trend of the stock and the general market in recent days: lean against it in direction and degree. If the stock and/or major averages have been up several days running (remember the discussion of extended runs in Chapter 21), any further upside attempt with a stop-sell above current levels should be quite limited. On the other hand, if the stock or market has fallen several days running but has not destroyed important uptrend lines or support levels, look for some rebound and place the order a bit farther away from present prices, that is, higher.

Another strategy for placing the stop-sell is to measure actual recent daily fluctuation. Calculate the actual daily price ranges for the last two to four weeks from daily newspapers, by consulting an on-line electronic data source, or from a detailed daily-basis chart service. Suppose that this discovery process reveals your stock to have an average daily range (high minus low) of $1\frac{1}{4}$ points. And suppose it is found that on well over half of the days in the study window this issue moved by at least $\frac{5}{8}$ of a point during the day (measuring total daily range here, not net change from close to close).

In this example, you might place a stop-sell about $^3/_4$ to $^7/_8$ above the current close, assuming that the latest close was roughly in the middle of its daily range. On average—assuming that the whole market does not collapse and that the company does not suddenly issue bad news—a few days' or a week's patience should get a better price than would an unnecessarily rushed market order.

SUMMARY OF CONTRASTING STYLES AND RESULTS

The degree of aggressiveness in order placement compared with the actual fluctuation pattern is influenced by the direction of the stock and of the overall market. It bears repeating that if the reason for sale is bad fundamental or technical news for the company or if an exit is considered because the overall market is creating tension, an above-market sell stop is a long-odds bet against yourself.

The major message of this chapter is that above-market sell stops give a reasonable chance of better sale proceeds if there is more to be had; below-market stop-loss orders guarantee a worse price than is available right now. Do not use arbitrary percentage stops, and do not use stop-losses as a mental crutch. Instead, face each selling decision head on, and do what is necessary in real time. This discipline will serve well in current dollars as well as in greater wisdom about and feel for the market in future situations.

24

Use Special Rules for Selling Low-Priced Stocks

KEYS TO INVESTMENT SUCCESS

- Consider Brokerage Firms' Policies
- Understand Margin Loans
- Be Aware of Maintenance Margins
- Watch for Nonmarginable Stocks

Three key dollar levels must be kept in mind when buying or selling low-priced stocks: $2.00, $3.00, and $5.00. Their effects are different, depending on whether the low-priced stock is rising or falling through these price levels. Because the extent of their effects is more pronounced on the downside, it is important to pay close attention to selling tactics in this price category.

First consider the $2.00 price level, thought of as the badge of respectability by most brokerage houses. Investors wishing to buy a stock trading below $2.00 per share will usually be required by a full-service brokerage firm to sign what is called in the trade an "unsolicited letter." This is a prewritten form letter from the client to the firm saying the stock was picked by the client, who realizes that trading in low-priced stocks is a risky business and who will not blame the firm if this stock loses money.

Because of the nature of the letter, there is no requirement to sign it to *sell* a low-priced issue. Theoretically, the firm is supposed to have the letter signed and on file before purchase, unless the client is known and trusted. The terms of this letter requirement should serve as a mild deterrent to buying stocks under $2.00 a share.

In practice this has only a moderate effect in bull markets, when people are optimistic rather than fearful.

By contrast, in bear markets the letter requirement has a chilling effect. With media headlines covering layoffs, recession, bankruptcies, and similar dark omens, many investors hesitate when their broker tells them about the requirement. And that means that chances are low that the buy order will get placed, for several reasons.

The hesitant investor muses about the bear market, the fact that his broker seems not to want a commission, and that it appears legal defenses are being erected in advance as a condition of accepting the trade. So the effect of the unsolicited-letter rule can be a depressant on price in a bear-market climate as stocks slip below that $2.00 level. The converse, however, is not true: when a stock goes above $2.00 per share, that fact does not encourage additional buying; there is merely the removal of a constraint as brokers need not exercise the unsolicited-letter routine.

Many brokerage firms waive the rule if the stock in question is traded on a major stock exchange, so you should ask in advance. Ironically, an investor who buys stock in a profitable, dynamic company trading over-the-counter at $1.75 is required to sign an unsolicited letter. But if he buys the most shaky, debt-ridden, exchange-listed company whose sales are shrinking, whose equity is negative, and whose prospects of turning around are between slim and none, selling at $0.25 per share, no letter is required.

CONSIDER BROKERAGE FIRMS' POLICIES

Another aspect of trading in lower-priced stocks is also worthy of note: the way in which brokers are compensated significantly affects their attention, which directly changes sponsorship for a stock.

Brokerage firms are becoming increasingly sensitive to legal risk, so they are taking more action to reduce exposure. One defensive brokerage weapon is the method by which firms pay their brokers. Some firms have become so risk averse and image conscious that they do not pay brokers any commission on buy orders for stocks under $2.00 per share. (An exception is made in the very rare instance when the research department is recommending the stock.)

Obviously, a broker would rather have clients investing in stocks that will generate buy-side commissions. Needless to say, if brokers are not paid for buy orders in unlisted stocks below $2.00 per share, those issues have little sponsorship in the market. If and when the price slips below that magic level, further erosion is predictable since a major source of demand—sponsorship—dries up. (See Figure 24–1, which features several charts from 1987, the most recent period of widespread margin calls.) After that point, it may take an unusually large amount of positive news to get the stock to move up. So keep the $2.00 level in mind as a mental quitting point on stocks, especially when the overall market tone is negative and cautious. In fact, in a fear-driven market, you should plan to bail out earlier and thereby beat the crowd.

The critical $3.00 and $5.00 levels both derive from the same basis. These price levels have considerably more significance in terms of price effects because of the way brokerage rules work. The reason is that while the $2.00 level affects a stock's market "respectability," the $3.00 and $5.00 levels determine marginability. And marginability is very important to a stock.

The unsolicited-letter effect is mostly psychological, but the effect of margin requirements is very real and urgent. It definitely moves stock prices, mostly to the downside—an important effect to factor into selling and holding decisions.

MARGIN LOANS

The power of a brokerage firm to make margin loans to purchasers of securities is governed under Regulation T of the Federal Reserve Board (under Regulation U for margin loans from commercial banks). The Board can change the rules of the game

F I G U R E 24–1

Price Drops Through $5, $3, and $2

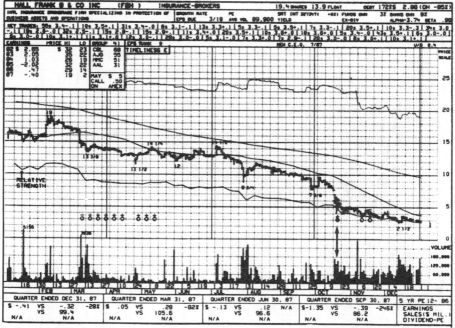

Courtesy of *Daily Graphs and Long Term Values;* P.O. Box 66919; Los Angeles, California 90066–0919.

F I G U R E   24–1 (continued)

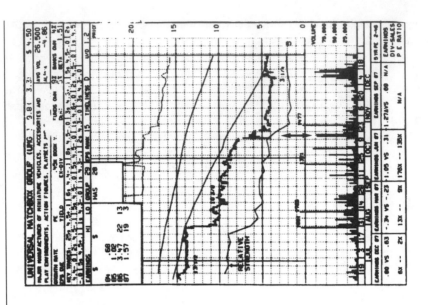

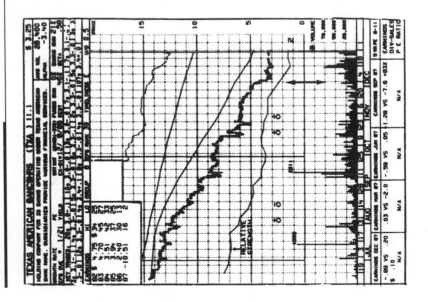

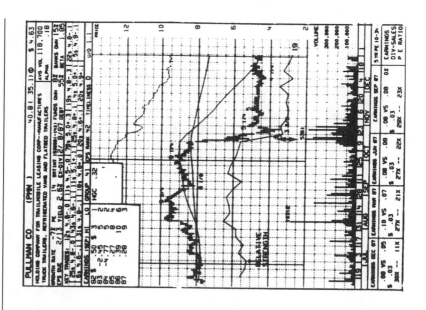

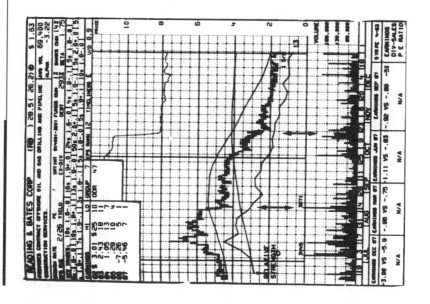

F I G U R E 24-1 (continued)

FIGURE 24-1 (concluded)

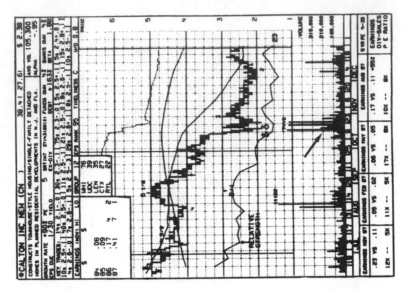

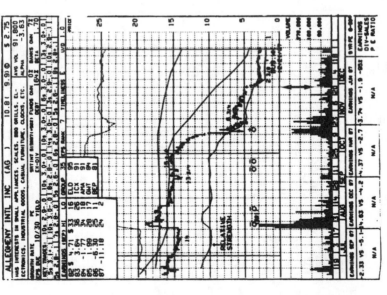

T A B L E   24–1

Margin Loans and Maintenance Margins

	Price	Value	Less Debit	Equals Equity	% Equity
Situation #1 Just bought 1,000 at $10 borrowed $5,000	10.00	10,000	5,000	5,000	50%
Situation #2 Stock drops to $9	9.00	9,000	5,000	4,000	44%
Situation #3 Stock drops to $8.50	8.50	8,500	5,000	3,500	41%
Situation #4 Stock drops to $8.25	8.25	8,250	5,000	3,250	39%

whenever necessary, although in recent years there has been less tinkering with margin requirements than in the past.

Basically, the Board sets as a policy the percentage of a purchase price that a brokerage firm (and, technically, a member bank) can loan to the customer. For historical reasons dating from abuses before the Great Depression, this power has been used to regulate speculation and to allocate credit within the economy.

For many years, the going percentage has been 50 percent. An investor wishing to buy $10,000 worth of stock can do so with as little as $5,000 of his or her own equity. The brokerage firm loans its customer the remainder (and charges interest on the borrowed balance). This is a very convenient type of loan because it requires no credit check or qualification nor any monthly payments against principal.

As long as the value of the collateral (i.e., the stock bought and held by the brokerage as security) is not badly impaired, the brokerage firm allows an investor to continue carrying a margin loan as long as the stock is held. When the stock is sold, the loan is automatically paid off out of the proceeds. (See Table 24–1.)

MAINTENANCE MARGINS

The level called "maintenance margin" is generally at 40 percent, which means the brokerage firm can let the investor's margin of equity shrink to the 40 percent level before it is forced to call for more cash (margin call).

Here is how the 40 percent maintenance margin rule works in practice.

Suppose that someone buys 1,000 shares of XYZ common stock at $10 per share and puts up the minimum 50 percent required. (Here, commissions are ignored for the sake of simplicity; in actuality the commission is allowed as part of the gross amount, so the investor can borrow half of it, too.) He borrows $5,000 from the brokerage firm and sends in the other $5,000. If the stock holds steady at $10 per share, obviously his equity stays at the 50 percent level (before the monthly subtraction of interest charges).

But if the stock declines, the customer's percentage of equity in the position decreases. Assuming that interest charges have not been taken yet (which increase the debit balance and thereby reduce equity), our unfortunate investor's equity will fall to the 40 percent level when the stock has declined to $8.33 per share.

To calculate, take the amount of the debit or loan balance, and divide by 60 percent (the complement of 40 percent) to get the minimum market value allowed. If the stock is worth $8,333 (1,000 shares times $8.33 each) and the loan is the original $5,000, the customer's remaining net equity is now just $3,333, or the new gross market value less the loan balance.

Below that point, the broker must demand that by the next business day the client deposit more money to reduce the loan balance. If the investor fails to do so, the broker is required to sell sufficient stock out of the account to restore up to at least a 40 percent position.

For the sake of simplicity, the account shown consisted of just one stock. In actual practice, all of the stocks in the account are valued together, and the total loan balance against the stocks is calculated as a single figure. The effect of one stock dropping from 10 to $8^{1}/_{4}$ is softened by the possibility that some other stocks in the account stayed steady or rose in value. Most brokerage firms produce computerized analyses of all accounts every night; brokers get notified in the morning if any accounts need a call. The compliance department makes sure that the brokers enforce the rules by forcing their clients to meet margin calls promptly. The alternative, to stay within the rules and to protect the firm's capital, is to sell off some of the stocks. If a client does not choose which stocks to sell, the firm does it for him—without delay.

NONMARGINABLE STOCKS

One other critical aspect of margin rules directly affects the calculation of equity margin: the marginability of specific stocks. The Securities and Exchange Commission or the listing exchange sometimes designates certain securities as "not marginable," usually because their price behavior has become highly erratic. With sharp fluctuations in prices, values in margin accounts gyrate daily, causing margin calls and adding to market instability. To reduce this effect, some highly volatile stocks are declared nonmarginable. This act in itself tends to dampen their volatility because some speculators' purchasing power is halved.

Regardless of its volatility, any stock can become nonmarginable for another reason that serves (for our purposes) as an important warning: price alone can get the stock into marginability trouble. In the past, the standard rule was $5.00 per share. In recent years, during the trend toward less government regulation, determining the key price level has been left to the discretion of brokerage firms. Many have retained the traditional $5.00 rule, while others have adopted $3.00; both have implications for the price behavior of stocks.

The $5.00 and $3.00 levels can signal significant price danger for stocks in a declining market. When a stock falls through either of those levels, its decline is likely to accelerate because of margin rules. First, the stock immediately becomes 100 percent worthless for calculating margins. That, in turn, causes the brokerage firm to send out margin calls to clients who own the stock in margin accounts and whose calculated equity has been impaired by the sudden exclusion of the stock from the margin formula.

To illustrate, suppose an investor's account consists of 2,000 shares of a stock bought at $5 per share; the minimum 50 percent or $5,000 was put up and the other $5,000 borrowed from the firm. (A broker would be irresponsible to allow this, knowing that an urgent and major problem lurks just $1/_8$ point away.) The morning after this stock declines to close at $4^7/_8$ or lower, a printout is placed on the broker's desk, highlighting the client's account. This one-stock portfolio has dropped below the marginable level.

Per the house rules, our investor now has a loan of $5,000 outstanding with zero allowable collateral behind it. He has not been wiped out because at $4^7/_8$ the stock is worth $9,750; equity is $4,750 after subtracting the loan. But the rules render that stock suddenly worthless for margin calculation. He is not broke, but his credit line has been pulled.

The investor has four choices; unfortunately, none of them is to call for a time-out. First, he can send the broker $5,000 to pay off the loan immediately. Second, he can send in stock certificates of other companies that are marginable. But those certificates must equal $8,333 in market value of marginable stock. This strategy leaves $8,333 in countable assets to secure the $5,000 loan and a countable equity of $3,333 after the loan is subtracted; it thus restores the minimum 40 percent maintenance margin level.

A third choice is to sell without delay at least $5,000 worth of now nonmarginable stock, or a little more than half the total position, to satisfy the compliance department and the federal regulators. A fourth option is to sell from the account at least $10,000 worth of other stocks that are still marginable, if any such are available.

Whenever maintenance calls occur, at least some traders sell part or all of the stock, which creates a sudden avalanche of shares coming into the market for sale at quickly declining prices. Because knowledgeable market players see the situation plainly, very few people bid to buy the stock. If it trades over-the-counter, market-making firms lighten inventory to a minimum to control their loss exposure and bid only cautiously and in small size. In a listed stock, the floor specialist is less willing to take stock except at a price concession.

The psychomechanics of the market dictate that this process unfolds a fraction above the key $5.00 level. Knowing how margin rules work, few informed investors are willing to buy or hold a stock that has fallen from $6.00 or above toward $5.00; this itself adds to the weakening market.

There are three refinements in this example. First, most investors own more than one stock in their margin accounts. So the decline of one stock below $5.00 does not wipe out their marginable assets. Second, not all margin accounts are down to minimum equity, so a drop in one stock—even from $5.00 to a countable zero—may not cause an immediate problem. Third, when one stock causes a problem in a margin account, no rule says this particular stock must be the one singled out for sale to satisfy the margin call.

In practice, of course, the offending stock often is thrown overboard for psychological and financial reasons. First, when the broker says there is a margin call on XYZ stock, the investor examines his options and discovers that selling any other stock generates half its dollar value toward equity and the rest toward the loan because of the 50-percent rule and the fact that once the stock is sold, it is no longer an asset in the account against which to borrow.

But selling the offending stock, which suddenly has zero loan value, nets full, dollar-for-dollar relief. Since this is the troubled stock, the broker is quick to point out that this stock is likely to feel pressure as other people sell it to meet their margin calls. The investor is wise to sell as soon as possible to get the best price.

Against these forces, an investor must be extremely stubborn or highly convinced that the intrinsic value of XYZ makes it worth holding through the storm. While there is no rule that XYZ stock must be sold, clearly it is the top candidate for dumping.

All facets of the $5.00 level apply equally at the $3.00 level for the market and for some brokerage firms. Some investors do not face a margin call generated by the $3.00 scenario until their stock slides below $3.00. But there are dozens of other brokerage firms that still adhere to the $5.00 rule, so their clients sell stock at that level, driving the price down. These price declines at both margin-call levels have no less wealth-reducing effect on investors who have no margin accounts. Foregoing a margin account certainly protects an investor from margin calls, but it does not protect against the downdraft in prices when *other* investors get *their* calls.

In a general bear market—as opposed to a situation where just one stock is distressed due to specific news—the effect is intensified. Players are apprehensive, so fewer come up with added cash to meet their margin calls. The instinctive reaction is to sell out now. In addition, weakness in other totally unrelated stocks can cause selling in issues you own, as other investors meet their margin calls.

There is no converse side to this $3.00 and $5.00 phenomenon, no automatic burst of buying. The only benefit of having a stock trade a safe distance above $3.00 or $5.00 is that it is safely marginable. Thus, at a safe distance above those levels, some buyers might buy extra shares using credit. There is no automatic surge in price when the stock edges through $5.00 on the upside. Aggressive and informed players know that using margin then is fraught with peril because the stock easily could slip back to $4^7/_8$.

The bottom-line implication is that investors must draw a red zone at all times around stocks as they slip toward the $5.00 or $3.00 levels. Use perhaps a half-dollar safety zone in a normal market and a wider buffer in a bear market, particularly if it has started to become violent. Be realistic and expect the worst; anticipate trouble before it starts. Getting out at $5^1/_2$ can prevent a quick slide to $4^1/_2$ or 4. And regardless of the fundamental merit of a low-priced stock, it is in imminent price danger at the $5.00 and $3.00 levels because of marginability problems.

25

Sell Smart on Good News

KEYS TO INVESTMENT SUCCESS

- Know the Definition of Great News versus Huge News
- Act Appropriately on News

Prior chapters have dealt with technical phenomena like volume and price as clues to finding market tops. Fundamental events such as the publication of positive news also accelerate intermediate or final market tops. Thus, ironic as it may seem, good news can often provide a very opportune time to sell. Actually, controversies find this not at all surprising.

For purposes of this discussion, there are three kinds of positive news. One is such unsurprising positive news as earnings coming in on-target with estimates or the declaration of moderately higher dividends on schedule. These events typically have no effect on stock price, although if they are expected their *absence* causes a drop. The mid-1990s have seen highly increased institutional sensitivity to the slightest shortfalls against consensus estimates, resulting in wild downside price volatility. Expected events seldom coincide with an interim price peak unless such a high proves to be reversed by a general market retreat.

The two other types of positive news—or impact news—are important to price behavior in the short term. These are events that are big or surprising enough to have an immediate effect on stock price. Within the impact category, also, the two types of news must be distinguished accurately by the alert market player, in real time, in order to determine proper action.

GREAT NEWS VERSUS HUGE NEWS

The factor that determines impact is the true, long-term importance of the news. Thus, what we are calling impact news includes "great news" and, by contrast, "huge news." Great news refers to positive developments that have no major fundamental long-term significance to a company. Examples are a quarterly earnings report that comes in well above expectations or the receipt of a major contract.

Sometimes a contract award has long-term impact by signalling superior technology or a series of follow-on contracts. Sometimes the directors' declaration of an unexpectedly large dividend is "great news" that has a short-term positive effect on a stock's price.

Any of these events is welcomed by investors and usually causes a near-term rise in the company's stock price. However, in judging their significance, be coldly objective to compensate for the natural tendency toward stockholders' positive bias. Existing holders generally are in a positive mental state about owning the shares when recent price action has been rewarding. In the spirit of Chapter 9, one must be very careful not to let confusion between the stock and the company intrude. Likewise, one must not double count expected positive news.

To make an accurate and meaningful judgment about a current piece of positive news, take an imaginary look back from the future. Move forward 10 years in time, and then look back at company and industry history over that period. Your key filter is the true importance—in a *long-term* context—of the news that looks so positive today. Is it certain that today's item will be judged as one of the two or three most significant events in a decade for the company, or is it among the top dozen events in its industry? By definition, the answer in virtually every case is negative.

Thus, in very many cases today's news is great but not huge. In contrast then, what *is* a huge news event? These are developments or announcements with true long-term fundamental and strategic importance to the company: usually management, technology, or strategy issues rather than current financial results or growth rates, certainly not an analyst recommendation.

Changes in these nonfinancial areas have much greater long-term significance and generally fall into the categories of blockbuster events or major unexpected changes. Examples of huge news in management are items about key individuals and shifts in types of corporate governance or management: Lee Iacocca's appointment in 1979 as head of Chrysler Corporation was a crucial turning point in the survival and revitalization of the number three U.S. automaker, for example.

A key transition in management is often necessary as a company built on entrepreneurial spirit reaches maturity. An excellent example occurred in 1983 when Apple Computer founder Steve Jobs—a technology genius—was replaced as chief executive officer by a veteran marketing executive, John Scully, from PepsiCo.

Sometimes the retirement or death of a company officer and major stockholder proves to be huge news: management power changes, and a block of stock transfers control, triggers a merger, or signifies a significant change in corporate direction. Dr. Armand Hammer's death in December 1990 began a new era at Occidental Petroleum. A 1996 announcement that T. Boone Pickens would relinquish control of Mesa may prove of parallel importance. Critical technological advances can also constitute huge news: one example was the issuance of an early patent on a test for AIDS to Cambridge BioSciences.

Finally, strategic changes in a company's direction can be huge news: abandoning a money-losing or highly competitive business, halting acquisitions in a debt-laden firm, selling off assets, working existing businesses harder, and paying down debt, for example. In January 1996, Xerox Corporation announced it would withdraw from the financial services arena; investors mistakenly reacted negatively to the related write-off because the decision implied higher returns on equity and faster growth, as indicated by a 16 percent rise in the dividend announced at the same time. The decision to cut and run was an important winner, a *buy* signal!

Strategic acquisitions or alliances that create vertical integration, a broader product mix, or strong distribution overnight are other examples. In 1988, Georgia-based Colorocs—which had developed an inexpensive, high-quality color photocopier—made what appeared to be a critical positive move by acquiring control of Savin Corporation instead of risking time and capital in the creation of its own distribution infrastructure. That decision removed a major risk factor for investors and, therefore, was huge news at the time. (Unfortunately, later problems with supply from Japan undermined success.) In the mid-1990s, Research Frontiers, developer of continuously variable light-sensitive glass, sharply improved its prospects by licensing giant General Electric to sell its products rather than going it alone.

ACTING ON NEWS

The critical distinction between great and huge is important because it indicates the proper tactical action to take in response to news: whether and when to sell on strength. Great news is usually good for two or three days of rising stock quotes, assuming a reasonably hospitable market climate at the time. Because great good news is not long-term in significance, a good short-term rally triggered by such news often provides an attractive near-term opportunity to cash in on strength by selling. This is the old "buy on rumor, sell on news" pattern.

This is especially true if a significant trading volume buildup takes place following the news. Remember that a rising pace of volume is required to sustain further price increases. Given that surprising great news has already become known, how much more can be expected realistically? Where will even higher trading volume and more excitement come from?

The mechanics of news dissemination and the timing of broker and investor reactions help create a typical two- or three-day pattern of rallying prices following great news. The day news is announced, assuming it is during the market session and is carried promptly on news wires, professional traders and boardroom ticker watchers act virtually immediately, as do a few other investors whose alert brokers call to relay the developments.

That same news is printed the next day in most daily newspapers and in the national financial press. Now more people can and do react. By the third day, those who got the news late or who typically are slow to act finally jump onto the bandwagon. Beyond that, there is little left in the short term. If an investor cannot justify being a buyer *after* seeing such a runup, this is a perfect signal to sell.

The occurrence of huge news poses a more perplexing tactical challenge for the stockholder because there are likely to be two positive reactions in the stock price. In addition to judging the possible strength of the two price moves, the savvy investor confronts a psychological test: she is so pleased by the enormity of the positive development that she is in danger of losing perspective and cool judgment.

The first price reaction is a short-term burst, similar to that from great news. But there is also likely to be a second, less dramatic effect. Because of the true import of huge news, the company, in effect, rises to a new and higher level of esteem among investors—particularly among those professional money managers who look at the big picture rather than at short-term earnings momentum only.

Even if the stock continues to exhibit gradual further price strength after its initial upside burst from the huge news, the tactical problem is to make a judgment about *when* the second effect has run its course. Clearly, this is an art rather than an exact science.

In general, remember that the occurrence of huge news should cause an investor to ease back on the selling trigger. And once the stock takes a rest and declines, expect it to decline less deeply than it would have before the huge news. Not only will there have been, in effect, a one-time markup for the new information, but there will be some institutional investors who did not jump in right away, waiting for a correction before accumulating their positions. These investors will provide the buying support for future basing and rallies in the stock.

If the stock develops a classic volume mountain and an extended string of consecutive daily rises after great or huge news, it is advisable to sell on the crescendo in trading (review Chapter 21). No matter how fundamentally important or long-term significant the news is, the stock cannot be expected to rise uninterrupted for an indefinite time. The formation of a flagpole advance on a volume mountain is a signal that the strength is unsustainable for at least the short term and that the stock should be sold on the rise. It can always be bought back, probably lower, at a later time. The experience of selling and then buying back in successfully will add to your confidence about implementing this maneuver again in the future. Each time you sell well, it helps you have the courage to overcome old subconscious biases and do it more easily thereafter.

In summary, great good news often provides a near-term selling opportunity for disciplined contrarians as naive players buy after good news. Huge news allows the fortunate or foresighted holder to raise her target for long-term value. But if huge news triggers a huge mountain of volume and an extreme advance, this too should be viewed as a gift worth accepting. Price runs do not last very long, and you can always buy back.

26

Understand How Bad the Bad News Is

KEYS TO INVESTMENT SUCCESS

- Differentiate Between Two Types of Bad News
- React Intelligently to Bad News

Bad news travels fast in the computer age, and this truth has important price implications when a company's news is unexpected or highly disturbing. Too often, investors give in to emotional market swings by selling out when all seems lost, only to find later that they were part of a selling panic bottom. And, especially in recent years, institutions have become extremely short-term oriented; their knee-jerk dumping on the slightest bad news drops prices sharply, adding to the sense of fright that individuals must assess and learn to deal with.

Before describing bad-news selling tactics, it is necessary to identify the "bad news" characteristics covered in this chapter:

- Relate only to company-specific news, not to market trends as measured by averages.
- Concern sharp price declines driven by negative news, not routine price declines that are merely technical corrections.
- Exclude acquisition situations, in which the ongoing sequence of news is highly unpredictable and where events and emotional responses are dramatic.

- Exclude situations driven by continuous (nondiscrete) outside influences, including commodity-price collapses (for mining companies), which have a life of their own and, therefore, are not discrete, one-day news items.
- Apply in the context of a sideways or higher market environment in which price reactions to bad news are worse in total but are not initially as severe as during bear markets.

DIFFERENTIATING BETWEEN TWO TYPES OF BAD NEWS

This chapter explores material, unexpected, and discrete bad news for a company. "Material" and "unexpected" are important qualifiers because other negative information does not tend to move stock prices.

For purposes of this discussion, news discreteness is important conceptually because it affects the validity of certain ideas. (Discrete news developments are one-time items that do not breed suspicions of further negatives to come.) Discrete bad news usually causes two to three days of sharp declines. (See Figure 26–1 on page 240.) Sometimes an apparently discrete negative item is followed quickly by another unrelated and unpredictable piece of bad news. In this sort of situation, the count of reaction days begins running again. Quite often, because suspicions now have been kindled, this newly emerging apparent pattern of clustered bad news means that the stock will react as it would to a non-discrete piece of bad news.

Some examples of material, unexpected, discrete bad news (or MUD for short) are as follows:

- For an insurance company, a major natural disaster that raises loss expense beyond normal expectations.
- For a high-technology company, the resignation or death of a key scientist or inventor.
- For any small company, the death of a senior officer, especially the founder or other person whose identity is central to the investment community's concept of the company.
- For a fast-growth company, the announcement of a competitor's major new product or technology that reduces the lead time or exclusivity enjoyed by the first company.
- A one-quarter earnings surprise caused by nonrecurring factors such as a supplier's strike or storm damage, or by write-offs that do not form part of an established company or industry pattern.
- A dividend reduction (or, in rare cases, an omission), because it usually follows other bad news.
- Damage to plant or other assets clearly caused by an outside force such as

a storm or the explosion of a nearby plant—a case in which no fault is likely to be attributed to the company.

In contrast, these are nondiscrete negative events:

- For an insurance company, a new law or court ruling that creates broader concepts of liability with true costs that cannot yet be calculated.
- Issuance of a qualified opinion by independent auditors.
- A major workplace or ecological accident in which the company will probably be found, at least in part, at fault.
- For any company, the unexplained resignation of a very senior executive or financial officer with any hint of mystery or scandal.
- For a high-tech company, failure to secure a patent on a device or technology that had been represented to Wall Street as critical to success.
- For a high-tech or fast-growth company, delayed or canceled introduction of a previously announced or expected new product.
- Announcement (or the expectation) of a decline in earnings for reasons that reflect management weaknesses (poor control) or unrecognized competitive pressures in the business (lack of foresight).
- Government probes of the company for possible antitrust violations, bid rigging, contract overcharging, or false documentation.
- SEC investigation into possible securities violations on the part of the company or one or more of its officers.
- Disclosure that one or more past financial statements were inaccurate and that some time will be required for an investigation before issuing revised reports.
- Announcement that the company's board is considering or will consider reducing or omitting the dividend or declaring bankruptcy.
- A news announcement that, while appearing to be discrete, represents a contradiction of previous management representations to analysts or the press.

The key difference between these groups of examples is the apparent degree of closure versus uncertainty on the bad news. There is an old traders' cliché that the market can handle good news and can even handle bad news, but uncertainty drives it crazy. Highly institutionally owned stocks are especially vulnerable to deep price wounds from nondiscrete problems because portfolio managers are driven by short-term performance, do not want to list out-of-favor or tainted names on their quarterly statements, and fear 20/20 hindsight misfeasance suits if they retain stocks with clearly questionable fundamentals. Widely held stocks present individual investors with a special challenge when a pattern of problems arises: while

FIGURE 26–1

Two-Day and Three-Day Drubbing from Bad News

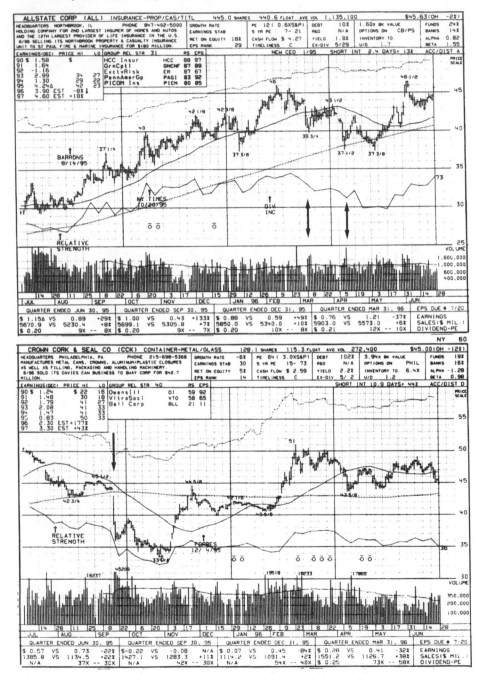

F I G U R E 26–1 (continued)

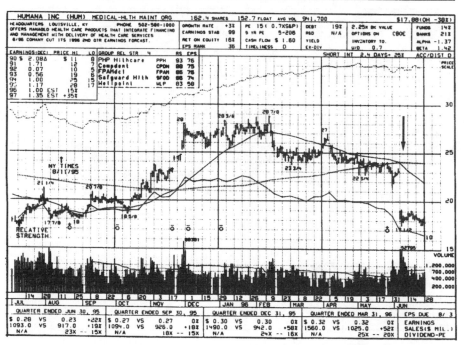

F I G U R E 26–1 (concluded)

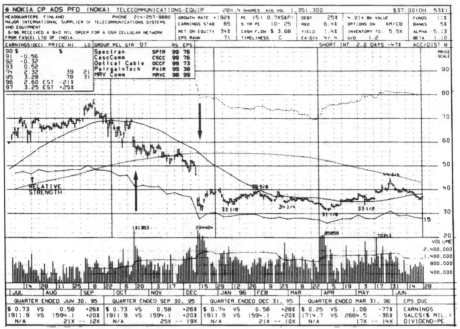

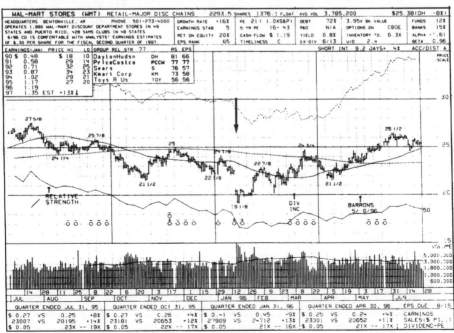

Courtesy of *Daily Graphs and Long Term Values;* P.O. Box 66919; Los Angeles, California 90066–0919.

one might feel the problems will not be fatal to the company, its reputation with analysts will usually require a lengthy healing process, implying deep and long stock-price injury.

REACTING INTELLIGENTLY TO BAD NEWS

The difference between finite, known bad news and uncertain, bad-portent news is reflected in the way investors react to it. The market's reaction to open-ended news with bad implications is painfully drawn out. This is because while uneasiness creates less severe selling pressure at first, it leaves a psychological dark cloud lingering for a long time afterward. When the bad news is discrete and appears to imply no further shocks, the price reaction is usually sharp but relatively brief.

MUD bad news typically imposes a two- or three-day price drop on a stock, which is often quite sharp in percentage terms. In effect, it is a private crash. There are psychomechanical reasons for this pattern of typical duration, and they concern news dissemination and investors' rate of absorption and reaction to it. The sharpness of the price reaction has been compounded in recent years by the twin demons of short investment horizons and a rising high concentration of institutional holdings. In very strong bull markets, such as in the 17 months that started at Thanksgiving 1994, bad news sometimes triggers merciless instant selling—since investor expectations are so high and other attractive opportunities are seen everywhere, few have patience for holding tainted issues in hope of recovery.

When news is announced, it typically has a two-day life in the media unless it is so major that prolonged follow-up coverage ensues. Major examples of the latter were Three Mile Island, the Bhopal chemical disaster, the Exxon Valdez accident, and various spectacular plane crashes such as ValuJet's flight 592 in May 1996. On the day of the announcement, unless the company can arrange to have the bad news released after the market closes, the item runs on the wire services and perhaps on stock market shows (e.g., CNN Business News or Bloomberg TV) televised during the session.

Some investors and traders react immediately. The next day, the story runs again—perhaps in greater length and detail—in national and local daily newspapers. If it makes "good television," like a spectacular physical disaster, it plays overnight and next morning. Then even more people react. Thus, on any meaningful negative news, generally expect a two-day price reaction at a minimum.

If the bad news occurs on a Thursday or Friday, a three-day reaction is likely because weekend researchers/investors react on reading the stock quotations in the Saturday and Sunday papers. They call their brokers on Monday and ask what caused the big drop the prior week, often creating a minor third wave of selling pressure. The weekend itself allows longer time for a brooding sense of panic to develop, and, in some cases, ready replacement-buy candidates are identified, adding to Monday selling orders.

In cases when major bad news occurs on Friday, the three-day rule emerges if the market happens to take a serious dive (related to the company's news or otherwise) on Monday. This is followed by a Tuesday morning rout that lets further air out of the stock that has suffered the bad publicity.

An important issue in the two- or three-day reaction to MUD bad news is the extent of the damage, specifically during the period of sharp price decline before stabilization takes place. There usually follows a period of time (perhaps two days to a week or longer) during which the stock steadies and sometimes tries to rally.

Later there is most often a renewed price decline, but it is usually less dramatic than the first. (See Figure 26–2.) The second decline occurs, typically, because the stock has run out of gas from bargain hunters attracted by the first crack, because the technical chart pattern looks weak (probably a rally on low volume or a rise into supply), because holders who refused to sell during the initial bashing wait and then try to sell slightly higher later on, or because of any coincidental general market weakness during which an already wounded stock cannot hold on.

With all these caveats, selling seems obvious if not easy; a preplanned selling scenario will provide the savvy investor with necessary guidance on specific selling tactics in this environment. For an effective sale,

1. Distinguish carefully between discrete bad news and nondiscrete bad news—which have very different longer-term implications for your hold/sell decision.
2. Create a mental scenario about the decline and stabilization; this will help you keep from reacting emotionally as events play out. It is useful to know that, while the price probably will not recover to its pre-news level soon, it will stop declining shortly and then provide at least two days' stability during which a better sale can be executed. If, due to inattention, lack of broker service, indecision, or denial, the stock has not been sold on the first day of bad news, one must understand that by the third day's arrival it is already too late; while it will be painful, at that point holding will provide a modestly better sale opportunity sometime during the several days following.

What is the usual internal decline pattern on MUD bad news? The first day's price decline is usually the worst unless the news is released late during the trading session. In that case, the second day is the worst because it absorbs the greatest barrage of selling volume. Otherwise, the second day shows a decline of from one-half to two-thirds the amount on the first (full) day, and volume starts to contract.

If there is a third day, a reversal can occur in which morning selling drives the price lower, followed around midsession by an abatement of selling pressure and some price snap-back. Again, volume is usually lighter. The depth of the most im-

FIGURE 26-2

Shock, Digestion, and Partial Bounce

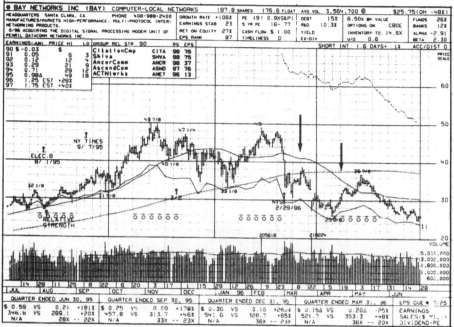

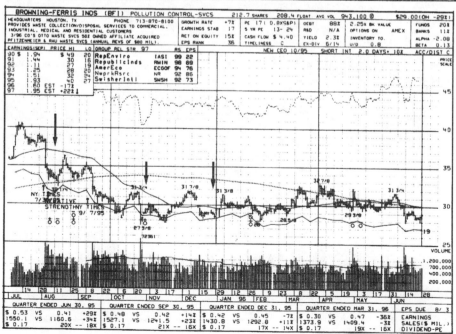

FIGURE 26–2 (continued)

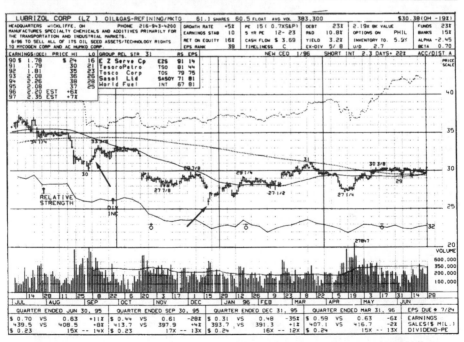

F I G U R E   26–2 (concluded)

Courtesy of *Daily Graphs and Long Term Values*; P.O. Box 66919; Los Angeles, California 90066–0919.

mediate decline can vary significantly, for any actual news severity, depending on the interaction of such factors as:

- Large institutional holdings (implying volume sales).
- Bad news occurring shortly before the end of a calendar quarter (institutional window dressers do not want to show a "bad" holding in quarterly portfolio lists).
- A lengthy past period of rising EPS (implying that the shock of bad news will be harsh, as with Wal-Mart in January 1996).
- Stocks that traditionally trade at a high P/E (implying widespread bullish consensus of expectations and therefore deep disappointment).
- Stocks having recently performed very strongly rather than sideways or lower, driving a sudden scramble to lock down profits (computer, semiconductor, and related issues in late 1995).
- Coincidence of a sharply weaker market at the same time company-specific news hits the stock itself (possible bargain hunters will stand aside).

- Stock price fall creating a technically significant chart flaw such as a breakdown from a channel bottom or the downward resolution of a triangle (bringing in technician dumping as well as fundamentally disappointed sellers).
- Bad news or any hint of possible unwinding of fortunes for companies controlled by charismatic wealthy persons (Donald Trump was a victim in the early 1990s as the tabloids dragged out his real-estate woes).
- Bad news smacking of a currently sensitive subject such as insider trading, ecological problems, health scares, or other hot topics.

When seemingly discrete bad news is followed shortly by a second news item, the reaction clock starts running again for two or three days; now the situation must be considered as an erosion problem in which other investors may come to see the second announcement as no longer discrete. It begins to look like a process of going from bad to worse.

A good example occurred during the early stages of the savings and loan crisis when Phoenix-based Pinnacle West Capital, the parent company of Mera-Bank and Arizona Public Service, announced a dividend omission late one afternoon. The stock moved fractionally lower to the close and broke sharply the next day. The second full day of post-news trading brought a further drop on lower volume.

Normally, a stabilization and a bit of a snap-back rally could have been expected. But then a major newswire interviewed a company spokesperson, who mentioned the possibility of a Chapter 11 bankruptcy filing to rid Pinnacle West of its troubled thrift unit. This second piece of bad news lengthened the period of sharp price drop for another two days. It was arrested only when an 80-point morning smash in the Dow Jones Industrials reversed itself to just a 4-point drop by the close.

For anyone not already familiar with the Pinnacle West story, the second item created a new cloud of ongoing uncertainty and, in effect, a potentially life-threatening situation: the stock was no longer in the discrete bad news category, and the news continued to worsen for a long time before being turned around.

Another lengthy painful sequence surrounded Morrison Knudsen, a once-prestigious worldwide engineering/construction firm. It reported large losses for 1994, and its stock was cut in half. Hopeful predictions of improvement during 1995 did not pan out; directors resigned and officers were fired. With the shares down to single digits, an attempted bank rescue was lined up but failed. The stock was already down from $29 to $2 before a Chapter 11 filing came in mid-1996. Often, as veteran observers say, the first bad news turns out not to be the last such.

The bottom line for investors deciding on tactics is that a two-day (three-day if over the weekend) price crack is to be expected on major bad news, followed by calmer trading and probably a slight recovery from panic lows. A different response is called for if the bad news is open ended or if it represents a pattern of deterioration. Without hesitation, sell when the news indicates general corporate decay, smacks of dishonesty, or falls into a pattern in a weakening industry.

CHAPTER 27

Sell on News Delays

KEYS TO INVESTMENT SUCCESS

- Know How to Act on Scheduled Announcements
- Anticipate Dividend Declarations
- Prepare for Earnings Reports
- Act On Implications of Other Delays

In the investment arena, no news is usually *not* good news. Expected but delayed news often falls into this category. There are three categories of expected news from a company:

- Scheduled announcements.
- Dividend declarations.
- Earnings reports.

SCHEDULED ANNOUNCEMENTS

The smallest and most unusual category is scheduled announcements. Managements of most companies do not box themselves in by committing to an announcement on a predesignated timetable because too much can go wrong that might require delay. Most managements say only that they are "preparing a statement and will release it as soon as possible under the circumstances."

An expected or anticipated announcement (other than periodic dividend and earnings news) usually occurs when the company is under some pressure. Something has gone awry, and a response is needed. Occasionally, under such pressure, the company attempts to control the public relations damage and to ward off further telephone barrages by saying it expects to make a statement on the matter by a certain date or time.

By making this commitment, a company has put its reputation on the block; if the deadline passes with no further announcement, presume that the situation is more difficult or that the response will be more drastic or far-reaching than shareholders would wish.

Suppose a corporate treasurer suddenly resigns, and the audit committee of the board suspects foul play. The company makes an announcement of the resignation. Under generally accepted standards of full and prompt disclosure, the fact that an internal investigation exists is considered material, so the company most likely feels obliged to release this information at the same time.

If management announces that it expects the investigation to last for a certain number of days and will issue a statement at that time, expect it to make good on the announcement unless the problem turns out to be particularly thorny. A delay past the appointed time without a timely and specific announcement is a danger signal.

What requires extra time? Management may have to call in independent auditors or a legal investigative agency to uncover the full extent of a problem. Or there may be legal subtleties that require careful review because of potential litigation. Or the situation may be so significant that management wants to complete a Form 8-K filing for the SEC that covers the news before making a statement.

Whatever the cause of delay, the outcome is much more likely to be surprisingly bad rather than happily benign or good news. Because money has a time value and because avoiding losses is very important in investing, lean to the cautious side and anticipate bad news by selling out on the delay itself instead of waiting for some other shoe to drop.

This is an occasion when commission phobia can get in the way. If an investor's suspicions or worst fears are proven wrong and the late news is no worse than expected, the stock is unaffected. In such a case you will have spent a round-trip commission as insurance to be safe rather than sorry. (Possibly you will see the company more objectively from a nonholder's distance and decide not to re-enter, in which case only a single commission will have been paid.) If the news only gets worse as it emerges, you may see a gap opening of several points down (dwarfing any commission), followed by further erosion. If the news is worse than it was earlier, management credibility will have become tarnished, delaying and limiting prospects for price recovery.

This admonition to be safe rather than sorry is even more forceful when the stock is widely held by institutions. In today's short-term money management culture, there is a rush to exit with huge sell orders whenever any news is bad. Chapter 10 dealt with that problem, and with necessary adjustments for wise individuals, in greater detail.

When the time period of news uncertainty is open ended, investors collectively are prone to suspect the worst and to invent or listen to rumors. While a delay for clarification is in effect, the stock price is likely to erode anyway. Thus, the delay in releasing follow-up news quite often means a lose-lose situation for stockholders: continued holding simply puts money at unnecessary risk.

While not all investors wish to, or should, take a short-term approach to the market, it is nearly always true that the first loss is the best loss. Therefore, when something goes wrong, it is most prudent to exit and re-examine the situation from a distance. By holding on in hope that the bad news will not be too bad after all, you are (1) playing a game for minimized loss and (2) exposing yourself to the heavier emotional baggage, greater financial loss, and more painful decision that will follow if the stock later in fact takes a big dive.

DIVIDEND DECLARATIONS

A second major category of news delays involves dividends. Not all delays are dangerous, so it helps to do some homework and have references available to help distinguish between alarming and forgivable delays in time to take action.

Corporate boards of directors usually meet on a predictable schedule, especially for dividend declarations (boards usually meet more than four times a year, even though shareholders seldom see any evidence of most nondividend meetings). As a courtesy to the board members, a company schedules board meetings on a standing basis so members can anticipate travel well in advance, for example, the third Tuesday or fourth Monday of the month.

How does an investor know when the board meets? When curious or concerned—and generally there is little cause to be worried if the latest earnings reports have been favorable and there is no pattern of trouble elsewhere in the industry—she can call the company. There are also several sources of accessible information. One is Standard & Poor's individual stock reports. For dividend-paying stocks, a table shows the meeting, stock-of-record, and payable dates of the last four quarterly dividends.

Be aware of two wild-card factors, however: the meeting after year-end is often further into the quarterly cycle than other meetings, and, in the summer, meetings are less regular because of vacations. Use the spring and fall meeting dates for the best guidance as to likely schedule patterns.

A second source that is widely available is The *Value Line Investment Survey,* although its coverage of large-capitalization companies is narrower (only about 1,800 stocks.) (Most public libraries subscribe to *Value Line* as do many brokerage offices.) *Value Line* makes a notation in the lower left corner of its page, or sometimes at the lower center, indicating the date of the next expected board meeting.

A third and highly comprehensive source is Standard & Poor's *Dividend Record.* Fewer libraries and brokerage offices subscribe, but give it a try and become familiar with it. This service tracks and reports declarations on both pre-ferred and common stocks. Its annual, soft cover, 8 $\frac{1}{2}$ × 11-inch volumes give the same data as the S&P sheets described earlier. The monthly and weekly update sup-plements track the most recent declaration dates. These sheets are looseleaf and usually filed in front.

Numerous on-line database sources are becoming available, often at little or no cost. Any broker with access to a Bloomberg terminal can readily provide needed dividend meeting data.

The reason for looking at delays in dividend meetings is cautionary. Although a delay can be innocent, it more often results from problems. Before calling the company, check with a broker; ask to have the day's news headlines scanned. If a news release came out too late in the afternoon yesterday, it will miss the morning papers and appear a day late. The dividend item will run on the ticker as soon as possible.

To call the company, try the corporate secretary's office rather than the public relations or stockholder relations department. It is an official duty of the corporate secretary's office to schedule board meetings and notify members, so that office has the timing information readily at hand.

EARNINGS REPORTS

By far the most perilous reason for delayed reports is bad corporate earnings. Late earnings releases most often mean trouble, but before concluding that a suspicious delay is occurring, check the facts and remember seasonal exceptions. Note that af-ter fiscal year-end it takes longer to release earnings (requiring auditor blessing) than it does following ends of the first three quarters.

Quarterly numbers usually are unaudited. Small adjustments can be pushed from one period to the next between quarters in case something slipped by earlier. Year-end numbers are audited, however, and there is no way of taking back a year-end number once it is released without embarrassment and loss of credibility. Therefore, expect those releases to come more slowly.

How does an investor find out when to expect earnings? A majority of broker-age firms capture and store the last 90 days' headlines from the Dow Jones wire on their quotation machines. To anticipate the release schedule rather than waiting un-til the news is out (always a highly useful mind-set for an investor), call just after the end of the quarter and ask on what date the prior EPS announcement was made. Add three months and mark your calendar. After more than 90 days have elapsed, the prior headline and its date are wiped off the quote machine.

Another excellent source is *The Wall Street Journal Cumulative Index,* which can often be found in a public library. It cross indexes the past year's articles in *Barron's* also, giving headline, date, page, and column. The release runs on the news wire one market day earlier. This source saves the amount of time it takes to look at every day's back issue in the month of the prior report. Similarly, you can narrow a daily search by looking back three months in *Barron's* and noting in its stock tables which week the previous quarter's information first appeared.

Another handy source is a chart service, for example, Daily Graphs by William O'Neil. (See the Appendix at the end of the book for addresses.) In small print in the narrow lines above the charts are the words "EPS due" and a date. This chart service monitors past news release dates and adds 3 or 12 months to create due-date estimates.

Several computer-based services such as Prodigy, Dow Jones News/Retrieval, and CompuServe provide dates of past quarterly reports (and other news items) via personal computer, but such information is not free.

Why does a company delay its announcement of earnings? If the company made an acquisition or divested a business in the last one or two quarters, the accounting department is very likely still in scramble mode, putting together revised numbers. On rare occasions, the summer vacation season might be a real excuse. Another legitimate delay is the imposition of new accounting requirements by the SEC or by the Financial Accounting Standards Board (it takes a lot less time to change a rule than it does to comply with new ones). If many companies are noting the effects of new reporting rules, some delay is tolerable.

OTHER DELAYS

Other delays are often harbingers of trouble. A new computer system may have been installed, which can bring a company at least temporarily to its knees. Sometimes records get lost and management loses control of operations until the loss is rectified.

If it is not a new computer, it could be a new accounting treatment that the company has voluntarily decided to adopt. Analysts usually greet such news with suspicion; sometimes the revised methods of accounting are more liberal or allow the company to cover poor performance for awhile because of lack of comparability. New accounting standards can also be more conservative, resulting in downward restatements of prior results and a drop in stock price. A delay due to new standards voluntarily adopted usually is a cause for concern.

There can be really serious problems: a cash or inventory shortage is discovered, accounting records are falsified, or operating problems have occurred and management is assessing the degree of damage and deciding how to explain what happened. Another possibility is a write-off or write-down of assets that can take extra time when independent auditors are called in to give advice and/or approve the charges.

Be aware of the regulatory deadlines for filing SEC reports. Public companies are expected to report quarterly results no later than 45 days after the period ends; annual numbers are due not more than 90 days after year-end. In practice, the SEC is understaffed and typically has more pressing matters to police than late reports. However, company managements, lawyers, and auditors are well aware of the rules; failure to meet a regulatory deadline is usually a sign that something meaningful is wrong.

One other source of concern is not an actual delay: a few companies routinely report results at the last possible date (the SEC deadline). Typically, such companies are extremely secretive and report only what is required and when it is required—neither more nor sooner. They tend not to give much or any useful interim information to analysts, heightening the potential for surprises. It is often advisable to avoid investing in such companies from the beginning.

However, if giants such as AT&T can get their quarterly data out in 10 days or less, surely a small company that has chosen to be publicly traded should be geared to do it in fewer than 45 days. If not, their accounting function is dangerously understaffed, and management is at risk of not being in the know and in control.

28

Selling versus Holding in a Crash

KEYS TO INVESTMENT SUCCESS

- Recall and Understand Earlier Panics
- Weather a Panic
- Pre-Identify Stocks That Don't Fare Well
- Know Panic-Resilient Stocks

Recall the chaotic pace of trading on October 19, 1987, when the Dow Jones Industrial Average lost 508 points (23 percent) and made its bottom for the move on then-record volume. Even considerably less dramatic important bottoms are typically referred to as climaxes because they consist of prices falling in a cascade or waterfall shape (if plotted on a graph against time), accompanied by a sharp concentration of heavy trading volume as investor emotions take hold and outrun logic.

RECALLING AND UNDERSTANDING EARLIER PANICS

On the way down, each temporary bottom is typically characterized by increases in fear and therefore in trading volume, with a bit of panicky dumping to mark each new interim low. The final downside climax is most violent and usually sees the greatest trading volume. Selling pressure becomes so intense that it literally cannot be exceeded; it becomes exhausted as large numbers of the previously brave finally jump overboard simultaneously—which is why, and when, prices hit a bottom. This is the profile of a final bottom, that is, the end of a selling trend and the end of a downward movement in prices.

This stage is usually followed on lower volume by timid bargain-hunting. When that process runs its course and the bulls run out of guts and/or ammunition, the initial base-building or rally falters. Such failure to hold ground leads to renewed fear, which builds in a minor crescendo to a new, oftentimes lower, cascade-shaped bottom on moderately high volume. The key to note here is the less dramatic price drop and volume rise than those seen earlier; the difference proves that the prior low was one of psychological exhaustion or washout.

In any discussion of holding versus selling stocks in normal market conditions rather than only during a panic, the circumstances under which it is best to sell should be outlined first. *Holding (which is really commission-free buying for a further holding period) should occur only if no tests for selling are failed.* The company-related reasons to sell are as follows:

- Sell if the news seemingly cannot get any better.
- Sell when your original scenario has been fulfilled.
- Sell if things did not go as planned.
- Sell when the broker's advice goes from "buy" to "hold."
- Sell if company fundamentals are getting sick.
- Sell on the rebound in the aftermath of material, unexpected, discrete bad news.
- Sell in certain cases when expected news is delayed.

The general market-climate indicators for selling are as follows:

- Sell some stocks when an extended market advance has exceeded realistic growth rates.
- Sell more stocks when you note general euphoria and unusually widespread public participation (strong final-stage indicators).

The stock-specific conditions for selling are as follows:

- Sell when the stock reaches your original price target.
- Sell on an unsustainable upward price spike on big volume.
- Sell when your portfolio shows all gains.
- Sell if the stock is lazy money and likely to stay that way.
- Sell when the stock is unusually far above its moving average.
- Sell using above-market limit orders, letting the market come to your price and free you from a decision while greedy and celebrating.
- Sell with a stop-loss order, but never remove or lower it.

Investor-related reasons to sell are:

- Sell if you would not buy the stock again now at today's quoted price.
- Sell after gloating or counting the chips.
- Sell rather than hope against hope for a "maybe" bailout.
- Sell and step aside when experiencing a personal losing streak.

Investors selling stocks in a disciplined manner using the preceeding signals are likely to end up with a good deal of cash before the market moves into a bear cycle. Relatively few of one's holdings will fail to hit one of the 20 triggers noted in those lists. Those stocks that do survive will tend to be high-quality growth issues that have continued to perform fundamentally and have not yet run up to unreasonable price levels. Some experts refer to these as core holdings or "businessman's risk" foundation stocks. They are stocks that have given consistent indications that they can be held through good and bad in the market.

All other stocks will have become sales before a panic bottom because:

1. They worked as planned.
2. They acted too well for a brief period of time.
3. They gradually became unreasonably priced.
4. They were wasting the time value of money by going nowhere.
5. They developed significant fundamental problems.

Very few stocks can escape all such screens for a long period. Thus, as an investor cashes in as prescribed and follows a buying discipline that rejects new positions when valuations get too pricey, she ends up still holding very few stocks as the market gets toppy. That, of course, works very nicely by protecting capital. Moving to increased cash will make her feel a bit lonely in a bull market's late stages, as certain speculative stocks skyrocket and give her regrets of being left behind. However, she should be assured that her selling discipline will be rewarded when the psychological climate, seemingly overnight, turns surprisingly nasty and others suffer sudden sharp losses.

To understand the big-picture perspective, review the descriptions presented in Chapter 7 of the mechanical supply/demand processes and factors such as sponsorship that make stock prices rise. Recall that if these processes and factors supporting further price advance are absent, an investor should not hold because the stock will not go up.

Looking now at stock-price trends not from a mechanical viewpoint but from a big-picture perspective, there are two major price-driving forces: fundamentals (which control the long term) and psychology (which rules the short and medium term). Review Chapter 13, as well as Figure 8–1 in Chapter 8.

Fundamental and psychological factors affect stocks in both directions. As an overlay, understand that they can affect a stock either directly (because of the company behind the stock itself) or indirectly (because the industry group's or the over-all market's trend is so strong that virtually no stocks can buck it). However, the indirect effect is much stronger on the downside than on the upside: fear is a more powerful driver than greed.

WEATHERING A PANIC

The central concept in this chapter is the occasional need to play when it is painful. But this concept specifically and only means to hold stocks that are being affected just by the overwhelming negative psychological forces that occasionally cause selling routs or panics *in the whole market.*

To put this very important limiting caveat another way, when a crash or panic occurs, stocks should be held only if they are going down solely because of market factors and not at all because of company factors. This should relate to only a few issues, however, because investors following the suggestions in this book should have already weeded out their bad performers and taken profits and closed out their stellar performers well before a bear market arrives, let alone reaches climax proportions.

Thus, when appropriate selling has left an investor with only a few, high-quality stocks, he can and should hold onto the gems and play through the difficult experience of a panic or crash. He will be holding only a relatively small portfolio (having followed the other cashing-in suggestions well before the bottom nears), so his level of pain will be no worse than moderate. His cash holdings will give emotional comfort and provide the resources for acquiring stocks advantageously when prices get really low. A comforting perspective for those less than 50 percent committed to stocks is that each decline means their cash is gaining stock-buying power faster than their remaining holdings are losing cash value!

Some investors may see a contradiction in this advice because earlier they were counseled that avoiding losses is the first priority and the best reason for selling. But taking a short-term dose of paper losses in a crash—by holding quality issues—is a lesser risk than selling out during the fury and hoping to have the courage and good trade execution to get back in at lower prices shortly afterward.

If an investor is down to just a few core holdings anyway, he is better advised to tough it out. The very experience of playing in pain through a temporary crash (think of the October 1987 and October 1989 bashings and the smaller one-day drubbings during the early and middle 1990s) is of enormous instructional value actually worth the modest monetary cost involved. The process of crisis thinking and the need to make wrenching decisions that prove valid in short order will serve the investor well for the rest of his or her investment career.

Once an investor has successfully navigated the worst of the choppy investment seas, she will have learned survival lessons and will have internalized feelings and taken in an experience that will be of permanent psychological and instructive value. That experience deepens her understanding of the way the market works. Probably most of all, having won at a difficult game, she develops the wisdom and courage to succeed in similar circumstances in the future. And that provides the opportunity to make big profits in the handful of similarly dramatic times that will occur in future years. She will know beyond any shadow of a doubt, from personal experience, that contrarian investing philosophy works.

When caught in a panic, the central question is whether capitalism in the United States and major Western democracies will continue to function after the panic ends. If the answer is yes, then there is no reason to sell at foolish levels. In fact, the only rational thing to do is take courage and make buys. Being gutsy enough to act on the contrarian test—refusing to sell good stocks cheap because Wall Street and Main Street have lost faith for a few days—ensures that your selling will be appropriate. It is difficult to buy in a panic. Those who can do so are demonstrably rational and calm enough to sell with discipline as highs approach.

There is one more qualifier on whether to hold or sell after a panic has passed. Once the panic subsides, there is a lift in the market. But its effect is significantly different for various kinds of stocks. For some issues, there is a sharp snapback rally; for others, there is very little improvement. Just as it is not advisable to sell into the panic, it is prudent to reassess positions after the selling frenzy has subsided and the lift in prices has begun.

The object, as always, is to decide what to sell and what to hold. Selling should not be urgent because pre-bear-phase tactics will have raised a lot of cash, so there is no need to sell to raise cash for margin calls or buying. But because the goal is always to maximize return on capital and to take advantage of the time value of money, look closely at what to hold and what to sell after the panic has cleared.

STOCKS THAT DON'T FARE WELL

Stocks that tend to be sub-par performers in a post-crash environment are the following:

- OTC issues.
- Low-priced stocks.
- Small total-capitalization issues.
- Thinly traded, undercovered, or noncovered stocks.
- Fundamental industry laggards.
- Stocks in recession-sensitive industries.
- Discredited groups.
- Panic-trigger related groups.

Because of fear, nervousness, and lack of speculative appetite after a crash or panic, the first five groups (some of which overlap) lack sponsorship. In addition, because market panics generate immediate scare headlines in the media, predictably there will be talk of recession (or depression) and parallels drawn with 1929. Therefore, recession-sensitive groups of stocks do not bounce back much for a period of time, even if later hindsight shows that no recession occurred.

There may, in fact, turn out to be no recession at all following the market's dramatic down-move (as in 1988), but perception and expectation drive stock prices in the near term more than facts do. Thus, cyclicals such as autos, steels, chemicals, papers, and capital-goods producers are not solid choices for participating in the bounce. Similarly, vacation-related (airline, hotel, and casino) and luxury stocks fare poorly.

The discredited groups vary from one market period to another. Their identity depends on what was in the headlines in recent months. Basic industry stocks were taboo in the early 1980s, known as the "rust-belt" period. High-tech stocks suffered through a private, one-industry recession in the mid-1980s. Banks were whipping boys in the early era of bad third-world loans. Savings and loans paid their dues in the doghouse during and after the scandals and bailout of the early 1990s. One might project that previously overblown expectations for Internet and telecommunications and software stocks will leave these as slow to recover from any big decline in the late 1990s.

Again, remember that longer-term perspectives may prove that the fear about leading companies in discredited groups was unfounded. More important from a tactical investment perspective in the healing phase after a crash is the reality that few will have the courage to sponsor tarnished-image-group stocks with either money or written advice. Such issues will always prove early-recovery laggards.

The final category should be off the hold list for similar reasons. Sometimes there is an industry or category of stocks related to the news that triggers the panic selling. In 1962, it was steel stocks sensitive to pricing confrontation with the Kennedy administration. Brokerage stocks would have been poor choices to hold after the 1987 crash because of all the controversy surrounding program trading. The 1989 crash was triggered by the collapse of the proposed buyout of United Airlines, so airlines and other proposed leveraged buyout candidates were identifiable as the trigger-related groups at that time.

In the post-decline phase that occurs after you read this chapter, carefully note the events on which the decline was blamed, and avoid for some time stocks associated with those concepts; they will have a difficult time regaining sponsorship quickly.

PANIC-RESILIENT STOCKS

There are, by contrast, several groups that tend to act well in a post-panic environment, especially if the crash itself drives prices to incredible levels. Of course, the more unusual the values created, the more brief the opportunity window and the quicker the upside correction. Some of the groups most likely to snap back are as follows:

- Recession-resistant industries (foods, drugs, utilities).
- Noncyclical blue chips driven well down (oils).
- Big names with corporate staying power (AT&T, Exxon, General Electric, Merck, McDonald's).
- Fortune 100 and similar companies with good yields.
- Trade-down concepts such as low-cost restaurants and discount retailers (recession "beneficiaries").
- Companies with low P/Es or low price/cash flow ratios not already in the preceding list.
- Companies selling below book value and with positive earnings estimates for the coming year (implying credibly sustainable book values).
- Companies with low debt/equity ratios (perceived as low in risk).
- Unleveraged closed-ended, non-junk bond funds.
- Panic-trigger beneficiaries (e.g., oil-service and insulation stocks after OPEC raised oil prices in 1973; temporary employment services and outsourcing manufacturers after a downsizing-driven recession such as that of 1991).

All of these stocks are recession resistant or perceived as among the most likely to survive hard times. They retain market sponsorship and are soonest to regain enthusiastic buyers. Related positively to the trigger event, they have high visibility because investors remember the concept vividly and relate to it readily.

It is highly important to make hold/sell calls with an eye on prevailing market expectations and not based alone on your personal judgment of what may or should happen. If the (correct) bet is no recession, the reward is smaller and slower than if the (correct) bet is market *expectation* of a recession (whether it comes or not). The investor must submerge his or her ego to the realities of the emotional climate (this may be one reason that women have become known as better investors). It is better to be richer today than to be vindicated slowly.

29

The Hold/Sell
Decision Checklist

KEYS TO INVESTMENT SUCCESS

- Use These 20 Questions to Focus the Hold-versus-Sell Decision
- Evaluate Your Answers Later, to Fine-Tune

This chapter contains a list of questions that summarize the points developed in this book to help investors create a selling strategy. The questions were originally adapted from a training session developed for brokers in a regional retail brokerage firm. They have proved useful for two reasons: they deal with a relatively unfamiliar facet of the investment process (i.e., selling stocks), and they help focus thinking in ways that encourage rational decisions and sometimes free up lazy funds for re-use.

Readers are encouraged to photocopy these pages of the book and to keep copies in three places: in your workplace, from where many broker conversations tend to take place; at home, where market studying and decision making tends to take place; and in your broker's office, so that he or she also might spend time thinking about these issues and be able to help a wayward reader/investor back onto the path should there be any straying from logical thinking.

Each stock should have its own separate checklist; keeping these in a notebook, especially after sales have been completed, will create over time a highly useful record that will reveal recurring patterns of strength and weakness.

20 QUESTIONS TO FOCUS
THE HOLD-VERSUS-SELL DECISION

At the Time of Purchase

1. Date stock bought?
2. Price paid? (For reference, DJIA level on that date?)
3. Price target? (What is the implied P/E ratio?) Sell order entered?
4. Target date to sell the stock? (Calculate projected return in percent per year from questions 1, 2, 3, and 4.)
5. What event(s) or change(s) should make the stock go up? (Specific expectations.)

Reviewing the Position at a Later Date

6. Are you currently more, less, or equally excited and sure about the company versus when stock was first bought?
7. Has the story expected in question 5 played out yet? If no, is there still a concrete chance the story will play? If yes, did the stock go up at all on the related or partial news? If yes, did the stock reach the objective in question 3?
8. What is stock's price now? (Compare with questions 2 and 3; note question 6.)
9. What is expected to happen fundamentally now? (Compare with question 5.) If discussed originally with friends, relatives, or colleagues, would the stock be discussed enthusiastically now and be purchased today?
10. Due to question 9, what price is expected now? (Compare with question 3.)
11. When is the price in question 10 projected? (Compare with question 4.) What is the revised estimated annualized percent return from questions 8, 10 and 11?
12. What is the downside price risk from current prices if nothing happens; that is, if the story or concept in question 5 or question 9 proves false?
13. Is the risk/reward balance favorable from current prices? (Compare questions 10 and 12 with current price.)
14. Where is the DJIA now? (Compare with DJIA level in question 2.) Is stock's relative performance surprising? Acceptable?
15. Have there been negative surprises from the company or its industry since purchase? How did these affect your thinking?

16. Since purchase, did you almost decide to sell, only to hold on for a little more? Was a mental or actual stop-loss point set and then reduced or removed as the stock weakened?

Analyzing Whether to Hold or Sell Now

17. Considering questions 9 through 12, why, specifically, should the stock be held now?
18. With your current knowledge, would you buy this stock again right now at today's price?
19. Have significantly better opportunities been identified for purchases right now?
20. Does the answer to question 17 square with answers to questions 3, 18, and 19?

EVALUATING YOUR ANSWERS

Written responses to these questions are recommended for two reasons: the discipline of thinking through the exercises in detail and the creation of an archival notebook record that can be used for later reference, comparison, and learning. Number a piece of paper from 1 to 20, put a blank for the stock's name on the top, and photocopy this answer grid in good quantity for future use.

Start filling out the sheet at the time of purchase by answering questions 1 through 5 immediately when the buy order is made. There will then be no need to search back for data for #1 and #2 and, most significantly, there will be no fudging of responses to questions 3, 4, and 5.

Later, answer questions 9, 10, and 11 with questions 3, 4, and 5 covered up: merely copying will render the exercise useless! The quality of your investment decisions will be enhanced by the rigor shown in carrying out this process.

Note that there is a built-in bias toward making one feel a bit defensive about holding a stock. This creates a presumption in favor of selling when things have not gone as planned. If a holding is not working, it needs to be fixed.

For starters, if time has gone beyond the period indicated by question 4 or if the stock actually has traded at or above the answer to question 3, something has gone wrong with the plan or the execution. If there are differences between the answers to questions 3, 4, and 5 as compared with questions 9, 10, and 11, study them again.

An affirmative answer to question 15 or to either part of question 16 indicates lack of decisiveness or consistency in dealing with this situation. Either greed arose when things went well or denial arose when things turned sour. It is only human to shift ground (rationalize) in an effort to be tolerant of the stock's performance (one's own judgment) or of one's less-than-perfect strategy and execution. Learn from past executions, and make a special effort to avoid falling into this pattern again. Continuing to do what is most comfortable will not improve results and is likely to hamper them.

The key question is question 18. If it cannot be answered in the affirmative with total honesty and enthusiastic conviction (use the subpart of question 9 as an acid test), then stop this deteriorating process by selling. If you would not buy today, why should you envision others doing so? If other investors cannot reasonably be expected to be buyers, such failure of sponsorship and support implies and forecasts lower prices.

How soon or how often this exercise should be conducted for each stock held is a reasonable question. It is advisable to create a tickler file in which you place each sheet for review 90 days from the buy date (or at the date noted in question 4, if that is sooner). If the review results in a hold decision, file the page for re-review at the date in question 11.

Use of this questionnaire is not guaranteed as a cure-all. Nor will it automatically make every position profitable. It will help to impose closure on situations that are not working out as expected, to generate urgency by examining and overlaying the time value of money, and to serve as a reminder that a decision to hold should be an active and reasoned act of the mind instead of a lazy default. A decision to hold should be every bit as active as a decision to buy or to sell, missing only the need to pick up the telephone and dial the broker's number.

To be successful, an investment must be not only bought right but also sold right. Until a sale occurs, the outcome is only a temporary paper result; a handsome profit can still melt away at any moment until it is actually closed out. This questionnaire should be used as a reminder, guide, and prompting tool to sharpen decision-making skills and sale executions.

CHAPTER 30

Summing Up:
The Winner's Test

KEYS TO INVESTMENT SUCCESS

- Define the Ultimate Test
- Consider the "Mother" Test
- Apply the Time-Value Test
- Apply the Ultimate Test: How Often?

You now recognize and understand the many externally imposed and internally created roadblocks to successfully selling your investments. To counteract those forces, you have begun to develop a newly activist mind-set about closing out your investment positions. A significant element of that revised way of looking at selling involves having adopted a contrarian's outlook toward the markets in both short- and long-term contexts. Prior chapters in this section have equipped you with several specific tactics for executing your position-liquidating decisions effectively and profitably—and under a variety of particular market circumstances. This final chapter names a single test that should be applied frequently to each of your holdings; its answer will sharply focus and define your choice between holding and selling.

THE ULTIMATE TEST

You own a stock; you've been watching its progress (or lack thereof) both in absolute terms and against the market background. When first buying, you had in mind a scenario or rationale that involved a view about future company developments, a time frame in which such events should materialize, and also a price target you envisioned as credible, driven by your story. No investor's crystal ball is perfect; unforeseen events in the world or specifically pertaining to your stock will have arisen since your original purchase action. Those now-known factors cannot be ignored, but neither should you be so totally focused on them that you mourn over (or continue to celebrate) them. What is of most practical importance in defining the remaining outcome of this investment position is the future. The future is all you can do anything about. This perspective defines, and highlights the importance of, the ultimate hold versus sell test.

Here is the test, followed by observations on why it is so critically important. Knowing all that you *now* know and expect about the company and its stock (not what you originally believed at time of purchase), assuming that you had available capital, and assuming that it would not cause a portfolio imbalance to do so, *would you buy the stock today, at today's price?* No equivocation—yes or no? Answers such as "maybe" or "probably" are not acceptable since they are ways of dodging the issue. No investor "probably" buys a stock; they either phone their broker and place an order or not. Here is the implication of your answer to that critical test: if you did not answer with an affirmative, you should sell; if you said yes, you should hold.

Some would object that this test is quite harsh. Indeed, it is sharply framed. But it is neither unfair nor less than 100 percent logical.

If you would not buy now, saying that you are nevertheless willing to hold amounts to playing a greater-fool game: holding in hope of higher prices implies your expectation that other investors will be more naive or less discerning than you since you have said that at present levels and with what you know, you would not be a buyer. Instead, as justification for your continuing to hold you would be counting on other investors to do what you would not do: buy the stock today and in the future, at present and at higher levels. Stock prices do not rise by magic or merely because people hope they will; rising prices require buying pressure that exceeds selling pressure. Buying pressure comes from buy orders generated by positive decisions. If you would not constitute part of the source of new buying orders, you are counting on others to make a decision you cannot justify. Such a decision to hold, therefore, is based on blind and unreasoning hope rather than on logic. Stating the point plainly: *what you would not buy, you should not hold!*

In case you harbor any doubts about whether holding is logically the same as buying, consider this: holding is redeploying capital for another time period, whether that be a moment, a day, a month, or longer. Purchasing an investment is deploying your capital by exchanging your wealth's form from cash (or a money market fund or margin buying power) into a certain number of shares of a given stock. When you have cash, becoming a stockholder requires deciding to exchange

your cash for the chosen security. When you are already an owner of a stock, holding implies a decision, namely, the choice to retain the security position rather than
exchange it back for cash at its current dollar value. Thought of in another (albeit
unusual) way, holding represents invisibly exchanging an owned stock for its cash
value and then deciding to immediately trade that cash back for the same shares to
hold for another moment, day, or longer. Holding is commission free and requires
no contact with your broker, but, in all other ways, it is a recommitment of capital
to the same stock for a further future time period. Since holding is every bit as
much a decision as was the purchase itself, holding should be an active choice
rather than a default due to inertia or inattention.

What you would not buy, you should not hold. Therefore, you should sell.
There is no other available choice. Avoidance by a nonholder is driven by the same
perceptions and expectations as sale by a current holder: cash or something else is
preferable to this stock. What you would not buy (i.e., would avoid if not already
involved with) is nothing other than a sale awaiting your action. Stripping away
questions of tax effects (dealt with earlier), for an owner to hold rather than to sell
what he would otherwise avoid (reject buying) is completely irrational.

CONSIDER THE "MOTHER" TEST

When considering the hold versus sell question, you might frame the issue in terms
of your author's "mother/mother-in-law" test. (Again: remember that holding is the
equivalent of buying!) Suppose your mother requested that you select a stock for
her to purchase today, and, for the sake of argument, assume that you share identical investment objectives and risk tolerances. Ask yourself whether you would recommend this stock (that you already own) to Mom for purchase (yes or no, not
maybe). You love her and you wish her success rather than grief and loss. You dread
the possibility that you might at some future date need to justify or explain away a
possible mistake in your selection. You realize you are human and therefore fallible
and can only exercise your best overall judgment for Mom's sake. But you would
really prefer to be right rather than wrong. Your mother might forgive you an error,
but you will still feel bad for having made it. This is a difficult screen for your stock
to pass, is it not? Well, treat yourself as well as you would hope to treat Mom! What
you would not suggest she buy, nor should you buy—and a hold is a commission-
free buy as noted earlier. How can you justify holding what you would not suggest
a loved one buy?

A variant of that test involving Mom is the mother-in-law version. Here, since
the relationship between you may have a somewhat different driving dynamic, your
attention is probably focused more strongly on first avoiding damage than on trying
to create success. In the real world of spouses and in-laws, of course, you would
most likely demur at the "opportunity" to render investment advice. But as a mental

measure of your true confidence in this stock, an imaginary mother-in-law test will serve well. Here, suppose that not only do you want her to think well of you and benefit rather than hurt from your advice, but also assume you will not have another visit for awhile. During the time you will be out of touch, the stock in question will be moving either up or down; your feedback will surely come at your next family gathering. Would you name this stock today as your buy choice for your mother-in-law? Again, only an unqualified yes or no is acceptable. If your expected risk of loss is not clearly overshadowed by your perceived likelihood of gain, you would not suggest buying. If you like the stock generally but would rather be a new buyer down five points from current levels, again you have defined a clear answer: you should sell now and place a limit buy at that level of greater comfort. Why willingly tolerate a suspected price retrenchment? Once again, treat yourself no less well than you would your mother-in-law. Avoid that anticipated remorse and that difficult review from 20/20 hindsight. What you would not tell her to buy, you should not hold either! What is not a buy is not a hold, and a sale is the only alternative.

Without question, investing is an art rather than a science. You should not expect to achieve near-perfect results; you must be able to forgive your own human imperfection. Your judgments regarding buying, holding, and selling must always be made under uncertainty and without sure knowledge of the future; diligent best effort at making a reasonably sound decision is all you can require of yourself, and desperately seeking all possible added information takes so long that the situation will have changed in the intervening time, requiring unending further reconsideration, and so on. (If you cannot function short of certainty, you are not well suited for investing, especially in individual stocks.) For these reasons, the preceding discussion of whether to sell versus hold must be interpreted in a fair and realistic context: given what you know, and exercising best available judgment while admitting that errors are a distinct possibility, what would you find seems best to do? In that spirit, another means of defining answers to your sell/hold question is offered next.

APPLY THE TIME-VALUE TEST

Always respect the time value of money. A due consideration of that factor can be very useful in your work on the sell/hold issue for any given stock. Occasionally reviewing Chapters 12 and 13 on this critical perspective may be of great value.

Considering your hold/sell choice with time value in mind should prove helpful regardless of where your stock's price has gone since purchase. Many investors are most careful to reconsider their positions when paper losses have occurred, and that discipline should be given due credit (whatever causes an investor to conduct an active hold/sell re-examination is healthy). But equally, a mental sell versus hold exercise should be undertaken if your stock has gone sideways and especially when it has risen smartly!

Your Stock is Down

Clearly, something has gone awry since you made that purchase. Has the overall economic or interest-rate climate deteriorated in a way that will take considerable added time for recovery? Did your original assumptions (price driven by story in an assumed time frame) prove inaccurate? Has the company jolted your thinking (and, clearly, the overall market of investor opinion) by producing one or more important negative surprises? Perhaps new competitors emerged or existing ones jumped ahead, leaving your choice in the shadows. Whatever has driven the downside price action, you need to reassess realistically. The basic and most fundamental test remains whether you would buy it today, knowing what you now do. If your added knowledge implies a more modest target price or, realistically, a longer period of time to justify your original goal, what is implied is a lower rate of return from today forward compared with whatever return you originally projected and also considered adequate for risking this purchase.

Given your inability to change past events, your only relevant consideration is a revised future whose shape you now find less attractive than you first thought. Is the implied return, starting from today, one that would cause you to buy the stock here and now? What you would not buy, you should not hold. Thousands of other investment possibilities exist, so do not remain stuck with a past choice merely to prove that you can come out without a loss or without having made a demonstrable mistake. Time is money. Holding this stock that so far has proved an underachiever should require you to find a compelling reason to expect (not merely hope) that events will now start unfolding rapidly and that a high rate of return is, therefore, predictable—a rate high enough to make up for time already lost and thus get your stock back to the target/time you first set out. If you cannot make such a case, looking elsewhere is likely to be a better choice than holding and hoping.

If Your Stock's Price Has Gone Nowhere

Assuming that price inertia cannot be blamed on the overall market, it would now appear that this stock may take more time to work out than you first thought. If that is because some expected news has failed to appear or because earnings growth has not materialized, you have some serious and honest re-assessing to do. Your stock has not treated you as badly as a decliner would have, but, in fact, it has failed to meet your original expectations, and it has wasted some of your valuable time. Putting it briefly, something (even if you don't know exactly what) has gone wrong—even if that something is not so severe as to cause an actual price decline. Assuming that an overall negative market environment has not caused your problem, the most likely reason your dollars have been asleep is that your original scenario was either overly optimistic or already obvious to much of the world by the time you jumped aboard at an inflated price.

Bottom line, as with that other stock that actually declined: you need to have convincing reasons to expect that this one will start making up lost time. Given that something has been amiss to date, such a scenario might well be on the optimistic side of real. Remember, something good enough must start happening to justify an annualized return on investment greater than what you originally projected in order for you to achieve your initial expectations by still riding this vehicle. Stocks sometimes do emerge from dormancy to act very well, but wishing will not make it so! What will be needed is better fundamental performance in a large enough dose to create sponsorship and, therefore, active buying pressure for these shares to rise. As elsewhere, would you actually buy it again today? Your answer tells you whether to hold or sell.

If Your Stock Is Up Ahead of Schedule

This is, of course, the most pleasant scenario: your purchase judgment has not only been vindicated but your pick has actually been working out more rapidly than you had originally hoped. Surprisingly, such a favorable experience contains very subtle but powerful aspects that can undermine your success. When your stock has caught fire, it is probably because of well-publicized good news, rotation of its industry into market leadership, or even just because it is a volatile stock doing well in a generally strong market. Psychologically, your tendency in such times is to be in love with both this stock/company and your own brilliance. The natural tendency is to project recent facts, with which we are now comfortable, into the future. What has done quite well we subconsciously condition ourselves to expect to continue rising. Just when a maximum number of investors (and traders) adopt this same belief, by definition, current buying pressure will reach a zenith, and price must soon thereafter begin to decline. Identifying the exact moment of maximum adulation for a stock is seldom possible, but an objective examination (such as a contrarian nonowner might make) can usually detect a period of bubbly enthusiasm unlikely to be long sustained.

Once again, the operative and defining question is whether you would buy it today. If the stock now sits well above that imaginary line of progression from your buy to your sell point (Figure 13–1 on page 124), only a highly significant, previously unimagined development should prompt you to raise your target and thereby justify continued holding. Expected good news or expected solid earnings progress does not count; those were reasons you bought and were already factored into your price/time target. Without that very significant new factor, when your stock is well above trend, it is most likely a timely current sell candidate from either of two perspectives. First, on a shorter-term basis, the thrust of its recent rise is very probably unsustainable. In the vernacular, this (good) can't go on like this! From a longer-term perspective, again without the fundamentally up-shifting development, the remaining path from today's advanced price to your original price/time target has a slope much flatter than your required rate of return. Therefore, while this stock might still go up in the long run, it will be a relative laggard from here to your target time and price.

Your comfort level about the company and how well you feel you understand its stock will tempt you to stay with a friendly vehicle you know rather than move elsewhere. Cold logic would say this stock is overheated and cannot be expected to provide an adequate return from here to your old target. The bottom line is that if you would not dare buy more atop this recent pleasant rise, you ought not hold it from here. Selling will reduce your risk of loss and disappointment and at the same time will take money off the table. You can use that cash either to buy another stock or to wait and repurchase this known winner a bit more reasonably after it corrects. The better a stock has treated you, the more strongly it will beguile you into holding at just those times when it is due for a price correction.

APPLYING THE ULTIMATE TEST: HOW OFTEN?

In the purest of theory, our "would you buy?" test could be applied at every moment the market is open. In fact, active day traders and other aggressive short-term market participants tend to do just that. But most of us are occupied with professional occupational pursuits throughout the market day, rendering such frequent testing impractical—all the more so when not just one stock but a list of holdings bears watching! Many readers do in fact look at their favorite newspaper's quotations pages daily. If your attention is actually that frequent, you should ask yourself what your intention is in doing that kind of intense watching. Checking stock prices daily should have a very different basis than watching the daily sports line scores to follow your favorite players. In the sports example, you are powerless to take action and are clearly a permanently passive spectator. With your stocks, daily tracking really should only be done if you are prepared to take action based on latest developments.

In at least two senses, daily tracking can be dangerous: (1) Unless you have a firmly disciplined contrarian's mind-set, close daily watching can lure you into following current trends: you will fall prey to selling in panic or to buying what has recently become too hot. (2) Daily tracking with absolutely no intention of taking counter-trend actions (selling up or buying on big dips) actually acts to numb your senses and to dampen the likelihood you will take action, particularly to sell. The more days you practice a habit of passively watching the market just to see day by day what comes next, the less likely it is that you will be in an alert, activist frame of mind and actually take action. Over-observing from a resting position makes you too forgiving and also fills your mind with myriad data elements that overload your circuits and contribute to confusion. A hundred days, half up and half down, will give you numerous paralyzingly equal reasons to hold and to sell, which will breed inaction from an overwhelming sense that there is no single clear answer since there are so many countervailing factors in the picture.

Much better than daily watching with no real intent of acting is the practice of regular weekend reviewing. Saturday or Sunday is a safe time since you cannot make an immediate transaction. This trading hiatus allows reflection, a trip to the library, or a scan of your favorite investment information databases. Also, net price moves for a week are larger than daily moves; bigger numbers are more likely to jar you into considering seriously whether a recent rise might be getting overdone, due for a correction. Finally, weekly portfolio work simply takes less time from your otherwise full schedule. Weekend market tracking presents a suitable balance (for other than active traders) between loss of perspective and overburdened time on the daily side, and being out of touch and too leisurely on the longer end of the spectrum. One may intend to be a long-term investor, but reality in an age of markets dominated by huge institutions' trades argues for vigilance more constant than one might actually prefer. A weekly review strikes a healthy balance.

Your review should include writing down the latest price for each stock held and probably also its high and low. Such a record becomes a ready reference, allowing you to recycle old newspapers promptly. Earnings and dividend developments can be noted, most easily in *Barron's* if not through an on-line data service. Company announcements can be noted and evaluated. Such news should be evaluated against your written plan for each stock. Are things going as anticipated, or is something perhaps beginning to smell a bit strange here? Has the stock reached your price target? Has it run well ahead of that imaginary progress line, implying that it is overheated and due for cooling down? Where is the stock on a chart; has it reached a supply area or a channel top (sell on the good fortune), or is it ominously breaking down technically (the world now knows something that you did not foresee)? The checklist described in Chapter 29 should serve as a reminder and guide about why you bought and what you expected to happen. Comparing latest information against your blueprint for each stock will go far in guiding you to a hold/sell decision for the coming week.

Finally, after sorting through the latest relevant facts and probably checking to calibrate with price trends of other stocks in the same industry group, you come again to the key test question: knowing all you know now, would you buy this stock again here at today's price? Your answer tells you whether to hold or sell.

A FINAL WORD

This book has been aimed at tuning you in, more sharply and insightfully, to how Wall Street really works and at helping you become intellectually and emotionally better prepared to pull that all-important selling trigger. Stocks are made to be sold as well as bought. Only a complete combination of those two actions, each reasonably well executed, results in a profit.

Much help (to be sure, of enormously varying true value) on the subject of buying is available elsewhere. Your author's intent has been to enrich you and your investment experience by making a measurable contribution to the sadly rather limited resources to which you can turn to make informed decisions about selling.

As you learn to do your selling more easily, your increased practice will produce more and richer feedback, enabling you to succeed at a task that many find elusive for a whole investment lifetime: selling when the time is right. Perfection is impossible, but a good batting average in this underemphasized skill is highly sufficient.

Useful Reading and Other Resources

The following is a powerful and yet highly selective reading and resources list on the subject of stock market investment. The items, grouped by subject, are useful to both a specialist and nonspecialist audience.

ORGANIZATIONS

American Association of Individual Investors, a not-for-profit educational association with chapters across the United States, offering investor-improvement tools. 625 N. Michigan Ave., Suite 1900, Chicago, IL 60611; (312) 280-0170.

National Association of Investors Corporation, the organizing force behind local investment clubs and a source of excellent stock-valuation worksheets ("Stock Selection Guide"). 711 W. 13 Mile Road, Madison Heights, MI 48071; (810) 583-6242.

CHARTS

Blue Book of 5-Trend Cycli-Graphs. Securities Research Company (13-year, monthly graphs of 1,100 stocks' prices, earnings, dividends); excellent for quick historical perspective. By subscription or single quarterly issues: 101 Prescott Street, Wellesley Hills, MA 02181. Phone (617) 235-0900 for rates.

Long-Term Values. William O'Neil & Co., Inc. (15-year, monthly graphs of 4,000 companies, showing EPS, dividends, and prices); great for perspective. Published on trial and subscription basis: William O'Neil & Co., Inc., P.O. Box 66919, Los Angeles, CA 90066. For current rate quotes, phone (213) 472–7479).

Daily Graphs. William O'Neil & Co., Inc. (one-year, daily NYSE, ASE, and OTC charts with price and volume plus dates of major published articles). Published on trial and subscription basis: William O'Neil & Co., Inc., P.O. Box 66919, Los Angeles, CA 90066. For current rate quotes, phone (213) 472-7479.

BOOKS ON SELLING

Fraser, James L. *The Art of Selling Stocks*. Burlington, VT: Fraser Publishing Company, 1983 reprint. A valuable pamphlet capsulizing wisdom from the single best source of contrarian investment publications. Phone (800) 253-0900.

Mamis, Justin, and Robert Mamis. *When to Sell: Inside Strategies for Stock Market Profits*. New York: Simon & Schuster, 1977. One of the few works devoted entirely to selling stocks (the last prior to this volume).

Rogers, Donald I. *How Not to Buy a Common Stock*. New Rochelle, NY: Arlington House, 1972. How and when not to buy is exactly when to sell!

CONTRARIANISM

Humphrey, B. Neill. *The Art of Contrary Thinking*. Caldwell, ID: The Caxton Printers, Ltd., 1954 to 1967. The classic; absolutely basic to the subject.

Dreman, David. *The New Contrarian Investment Strategy*. New York: Random House, 1982. Deals with both contrarian theory and self-understanding.

Ellis, Charles D. *Investment Policy: How to Win the Loser's Game*. Homewood, IL: Dow Jones-Irwin, 1985. Setting reasonable rules to help overcome emotion and illogic.

Browne, Harry. *Why the Best Laid Investment Plans Usually Go Wrong*. New York: William Morrow and Company, Inc., 1987. A lot of contrarianism here; easily his most useful volume.

HISTORY AND PERSPECTIVE

Galbraith, John Kenneth. *The Great Crash of 1929*. Boston: Houghton Mifflin Company, 1954. History now becoming dim, lest we forget.

Galbraith, John Kenneth. *A Short History of Financial Euphoria*. Nashville, TN: Whittle Direct Books, 1990. Documents several common threads signalling climactic stages of market blow-offs followed by crashes.

Sobel, Robert. *Panic on Wall Street*. New York: The Macmillan

Company, 1968. A very useful history of panics in the United States, 1792 to 1962.

Mackay, Charles. *Extraordinary Popular Delusions and the Madness of Crowds*. New York: Harrar, Straus and Giroux, 1932. Interesting history overall, but tulip-craze story most essential.

Fisher, Kenneth L. *The Wall Street Waltz: 90 Visual Perspectives*. Chicago: Contemporary Books, Inc., 1987. Long-term graphics from P/E ratios to Kondratieff waves provide a sense of perspective on cycles and the investor's need for perspective.

FUNDAMENTAL ANALYSIS

Graham, Benjamin, et al. *Security Analysis: Principles and Technique*. New York: McGraw-Hill Book Company, 1934 and later editions. The bible for the fundamental approach.

Graham, Benjamin. *The Intelligent Investor: A Book of Practical Counsel*. New York: Harper & Row, 1949 to 1986. The new testament; less a textbook, more an advisor; keep perspective.

O'Glove, Thorton L. *Quality of Earnings*. New York: Macmillan, Inc., 1987. Sobering insights into what the reported numbers can really mean.

Sharp, Richard M. *Calculated Risk*. Homewood, IL: Dow Jones-Irwin, 1986. A solid approach to understanding and measuring investment risk.

Miller, Lowell. *The Perfect Investment*. New York: E.P. Dutton, Inc., 1983. Although book focuses on buying, his lists' opposites are good as selling signals.

TECHNICAL ANALYSIS

Edwards, Robert D., and John Magee. *Technical Analysis of Stock Trends*. Boston: John Magee Inc., 1948 to 1979. The bible for the technical approach. Expensive but worth it.

Hurst, J. M. *The Profit Magic of Stock Transaction Timing*. Englewood Cliffs, NJ: Prentice-Hall, Inc., 1970. A strong time-value case for selling sooner versus holding long term.

Arms, Richard W. *Profits in Volume*. Larchmont, NY: Investors

Intelligence, Inc., 1971. A useful way of measuring resistance that helps define a top.

Granville, Joseph E. *A Strategy of Daily Stock Market Timing for Maximum Profit*. Englewood Cliffs, NJ: Prentice-Hall, Inc., 1960. Full of technical insights; from before the days of the author's celebrity.

PSYCHOLOGY OF INVESTING AND TRADING

Mamis, Justin. *The Nature of Risk, Stock Market Survival and the Meaning of Life*. Reading, MA: Addison-Wesley Publishing Company, Inc., 1991. Insightfully probes our innermost drives, motives, and fears, showing that the greatest risks lie inside ourselves.

Plummer, Tony. *The Psychology of Technical Analysis*. Burr Ridge, IL: Irwin Professional Publishing, 1993. Explains why technical analysis cannot be ignored; especially good on crowd dynamics.

Wyckoff, Peter. *The Psychology of Stock Market Timing*. Englewood Cliffs, NJ: Prentice-Hall, Inc., 1969. A valuable blending of psychology and technical analysis.

Koehler, David, and Gene Walden. *Winning with Your Stockbroker*. Minneapolis, MN: Longman Financial Services Publishing, 1988. Understanding each other; how to select and use one.

Anthony, Joseph. *The Stockmarket Saga*. Los Angeles: The Nowadays Press, 1972. Humorous little rhymes rich with wisdom about wrong market psychology.

COMMISSION DISCOUNTS

AAII Journal, January issue. (Annual; detailed tabular listings of updated rate structures and phone numbers.) From the American Association of Individual Investors (see address given under Organizations on page 279).

Coler, Mark D., and Ellis Ratner. *70% Off! The Investor's Guide to Discount Brokerage*. New York: Facts on File, 1983. Explains which fee schedules fit different order types best; lists phones and addresses.

INDEX